Entering the World of Work

Third Edition

Grady Kimbrell
Research Analyst
Santa Barbara School Districts
Santa Barbara, California

Ben S. Vineyard
Professor and Chairman Emeritus
Vocational and Technical Education
Pittsburg State University
Pittsburg, Kansas

Entering the World of Work

Third Edition

GLENCOE/ McGRAW-HILL
A Macmillan/ McGraw-Hill Company
Mission Hills, California

Send all inquiries to:
Glencoe/McGraw-Hill
15319 Chatsworth Street
P.O. Box 9509
Mission Hills, CA 91395-9509

ISBN 0-02-676730-9

3 4 5 6 93 92 91 90

We would like to thank the following teachers, supervisors, and specialists for offering freely of their time to review the manuscript for this third edition of *Entering the World of Work.* Their opinions and suggestions helped make this edition more interesting, informative, and readable for your students.

Ms. Chari Ann Allison
Teacher
Cincinnati, OH

Ms. Londa Appignani
South Brunswick High School
Monmouth Junction, NJ

Mrs. Carolyn Balsa-Hancock
Career/Vocational Specialist
San Jose, CA

Mr. William P. Caci
Hempfield High School
Landisville, PA

Ms. Lori Carlson
Amherst High School
Amherst, WI

Ervin Carpenter
Special Education Teacher
Oshkosh, WI

Ms. Rosemary K. Fransis
LD/ED Teacher
Amherst High School
Amherst, WI

Richard Gerchak
Staff Developer
Office of Superintendent
Bronx High School
Bronx, NY

Ms. Cathy Haner
SM Teacher
Cresco, IA

Mrs. Chiara Hodan III
Oakland School District
Oakland, CA

Ms. Karen Levine
Dunellen High School
Dunellen, NJ

Ms. Oretta M. Littrell
Pulaski County High School
Somerset, KY

Ms. Barbara Neely
Special Needs Dept.
Mark Morris High School
Longview, WA

Terry L. Reece
Northwest Cabarrus High School
Concord, NC

CONTENTS

Introduction

The World of Work! You have probably heard that phrase before. What does it mean to you?

"I will earn my own money."

"It is a big responsibility."

"I am looking forward to the change from school to work."

"I will get to do something I *like* every day."

"Wow! A full-time job sounds scary."

"Work means freedom. I will be on my own."

"A career means moving up the ladder."

"Hurray! I will be my own boss."

Working means different things to different people. Two things about work, though, are certain.

One, entering the world of work will be a big change. You want to make the change carefully. The more you know about the working world, the better. The change will go smoother if you know what to expect.

Second, work will be an important part of your life. You will be working many hours each week. You will be working for many years to come. Being unhappy at work usually means an unhappy life. A good work experience usually means a good life.

This book explains the importance of work. It tells how you can fit into the work world. It also tells how work fits into your life.

You will learn to make smart decisions, too. First, you will learn more about yourself. Then you will explore many different jobs. You will learn how to choose the right career for you.

Next, you will learn how to find the job you want. You will read tips on applying for and interviewing for jobs. You will learn how to get started on the right foot at work. You will learn how to be a good worker.

Finally, you will learn some everyday skills related to working. Your paycheck, taxes, managing money, and smart shopping are all included. You will learn much of what you need to know before living on your own.

The world of work offers you many choices. It offers you many opportunities. Take advantage of them. Make smart decisions now. Use your abilities to their fullest. This will make your entry into the world of work easier and more successful.

PART ONE

PLANNING FOR WORK

Soon you will be leaving high school. You will be entering a new part of your life. You and your classmates will go separate ways. You will do different things. You will follow different dreams.

You will not suddenly become a totally new person. Changing from a student to a worker is not a giant leap. It is a series of small steps. It includes learning about the world of work. It also includes understanding yourself, weighing choices, and making important decisions.

You need to look ahead and do some planning. Part One gives you a big picture of the work world. It also lets you take a good, close look at yourself. Then you will see how you best fit into the working world.

CAREERS

Chapter 1

You and Work

What's wrong here?

Words to learn and use

You will learn several new words in this chapter. The most important words are listed below. Do you know the meanings of these words?

work	identity
job (occupation)	lifestyle
self-esteem	leisure
career	cost of living
dignity	equal opportunity

Build on what you know

You already know:

- most people work to earn a living.
- some jobs have been known as *men's work.*
- people are often known by the work they do.
- people live very different lives.

In this chapter you will learn . . .

- three basic reasons for working.
- how work roles are changing for men and women.
- how adults are usually identified.
- the six parts of lifestyle.

The adult world is a world at work. In the movies and on TV, you see people working. In magazines and books you read about people working. You see people working every day.

Have you ever thought that people work only for money? In this chapter, you will learn why work is good. You will begin to see why people work to be happy. And you will see how your work will affect every other part of your life.

Why People Work

Why do people work? Most people work to earn money, of course. While money is a good reason for working, it is not the only reason.

There are three main reasons why people work.

1. Money
2. Contact with people
3. Self-esteem

First, you earn money to pay for the things you need and want. You need food, housing, medical help, and schooling. And most people *want* more. You may want a car, TV, and other things you could live without. These extra things are called *luxuries.* Luxuries help make life fun, but they cost money.

A second reason to work is to be with other people. Your job can be a way to meet some new friends. Doing things for and with others can help make a happy life.

Third, when others count on you to do a good job, it makes you feel important and worthwhile. When you do a job well, you feel good about yourself. You take pride in what you do and who you are. This good feeling is called **self-esteem.** It gives you confidence. Confidence is the belief that you can do well. You feel satisfied. You feel happy. Your self-esteem may be worth more than money.

Work, Job, and Career

You often hear the terms *work, job,* and *career.* While they all are part of earning a living, they are really quite different.

Work is any useful activity. For example, you rake leaves. You deliver newspapers. You wait on a customer. These are all types of *work.*

Each of these work activities is called a *task.* All the different tasks that a person does to earn a living make up a **job.** A bigger word for job is **occupation.** For example, a man may be a gardener. Gardening is his job. He gets paid for doing it. His work as a gardener includes many tasks. Mowing grass, trimming bushes, and hoeing weeds are some of the tasks.

Career refers to the work a person does and the jobs that a person holds over a number of years. Most people have many different jobs during their lifetime. They may change jobs to make more money. They may find a job they like better than the one they have. They may want a change of pace.

For example, suppose a woman works as a receptionist in a dentist's office. Then she goes back to school and becomes a licensed practical nurse. She takes a job as an LPN in a hospital. Then she goes back to school again and earns her degree. She then takes and passes the test to become a registered nurse. She then decides to take a job as an RN in a doctor's office.

You would say that this woman's job is *registered nurse.* Or you could say she is a nurse in a doctor's office. Her career is nursing or medicine. She may change jobs again within her field of nursing. She could work as a company nurse in a business or factory. She could become a home health nurse. She could decide that she wants to become a doctor. She would go back to school to earn her degree in medicine. Then she would get her doctor's license. She may decide to get out of the medicine field and go into business. Then she would be changing careers.

Right now you are learning to do many different types of work. A certain task that you learn to do could be useful in many different jobs. Take typing, for instance. You would use your typing skill if you were a secretary. Typing would be a helpful skill if you were a writer, too. Typing would also be helpful if you operated a computer. Or if you owned a business. How many jobs can you think of that need typing skills?

All of the work you do helps you decide what type of job you would like. All the jobs that you have help you decide on a career.

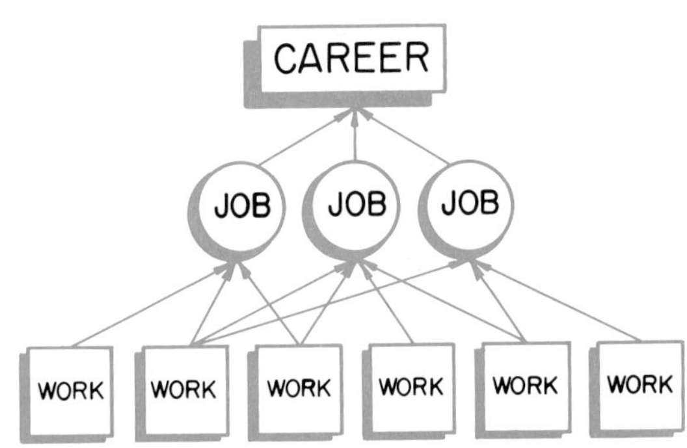

You do many different work tasks at each job you have. The jobs you have over a number of years are called your *career*.

Check Up:✓✓ True or False?

1. The only reason people work is for money.

2. *Job* and *occupation* mean the same thing.

3. Your career is the work you do and the jobs you have over a number of years.

A Desire to Succeed

Overcoming Shyness: Garrison Keillor

In school, Garrison Keillor was very shy. He went to high school in Anoka, Minnesota. His teacher says that Garrison was the most timid student he ever had in class. Garrison was afraid to sit where the teacher might call on him. In fact, he always walked to the farthest chair in the back of the room. He never answered the teacher's questions. He never said a word in class.

Garrison knew that being so shy was a problem in school. He also knew that it might be a bigger problem as a adult.

Garrison made a decision to change. He forced himself to talk to people. Talking was very hard at first. It was the one thing he was afraid of most. But he had to try. So he forced himself to keep on talking.

After several years, Garrison was less afraid of talking. But he still did not really enjoy it. Most of the time he still felt very shy. He thought he had to do something more. So, in July of 1974, he tried talking on a radio show. Garrison says that he never thought he was very good on the show. But his show, and Garrison, have both been very successful.

His show, *A Prairie Home Companion,* ran for thirteen years on the American Public Radio network. He told stories and sang. He had other musicians on his show. One of the regulars was the world famous guitar player Chet Atkins.

Garrison also wrote a book, published in 1982, called *Happy to Be Here.* It sold very well. So he wrote another one, published in 1985, called *Lake Wobegon Days.* It was the top selling book in America in early 1986. Garrison's picture was on the cover of *Time* magazine.

At age 44, Garrison retired from his radio show. He began traveling in Europe.

Garrison Keillor must feel very good about himself today. As a young person, he realized that he had a problem. But he worked very hard to overcome it. He succeeded. He added greatly to his self-esteem.

Identity Through Work

Your **identity** is the way that other people know you. For example, right now school is a big part of your life. Studying is an activity you do for school. You are a student. Adults may introduce you as a student. Your school name may be mentioned, too. Being a student is a large part of your identity.

When you have finished school, you will be identified, at least partly, by the work you do. If you teach children, you will be known as a teacher. If you repair cars, you will be known as a mechanic. If you clean hotel rooms, you will be known as a maid. Your work, your job, or your career will help identify you to others. So always be proud of the work you do.

You will likely work at many different jobs during your life. You will like some of them. Some you may not like. Your goal is to find work you like and can do well.

Today there are about twenty thousand different jobs. Each job is important. Each job helps other people in some way. Each worker is paid for doing his or her job.

Whatever job you choose for your work, it should give you **dignity.** Having dignity means that when you do your job well, you can be proud of yourself and the work you do. When you become good at one type of work, you may stay with it. Then it becomes your career.

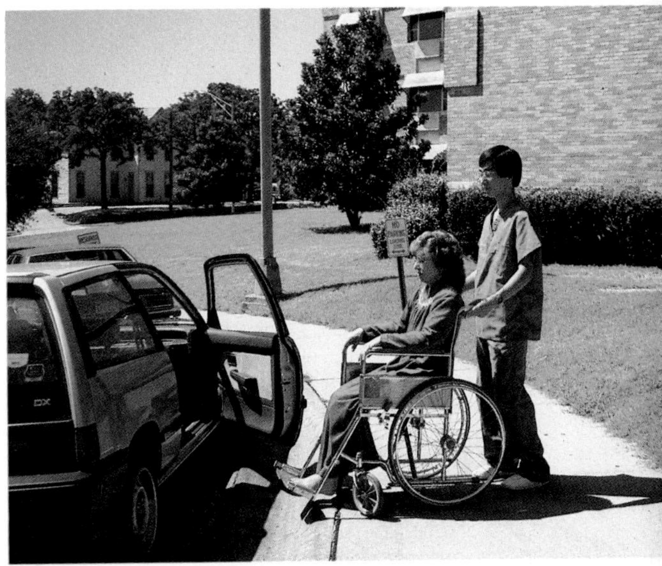

You will be identified by the type of work that you do.

Check Up:✓✓ **True or False?**

1. Today there are about 20,000 different types of jobs.
2. Most adults are identified by their family size.
3. All people should be proud of the work they do.

Lifestyles

Everyone wants to be happy. But each person looks for happiness in a different way. Each wants his or her own kind of life. The way you spend your time is called your **lifestyle.** *Lifestyle* is the way you live.

Parts of Your Lifestyle

For most people, lifestyle includes six parts:

1. Family
2. Friends
3. Leisure
4. Religion
5. Personal Choices
6. Work

Family. How many hours a day do you spend with your family? The time spent with family members is important to most people. Is this an important part of your lifestyle?

Friends. Having friends is important, too. They are people to talk with and do things with. Do you see friends every day? How important are friends to you?

Leisure. The way you spend your free time is **leisure.** Many people like to spend leisure time in some type of recreation. How do you like to spend your leisure time? Is recreation or a hobby important in your lifestyle?

Religion. Some people need a lot of time for worship and church-related activities. Others do not. Are religious activities an important part of your lifestyle?

Personal Choices. Personal choices are part of your lifestyle, too. Here are some of the personal choices you will make:

- Should you stay single or get married?
- Where should you live?
- Should you buy or rent? What kind of furnishings would you like?
- What foods should you eat?
- Should you buy a car? Would leasing a car save you money? Or is public transportation the answer?
- What health habits should you develop?

Work. As a student, you spend a lot of hours at school. As an adult, you will spend many hours at work. In fact, you may spend more hours at work than in any other part of your lifestyle.

Your Choice of Lifestyle

The parts of a person's life combine to form a "lifestyle pattern." This idea is shown in the lifestyle pattern at the top of the next page. Each part of this

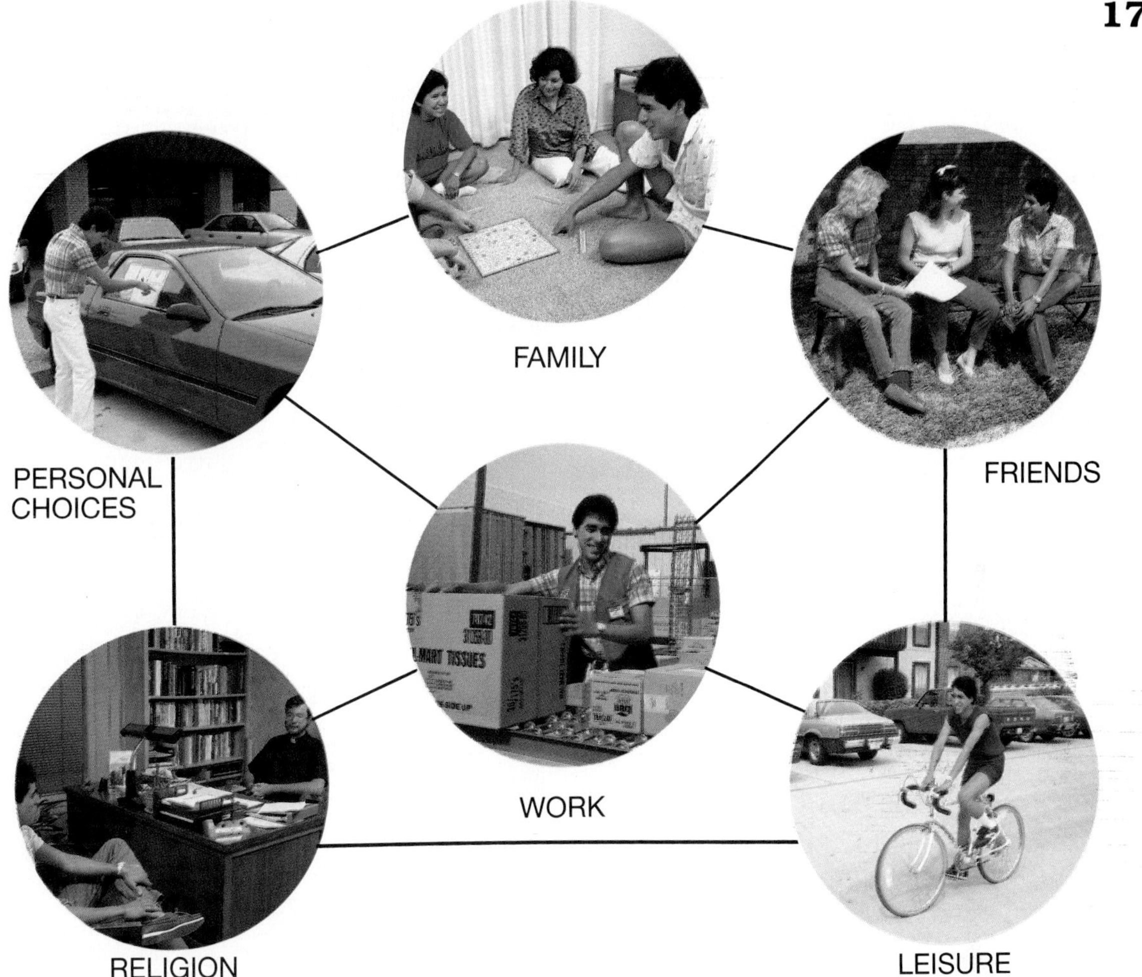

All six parts of this young man's lifestyle are shown the same size. This means that he values each part equally.

person's life is as important as every other part. So all parts are shown the same size.

For most people, though, some parts of life are more important than other parts. For example, many people think that a happy family life is most important. The same people may place little or no value on leisure. For others, religion or personal choices may be the most important. For many, work is most important.

How would you show your own lifestyle? Which parts are most important to you?

Your Work Affects Your Lifestyle

Each part of life affects every other part. For most of us, work has the greatest effect of all. We spend most of our lives working and sleeping. We also spend a lot of time going to work and coming home.

For example, when do you get up each morning? You probably get up early enough to be at school on time. When you finish high school, you may get up at a different time. It will depend on when you must be at work.

When do you eat your evening meal? Does it depend on when someone gets home from work? Most people plan their daily lives around their work. Work is the central activity of life.

The money you earn from your job will determine where you live. If you earn a lot of money, you can buy a big house. You may buy expensive cars. Of course, most people do not have a lot of money. So they have a less expensive lifestyle.

Your work also affects who your friends are. You will make some friends on the job. You may even meet your future wife or husband at work.

How you spend your free time depends on where and when you work. Some companies have bowling teams. A few even provide a swimming pool or tennis court for their workers. New friends from work may get you involved in new activities. All these things add interest to your lifestyle.

When you must go out of town on your job, you have less time for family and friends.

Plan Your Work to Fit Your Lifestyle

Do you sometimes daydream about the future? If so, you are trying out ideas for an adult lifestyle. This is good. It is the first step in planning your future. It gives you a starting point.

As you daydream, think about what will be important to you. Think ahead five or ten years. Think of how you want to live. Then set some goals. Working toward goals is one way to take control of your own life.

If you let it, work can control your lifestyle. For example, a truck driving job can keep you away from your family a lot. A night job can keep you from being with your friends. A job on weekends can keep you from attending religious services. If you work long hours, you may not have much time for recreation.

What does all this mean? It means that you need to know which parts of your lifestyle are most important. You need to know before you choose a career. Then you can choose work that gives you the lifestyle you want.

Is enjoying vacations and sports important to you? If so, you will need a job that pays well enough to afford these luxuries.

Check Up:✓✓ True or False?

1. There are five parts to every lifestyle.
2. For most people *leisure* has the greatest effect on their lifestyle.

Men and Women in the World of Work

Have you thought about how many years you will spend working? The average man works more than forty years. Many women work as many years as men do.

Of course, women do leave work, at least for a while, when their children are born. Just a few years ago, most women stayed home until their children were all in school. Then they went back to work. Now most women return to work just a month or two after the child is born. The average woman now works more than twenty-five years.

Do you know the stories of Cinderella, Sleeping Beauty, and Snow White? In the past, many young girls read these fairy tales. Then some thought that they would not have to work. They would simply marry a prince. They

Today more women than ever before are working outside the home. Many work at jobs that were once called "men's jobs."

would not have to go out into the work world. Working, they thought, was just for men.

The real world, of course, is not like the fairy tales. Cinderella, Sleeping Beauty, and Snow White are only make believe. Few real women marry a prince. In fact, few real men earn a living as a prince. Most men and women work very hard at what they do.

In the real world, the work roles of men and women have been changing. Years ago, when your grandparents were young, most women did not take jobs outside the home. In those days, men worked to earn the money needed for the family. Most women stayed home. Women's work was cleaning, cooking, and caring for the children.

Today many women work outside the home. One reason for this is the **cost of living.** The cost of living is the amount of money it takes to live. This includes such things as food, housing, clothing, and medicine.

Since the 1950s, the cost of living has gone up every year. This means you need more money to pay the bills than your grandparents did. So every year more women have gone to work outside the home. In the 1970s and 1980s most married women worked at paying jobs. Now, about half of all U.S. workers are men and half are women.

In most families today, both the husband and the wife must work to pay the bills. Because both spend a lot of time on the job, they need to share the chores at home.

Do you think of some jobs as "men's" work? And other jobs as "women's" work? A few years ago, many jobs were open only to men. Truck drivers and carpenters were almost always men. Most people hired women for other jobs, like nurses and secretaries. Most grade school teachers were women, too.

Truck drivers and carpenters usually earned more money than nurses and secretaries. In fact, most of the jobs men did paid well. Most women earned less on their jobs. This seemed unfair. So new laws were written. These laws made it illegal to hire only men or only women for any job.

Then the world of work began to change. More and more women felt they could do the same jobs men did. Now almost every job is open to both men and women. This is sometimes called **equal opportunity.**

Check Up:✓✓ True or False?

1. The cost of living has affected the changing roles of men and women.

2. Few married women work at paying jobs.

3. Men and women can both do the same jobs.

The words

Listed below are the important new words that you learned in this chapter. Next to each word is the page on which you will find the word in bold, black print. Turn back and read again the paragraph in which you find each word. Then write the word and its meaning on a sheet of paper. Also write a sentence of your own using each word.

1. career (12)
2. cost of living (21)
3. dignity (15)
4. equal opportunity (21)
5. identity (15)
6. job (occupation) (12)
7. leisure (16)
8. lifestyle (16)
9. self-esteem (12)
10. work (12)

The facts

1. What are three reasons people work?
2. How many years does the average man work?
3. How many years does the average woman work outside the home?
4. About how many different jobs are there in the U.S.?
5. How are young people in school often identified?
6. In what way are adults often identified?
7. What are the six parts of lifestyle? Briefly explain each one.
8. Which part of lifestyle is the central activity in the life of most adults? Why?
9. What is the first step in planning your future?
10. What is the major difference between a job and a career?

What's right here?

ADD TO YOUR KNOWLEDGE AND SKILLS

Talk about your ideas

1. Which reason for working is most important to you? Why?
2. Which part of your lifestyle is most important to you? Why?
3. Do you think that some jobs should be done only by men? Only by women? Why, or why not?
4. Imagine that a husband and wife both have jobs. Who should do the housework? Why?

Do some activities

1. Draw the lifestyle pattern you expect to have in ten years.
2. Find some old magazines. Cut out pictures that show the type of work you would like to be doing in ten years. Paste the pictures in the center of a large piece of cardboard. Then add pictures of other activities you would like to do. Add pictures of things you would like to own. Let some picture edges overlap.

Improve your basic skills

Articles about work appear in almost every newspaper. Look in your local paper for the next several days. Find two such articles. Read them carefully.

1. Write a paragraph about a, b, c, and d. (a) The two work articles you just read. (b) Something that has given you a feeling of self-esteem. (c) How you feel about the changing roles of women and men, both in the workplace and at home. (d) How you hope to be living five years from now.
2. Make a list of places where you have learned about work. Your list might include movies, TV, and books. Pick one source from your list. Write a half page about what you have learned from this source.
3. Suppose that you are 35 years old. You have a son or daughter who is 13. Write a letter to your child. Talk about some personal choices you have made in your own life.

5×7=?

1. Tom is taking lessons to improve his tennis skills. He pays $20 an hour for tennis lessons. Tom takes two lessons each month. How much will Tom pay for lessons for three months?
2. Jill earns about $200 a week. George earns $2000 a month. Ann earns $20,000 a year. Who earns the most in a year?

Chapter 2

Understanding Yourself

What's wrong here?

Words to learn and use

You will learn several new words in this chapter. The most important words are listed below. Do you know the meanings of these words?

career goals
values
interests
experiences
volunteer work
talent
aptitude
personality
self-concept

Build on what you know

You already know . . .

- work is a big part of your total lifestyle.
- daydreaming is the first step in planning your future.
- you must decide your own lifestyle.
- self-esteem is the good feeling you have about yourself.

In this chapter you will learn . . .

- how your career goal will affect your lifestyle.
- how your interests, values, and talents help you find your career goal.
- how understanding your personality traits can help you reach your career goal.
- how to overcome handicaps and build your self-esteem.

In Chapter 2, you will learn to understand yourself better. You will see how knowing yourself can help you decide what kind of work you would like to do. You will see how you fit into the world of work.

Setting Career Goals

You know who you are now. You have thought about who you want to be in the future. How will you get from the person you are to the person you want to be? Do you know what you have to do?

Now is the time to set some goals. *Goals* are aims for the future. You may have a goal of learning to swim. Maybe you want to go to cooking school. Maybe you want to marry and have three children. You may want to earn a certain amount of money.

Setting goals is important. It gives direction to your life. It increases your chances for success.

Career goals are decisions about the type of work you want to do. Without career goals, many people fall into careers by accident. They work for years at jobs they do not really like. They wait for opportunitites that may never come. If you plan, you can make your own opportunities! It is best to have two or three career goals in mind.

Do you know what things are important to you? Do you know what you like to do most? Do you know what you are good at doing? You need to know these things to set your career goals.

As a young child were you aware of your parents' goals? Are your present goals similar to your parents'?

Your Values

As you daydream about your future lifestyle, you will begin to think about your values. **Values** are things that are important to you. Everyone has values. Like lifestyles, everyone's values differ. Defining your values is another way of understanding yourself.

When you were a child, you lived mostly by your parents' values. If they thought good health was important, so did you. If they thought going to church was important, you did too. You probably imitated many of their activities.

In junior high and high school, we begin to choose our own values. We keep some—but not all—of our parents' values. But we add some new values of our own. Choosing values is part of looking at life to see how we will fit in.

You need to think about your values before you choose a career. Certain careers match up well with certain values. Some careers conflict with some values. You want to make a good match between your values and your career.

On the next two pages you will read about some common values. Try to decide which of these values are yours. Then, as you learn about careers, think about how each career matches your values.

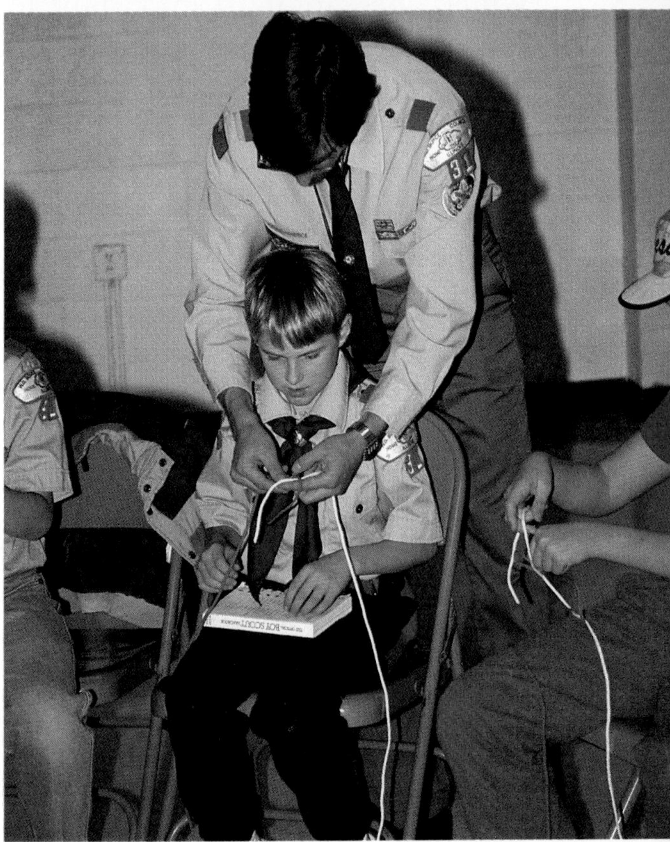

As you grow older, you decide for yourself what is most important in your life.

Check Up:✓✓ True or False?

1. *Career goals* are decisions about the work you will do as an adult.

2. *Values* are things that are important to you.

3. Your values will always be just like your parents' values.

Rating Your Values

Look at the values listed below. Which ones are most important to you?

1. Earning a lot of money
2. Helping other people
3. Raising a family
4. Having good health
5. Having a lot of friends
6. Being a religious person

Earning a lot of money. Will you need a lot of money to live the way you dream? If so, you will place a high value on earning a lot of money. Knowing this about yourself, you will want to learn about careers that pay well. If you dream about a simple life, money may not be so important.

Helping other people. Do you like to do things for others? Helping others is very important to some people. On some jobs, you can be very helpful to others. Many people spend some free time helping children or old people.

Raising a family Do you want to have children? Most people do. If a family is important to you, think about your family when you set your career goals.

Having good health Most people like to be healthy. How important is your health to you? Do you take great care to stay healthy? Do you eat the right foods? Do you overeat? Do you exercise in your free time?

If your health is important to you, you will not want to do some types of work. Some jobs are more dangerous to your health than others. Workers on some jobs breathe dangerous fumes or dust. On some jobs, workers must lift or carry heavy things. After a few years, some types of work can cause health problems.

Having a lot of friends. Do you like people? Do you need to have a lot of friends? Some people do. Some do not. Most people need at least one or two good friends. Friends may be members of your own family. It is important to be a good friend to family members. Husbands and wives often consider each other best friends.

For some people, keeping physically fit is an important part of their lives. You must decide what is important to you.

School is a great place to make friends. There are many people about your own age. After you are out of school, you will meet people on your job. Some of them may become your best friends.

Being a religious person. Are you a religious person? If religious activities are important to you, you may not want some jobs. You may not want to work on the days you attend religious services.

Some people do not like to work where alcohol is sold or used. Others do not like to work where vulgar language is used.

Being Proud of Your Life

How you feel about each of the values will influence the work you choose to do. You need to think about these values when you decide your career goals. You will not want to give up your values for a certain job. So think about your total lifestyle when you plan your career.

Most happy people are proud of their lives. They take pride in their work. And they enjoy what they do in their free time. They do not give up the values that are important to them.

You will want your parents to be proud of you. If you have children, you will want them to be proud of you, too. If you are not proud of your own life, you cannot expect others to be proud of you. Being proud of how you do your job is very satisfying. It carries over into other parts of your life. It makes you a happier person at home, too.

You may not be rewarded every time you do a good job. But you should be proud of whatever you do.

Check Up: ✓✓ True or False?

1. Everyone has the same values.
2. Your values have nothing to do with your career choices.
3. Being proud of your work carries over to other parts of your life.

Your Interests

Your **interests** are the things you like to do. Understanding your interests is another part of understanding yourself. You have already thought about some of your interests each time you daydreamed about your future lifestyle. Knowing your interests will help you set your career goals. It will help you plan other parts of your lifestyle, too.

School

You can decide what your interests are by thinking about what you have already experienced. **Experiences** are activities that you have tried. For example, what subjects do you like in school? Your favorites may be clues to a future career.

Do you really like math? Or science? Or geography? Or home economics? Or machine shop? There are many jobs in each of these fields. Take more courses in the fields that interest you.

Other school activities tell about your interests. They can help you see if you are interested in certain activities. For instance, you may belong to the photography club at school. There you will learn how to take pictures and develop film. You may find you have an interest in photography. If so, you might like a photography career.

Work

You can learn about your interests from the work that you do. Doing chores at home is one type of work. Do you enjoy cooking, sewing, doing yard work, or repairing broken items? Many people earn a living doing such work. Perhaps you would like a career doing one of these things.

A part-time job gives you a chance to try working at a certain job. So does volunteer work. **Volunteer work** is work that you do without receiving pay.

Suppose you have a Saturday job working in a fast food restaurant. You will find out if you enjoy restaurant work. By volunteering at your local library, you will find out if you would enjoy working there full time. By volunteering at a nursing home, you will see if you enjoy working with older people.

You may find that you enjoy one part of a job but not another part. For example, by working in a restaurant, you may find that you like waiting on customers. You may not like preparing food. Some young people try three or four types of work. This gives them a chance to see what interests them most.

Working at a part-time job can give you lots of experience. This experience will help you decide if you want to work full time at a job.

Leisure

How you spend your leisure time is a clue to your interests. Leisure interests can lead to a career. Most carpenters first enjoyed woodworking as a hobby. Many mechanics began by working on their own cars. Tennis instructors first learned the game for fun.

Overall, trying things is the best way to see if you like them. The more things you try, the better you will know what you like to do. Then you will have a better chance of finding a career that will make you happy.

Interest in a hobby can give you ideas for your career.

Interest Tests

There is another way to learn about your interests. You can take an interest test. An interest test is not like other tests. There are no right or wrong answers.

The purpose of an interest test is to learn which jobs have work activities that interest you. Your teacher can help you find out more about interest tests.

An interest test can help you learn which careers have work activities that interest you.

Check Up:✓✓ True or False?

1. You can learn about your interests from school, work, and leisure activities.
2. The best way to learn about career interests is to read about them.
3. Your leisure activities are part of your lifestyle.

Jack's father runs an auto repair shop. When Jack was in eighth grade, his mother took a job. She did not want Jack to be home alone after school. So Jack began to stop at his father's shop in the afternoon.

Soon Jack started helping his father. At first, he just cleaned up. But he asked a lot of questions. He asked about how to repair cars. He wanted to know how to fix brakes. He asked about tune-ups.

When Jack was in high school, he began repairing brakes. Then he started doing other repair jobs. One day Jack's father asked him, "Jack, after you graduate, would you like to work in the shop full time?"

Jack was interested in the car-repair business. He had become interested by spending some time on the job. But Jack thought maybe he could become interested in other jobs, too. He knew there was no time to try out a lot of jobs. How would he know if car repair was the right job choice?

Jack talked to his school counselor. Jack's counselor said an interest test might help. This test gave Jack a list of jobs he might like. Jack decided to try out one or two of the jobs. Then he would choose.

Your Talents

Understanding your interests is only the beginning step in choosing a career. You also must think about your talents. A **talent** is a natural gift. It is the ability to do something easily or to learn something easily. The more talent you have for something, the easier it is to learn. You can, of course, learn something for which you have little talent. But it will take more time and training.

Everyone has talents. Some people have more than others. Do you know what your talents are? To set career goals, you need to know your talents. Do not set a goal that requires talents you do not have. That would be unrealistic. It is better to set realistic career goals. These are goals that you can reach.

When you were younger, did you have friends who wanted to be movie stars? Or professional baseball players? Or singers? These careers require special talents. Without talent, even years of practice will not make you a movie star, or a good singer, or a baseball player. Without the talent to learn the skills, such a career goal is unrealistic.

Types of Talents

There are different types of talents. There are mental, physical, and social talents. How you use your mind shows your mental talents. Physical talents use your mind and your body. Social talents show your ability to get along with other people.

Mental talents. Do you work hard in school? If so, your grades will show some of your mental talents. If not, you may have more talent than your grades show. Many jobs require mental talents, such as math, reading, writing, and remembering skills. It is important to work hard at developing your mental talents.

How could this physical talent help you succeed at some jobs?

If you truly have a talent, you may want to start a career using that talent.

But don't try to start a career if you have no talent for it.

Physical Talents. Are you strong? Can you run fast? Can you throw a ball straight? Can you move your hands and fingers quickly? These skills show physical talents. Some jobs require physical talents. These jobs include such jobs as technicians, typists, and ball players.

Social Talents. Getting along with people is a social skill. Most people can learn to get along well. But it is easier for some than for others. Those who find social skills easy are understanding of others. They seem to have a social talent for saying things that make people feel good. Salespersons, social workers, and ministers are examples of people who need social talents.

Of course, many jobs require a combination of talents. For example, cashiers need mental talents to total customers' bills and to make change. They need social skills to please their customers and to get along with their co-workers.

Check Up: ✓✓ True or False?

1. A talent is an interest in doing an activity.
2. You show your social talents by getting along well with others.
3. Many jobs require more than one talent.

Ways of Understanding Your Talents

You can learn what your talents are by trying many different things. Is a certain subject at school easy for you? Do you find that you can do certain tasks easier than others? Are you good at sports, music, art, repairs, math, or something else? By knowing what you can do quickly and easily, you will learn what your talents are.

Sometimes other people can help you see talents that you never thought about. Notice when people say you did a good job with a certain task. Listen to what people praise you for. Have you ever won an award? If so, this may indicate talent. Do you usually get high grades in a certain subject? This too can mean you have some talent. Are you beginning to identify your talents?

Sometimes your parents or others may see talents in you that you did not know you had. Listen to these people when they tell you about your talents.

Simple things, such as conducting a meeting, doing research, or making someone laugh, are valuable talents.

There are other ways to learn about your talents, too. One way is to take an aptitude test. **Aptitude** is another word for talent. An aptitude test can help you set realistic career goals. That is, it may help you choose a career that will make use of your talents. Ask your teacher if you should take an aptitude test.

Each person is "one of a kind." Each is different from everyone else. And everyone has talents. You are born with them.

Some people have more talents than others do. There is nothing you can do about that. Do the best with what you have. You will be happier than the person with more talents who does little with them.

Check Up:✓✓ True or False?

1. Trying things and listening to what others say about you will help you discover your talents.
2. Aptitude means what you like to do.

Your Personality

Everyone is different. Everyone has different needs, wants, values, interests, and talents. The way all these things are combined is called your **personality.** How you choose to look and act shows your personality to others.

Your personality is important to your career for two reasons. One, an understanding of your personality helps you pick a career you will like. Two, having a pleasing personality helps you get a job. It also helps you get along well on the job.

Understanding Your Personality

No two people look exactly alike. And no two people have exactly the same personality. For example, some people are friendly with everyone. They like to talk. These people have outgoing personalities. They are easy to get to know. They might like a job working with people—such as a salesperson, a tour guide, or a performer.

Other people do not talk so much. They have more quiet personalities. They are harder to get to know. They often listen better than those with more outgoing personalities. People with quiet personalities might enjoy jobs working with plants and animals. Such jobs have little contact with people. Which type are you—outgoing or quiet?

Think of other parts of your personality. How do they make you suited for some jobs and not others?

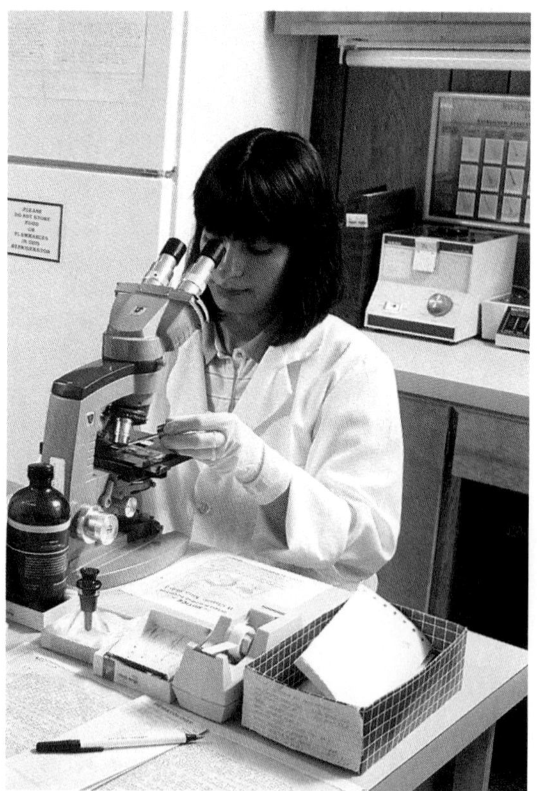

Knowing what your personality is like can help you pick a job you like. A person who is quiet and likes routine and detail work might like to be a lab technician.

Perhaps you like routine. Do you enjoy doing the same tasks over and over? Then you might like working on an assembly line or checking groceries. Do you like a variety of tasks? Then you might like working in a busy office or retail store.

Do you like to make your own decisions? If so, you might consider owning your own business. Maybe you would rather have someone else decide what tasks need to be done. Then you will probably want to work for someone else.

Having a Pleasing Personality

Have you ever heard that some boy or girl has a pleasing personality? That means that others like what they see and hear. People with good personalities are easy to like.

Employers like workers with good personalities. Here are some things employers said when calling a high school:

"Send me someone with a nice personality."

"I want a person who can type and has a good personality."

"I hired Maria because she has a nice smile and a pleasing personality."

"I need a person in the sales department. He or she will be meeting the customers. A nice personality is a must."

Some traits that make up a pleasing personality are

- being friendly.
- being polite.
- being courteous.
- being interested in others.
- being willing to learn.

Can you think of others? You will learn more about a pleasing personality in later chapters.

Smiling is one way to show that you have a pleasant personality.

Check Up:✓✓ True or False?

1. Understanding your personality can help you make the right job choice.
2. A pleasing personality may help you get the job you want.

Your personality affects how other people react to you. Their reaction helps you form your self-concept. Your self-concept shows through in your personality.

Your Self-Concept

Your **self-concept** is how you see yourself. It is how you picture yourself in your own mind. Your self-concept is important to your career.

Your personality, your self-concept, and other people's reactions to you all work together. Here is the way it works:

1. How you look, act, and sound shows your personality to people. People notice these things about you. They form an impression of you.
2. Others react to you based on what they see and hear of your personality. They may like you. They may want you as a friend. They may want to hire you for a job. Or they may prefer not to be around you.
3. You form your self-concept based upon other people's reactions to you. If people react kindly and friendly toward you, you feel good about yourself. If they do not, you may think you do not have much worth.
4. Your self-concept shows in your personality. If you have a good self-concept, you have many advantages. You feel confident. You will try new things. You will learn more. You will show a pleasant personality. You are more apt to succeed at school and on the job.

This action is like a never-ending circle.

You want to have a good self-concept. But it must be a *true* self-concept. Know what you can do. Do not be afraid to try new things. But know your weaknesses, too. Do not set your career goals based on a false image of yourself.

If you see yourself as a great baseball player, you may decide on a career with the Dodgers. If you really do have the talent, this is a good goal. But if you do not, your false self-concept may cause you some trouble. Your unrealistic goal can, indeed, cause you a lot of unhappiness.

Compare your self-concept with how others see you. This will give you a clearer picture of yourself. You can make good career choices if you know who you really are.

Check Up:✓✓ True or False?

1. Other people's opinions of you help you form your own self-concept.
2. Having a good self-concept may help you succeed in your career.
3. Having a true self-concept may help you pick a suitable career.

Handicaps

You can see that the work people do becomes their center of activity. Work is often the key to happiness. You will work most of your adult life. So you will want to choose your career with care. You will want a career that you will enjoy. You will want a career that you will be proud of.

No one can do every kind of work. But every person can do some kinds of work. Some things you can do well. Other things you cannot do well. That is because we are all handicapped in some way.

Kinds of Handicaps

There are four different types of handicaps.

1. Learning handicaps
2. Physical handicaps
3. Health handicaps
4. Social Handicaps

Learning Handicaps. Some people have learning handicaps. Those with learning handicaps may find it hard to do such things as

- understand directions or ideas.
- read.
- write.
- do math.
- make decisions.

Physical Handicaps. Some people are born with physical handicaps. Others are physically handicapped because of illness or injury. Physical handicaps make it hard to do such things as

- walk or run.
- lift heavy things.
- drive a car.
- throw a ball.

Health Handicaps. Some health handicaps can be seen by others. Many do not show. Many people who do not appear to be handicapped have health handicaps. For example, workers might have heart disease or diabetes. They should, of course, get medical help. They should take their medicine regularly. If they have limitations on the job, their boss and co-workers should know about them.

Social Handicaps. Social handicaps make it hard to get along with people. Most social handicaps are due to such things as

- having a poor attitude.
- being easily embarrassed.
- lacking self-confidence.
- not being able to carry on a conversation.
- being afraid to try things.
- not controlling anger.

Overcoming Handicaps

Some handicaps are small. They may not affect your work at all. Suppose you cannot throw a ball straight. This would not matter unless you wanted to be a ball player or a gym teacher. You could choose any career that does not involve throwing a ball.

Some handicaps are great. Many cannot be cured. But all of them can be overcome. How do you overcome a handicap? You simply find a way to do what you want in spite of your handicap. It may mean learning new ways of doing things. Blind people learn to read Braille. People without legs learn to walk with artificial legs.

Great people have overcome handicaps. Franklin Roosevelt's legs were paralyzed from polio. But he walked using leg braces. He was the only President of the United States to be elected four times.

Winston Churchill stuttered. But he overcame it. He became a great speaker and the Prime Minister of England. All through this book you will read about people who have "The Desire to Succeed." These people have overcome handicaps.

Franklin D. Roosevelt and Winston Churchill overcame great physical handicaps to become famous statesmen.

A Desire to Succeed

Living in Dark Silence: Helen Keller.

Everyone has some kind of handicap. Helen Keller was handicapped more than most people. She was blind, deaf, and mute after an illness when she was nineteen months old. She could not see, hear, or speak. But she was playful and active.

When Helen was six, Anne Sullivan came to be her teacher. Anne was partly blind herself and she understood Helen's handicaps. Anne was not able to teach Helen to see or hear. But Anne did help Helen learn to read and write. Then she learned to speak!

She learned to read using Braille, raised letters, and finger language. The finger language helped her learn to write. Helen had a great desire to learn.

Helen begged her teacher to help her as she practiced day and night. She was thrilled when she found out everything had a name. She felt this was the key to her learning to read and write. She wanted to know everything's name.

Helen learned to speak by placing her hand on Anne's lips. She felt the movement when Anne talked. She also put her hand on Anne's throat to feel the vibrations. It took thousands of hours of practice. Helen wanted so much to be understood by her friends.

When Helen was a teenager, she learned to read, write, and speak French, Latin, and German. She also learned geometry and algebra.

Helen enjoyed reading. She also enjoyed outdoor sports. She learned to row a boat and to swim. She canoed. She rode horses. Her favorite sport was sailing.

Helen graduated from Radcliffe College with honors. She wrote her first book, *The Story of My Life*, when she was in her second year of college. She traveled in every state in the United States and all over the world. She gave speeches and helped others who were handicapped.

Handicaps did not keep Helen Keller from learning and doing things. She succeeded in spite of them.

Preparing for the Future

You have learned about some things that will help you to understand yourself. You have thought about these things.

- *Your dreams.* Do you often daydream about your future lifestyle?
- Your values. Do you know what things are the most important to you?
- *Your interests.* Do you know which of your interests might lead to a job for you?
- *Your talents.* Do you know what your talents are?
- *Your personality.* Do you know how your personality will affect your choice of job?
- *Your self-concept.* Do you see yourself as others do? Do you feel good about yourself?
- *Your handicaps.* Do you know your limitations? Do you know how you will overcome your handicaps?

Did you answer "yes" to most of these questions? If so, you now have a better understanding of yourself. It should be easier for you to set career goals.

Understanding yourself helps you know what kind of work interests you. It should also help you know what you are able to do. As you prepare for the future, you need to know these things.

Make sure you understand yourself before you make a career decision.

The words

Listed below are the important new words that were used in this chapter. Next to each word is the page on which you will find the word in bold, black print. Turn back and read again the paragraph in which you find each word. Then write the word and its meaning on a sheet of paper. Also write a sentence of your own using each word.

1. aptitude (37)
2. career goals (26)
3. experiences (30)
4. interests (30)
5. personality (38)
6. self-concept (41)
7. talent (34)
8. values (27)
9. volunteer work (30)

The facts

1. What three things are important to understand about yourself before choosing a career?
2. What are six ways your career can affect your lifestyle?
3. How can you discover your interests?
4. Name three types of talents.
5. How does your personality affect your career choice?
6. Explain how others get an impression of you.
7. Name at least four types of handicaps.
8. Explain how your leisure activities can affect your career choice. How can your career affect your leisure activities?
9. What is an interest test? an aptitude test?
10. What does it mean to have a realistic self-concept?

What's right here?

REVIEW

ADD TO YOUR KNOWLEDGE AND SKILLS

Talk about your ideas

1. Do you know your talents? What do you think is your best talent for work? Why?

2. List five words that describe your personality.

3. How do you feel about yourself? Do you think others can tell how you feel about yourself?

Do some activities

1. Make a list of your interests. Include school, work, and leisure activities. Then write a 1 by the interest you like best. Write a 2 by your second choice. Write a 3 by your third choice. Make a folder of career information. Put your interest list in it. Later add other information that you gather.

2. Copy the list of values from page 28. Then show your list to three adults. Ask which are the four most important values to them. Then mark the four *you* think are most important. Save your list for class discussion.

Improve your basic skills

1. Find and read a magazine article on values. If you don't know how to find magazine articles, ask your teacher or librarian to help you. Take notes on the article and save them.

2. Think of a hobby or leisure activity that you enjoy. Look through old newspapers and magazines. Find an article about that hobby or activity. Read it. Tell the class something interesting that you learned.

1. Write a summary of the article on values that you read. Also write why you do or do not agree with it.

2. Write a half page telling about your personality. Tell how your personality will affect your job choice.

3. Write a paragraph telling about your strong points and your handicaps. Say how your strong points could help you on a job. Tell how you can try to overcome your handicaps.

5×7=?

1. Ann wants to buy a sweater that costs $50. She saves $12 a week. Will she save enough to buy the dress in 4 weeks? In 5 weeks?

2. Carlos has been reading ads for cars. The type of car he wants costs $5,000. Carlos earns $1000 a month. He thinks he can save half of what he earns. How long will it take Carlos to save enough to buy the car?

Chapter 3

Exploring Careers

What's wrong here?

Words to learn and use

You will learn several new words in this chapter. The most important words are listed below. Do you know the meanings of these words?

apprentice
technician
seasonal
mechanical
industrial
inspectors
accommodating
humanitarian
influencing

Build on what you know

You already know. . .

- your career will be a big part of your life.
- you must plan for your career and your lifestyle.
- you should consider your interests, values, talents, and personality when you plan your career.

In this chapter you will learn. . .

- the first step in choosing a career is to know what jobs people do.
- all jobs can be grouped into twelve interest areas.
- to explore careers by limiting your choices to one or two interest areas.
- how to pick several jobs to explore.

In Chapter 2 you began to understand yourself a little better. You also know by now that work will be a big part of your life.

In this chapter you will learn that there are many jobs to choose from. You will pick a work area that seems interesting to you. Then you will read about the small groups of jobs within that area. Last, you will choose several jobs to explore in detail.

Looking Around at Jobs

Can you imagine trying to order food in a strange restaurant without a menu? You would not know what foods were served there. You would not know where to begin.

The same is true for job hunting. You cannot choose a job without knowing what jobs there are. So your first step is to know what types of jobs there are.

You can learn something about the many types of jobs by keeping your eyes and ears open. Watch what people in TV shows and movies do for a living. Notice what the work is like. Listen to radio reports about different jobs that people do in your area.

Books and magazines often tell about jobs. They may tell stories about people in certain jobs. You can learn a great deal by reading these stories.

You can also talk with people. Start with your parents. Ask them what tasks they do in their jobs. Find out what they like about their jobs. Find out what they do not like.

Talk with your friends, their parents, your parents' friends, and your neighbors. Talk to anyone you can think of.

Today people work at twenty thousand types of jobs. It would be pretty hard to learn about that many jobs. Luckily, you do not have to learn about them all. You can choose a career by narrowing (limiting) your choices. Then you can find out more about the jobs that interest you most.

Narrowing your choices is like shopping for a new shirt. There may be a dozen clothing stores in your town. First, you narrow your choices by shopping in one or two stores. You pick stores that have clothes you usually like. You pick ones that charge prices you are willing to pay.

Then you look at all the shirts for sale. You narrow your choices again by pulling some shirts off the rack. You take a closer look at these. Then you pick three or four that you want to try on. You choose one or two that look good to you. Finally, you choose one you can afford, and you buy it.

Deciding on a career works much the same way. Experts have put all jobs into twelve areas. These areas match the interests of workers. Each area is called an *interest area*. Read about each of the twelve interest areas on the next few pages. Then choose one or two interest areas that you might like. Right away you will have narrowed your choice of careers.

Artistic

There are many jobs in the artistic area. Some workers in this area use their hands to make things. Some show their feelings and ideas to other people. They use their bodies, faces, and voices to do this. To work in the artistic area, you must be able to express yourself. Writers must be able to put their thoughts into words and sentences. They must get details right.

Painters and sculptors must understand colors, designs, shapes, lines, and balance. So must map makers, jewelry makers, photographers, and make-up artists.

Performers work in front of others. They are picked for their jobs by the way they can express themselves. They are also chosen by the way they look.

Some artistic jobs are helping jobs. Photographers take photos. Their helpers may help them set up the scene. Some artists draw pictures. Their helpers may add lettering.

How Would You Learn It?

For many artistic careers, school is important. College may be needed. Helpers need less training. A few courses may be enough. Many just learn on the job. Skill is very important for artistic workers. Dancers and models must be graceful. Comics must have a sense of humor. Artists must be able to use brushes, pencils, or clay well.

Is the Work for You?

1. Do you draw well?
2. Do you take good pictures?
3. Do you like to design things?
4. Do you like to go to art shows?
5. Do you like to write? Have you ever worked on your school newspaper or yearbook?
6. Have you ever performed in front of others?

Scientific

Coal miners, oil field workers, and rock collectors are scientific workers. So are helpers for doctors and engineers. All scientific workers must follow detailed directions. They may work indoors or outdoors. And some work in laboratories.

Scientific workers solve problems and find better ways of doing things. For example, scientific workers may study lake water to find out why fish are dying.

Some scientific workers are called technicians. **Technicians** often work with tools such as microscopes or test tubes. They must be good at detail work. They look for small differences in size, shape, or color. Then they write a record of what they see. Often they work many hours to learn what they want to know. They may do the same thing again and again.

Many scientific workers work out-of-doors. They may watch and report changes in the weather, moon, or stars. They may work with the earth or water.

How Would You Learn It?

To be a scientist, you need to be good with your eyes, hands, and fingers. Most scientific workers go to a special school. Many work as helpers. Often the training for helpers is on-the-job. Helpers must follow the directions of someone who has trained for many years. Math and science courses in high school are helpful.

Is the Work for You?

1. Do you like to follow directions?
2. Do you like scientific or medical TV shows?
3. Have you ever done a science project? Did you enjoy it?
4. Have you ever used a microscope?
5. Have you ever used test tubes for an experiment?
6. Do you like to take notes? Can you read charts and graphs?

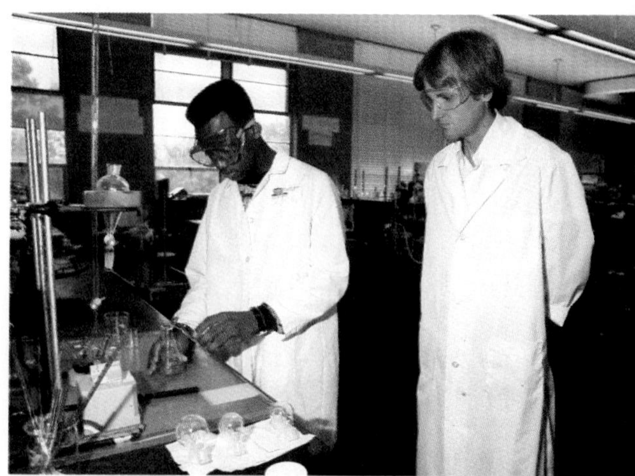

Plants and Animals

Workers in this area care for plants and animals. These workers need to be strong and healthy. They often do heavy work. They usually work outdoors and may work even in bad weather.

Sometimes this work is seasonal. **Seasonal** means only at certain times of the year. For example, few crops are grown in the winter. So more farm workers are needed in the spring, summer, and fall than in the winter.

Animal workers feed and groom animals. They check their health. Some train dogs or horses. This takes patience. Some people work in stables or circuses. Others may work on farms or in laboratories.

People care for plants, too. Farmers raise crops. Some workers plant trees in forests. Others cut down trees for lumber. Gardeners care for parks and gardens.

Plant workers use tools such as shovels and hoes. They may run lawn mowers or tractors. Workers do the same thing for many hours. They may work long hours during good weather.

How Would You Learn It?

Plant and animal workers often learn on the job. They may take courses. But for many jobs they do not have to.

Is the Work for You?

1. Do you like plants or animals?
2. Have you been a member of FFA or 4-H?
3. Have you mowed lawns? Would you enjoy work like this all day?
4. Do you like to go camping?
5. Are you physically fit?
6. Do you like hard work outdoors?

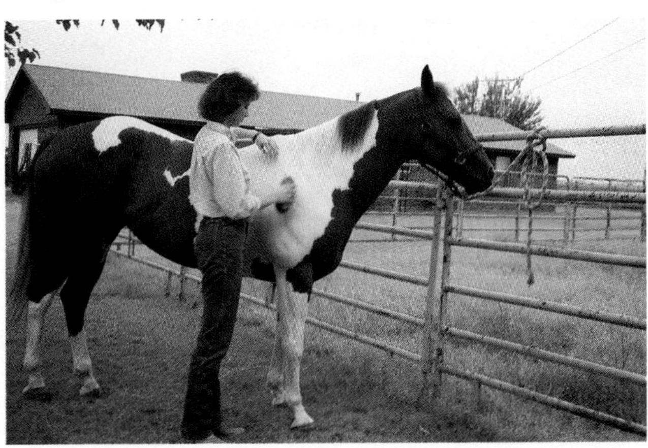

Protective

Workers in this group are police officers, fire fighters, and guards. They protect people and property. They put out fires. They help people in need. They see that people obey the laws. They catch and arrest people who break the law.

People who work in protective jobs must be able to think quickly. They must know how to talk with people easily. They must be strong to handle heavy equipment. They must be willing to work indoors and outdoors and in dangerous situations. They may work at night or on weekends.

They need many different types of skills. Some must be able to handle a gun. Others give first aid. Almost all must be able to drive cars and trucks. They must understand all the laws.

How Would You Learn It?

Most protective workers need to finish high school. Additional courses and training are helpful.

Protective workers often go through training. They usually have to pass tests before they are hired. Some tests are written or spoken. Some are physical tests. Most protective workers have to be a certain height and weight.

Is the Work for You?

1. Do you like to help people?
2. Are you able to stay calm in an emergency?
3. Have you ever given first aid? Did you do it well?
4. Were you on a school safety patrol? Did you like it?
5. Are you physically fit?
6. Can you decide quickly? Are your quick decisions usually good?

Mechanical

Mechanical workers use tools and machines. They work with their hands. Some of them work outside. Some work indoors. They make or fix things. They run machines or trucks. Some workers need much training and skill. Others do not. There are many, many types of mechanical jobs.

Some workers run machines. They might operate a boiler. These workers read dials. The dials may show too much steam in the boiler. If so, the workers adjust the steam.

Mechanical workers use all sorts of materials. Some use wood. Some use metal. Some use plastic. They learn about the material. They learn how to cut it. They learn how to smooth it. They learn which machines to use on it.

Mechanical workers do many other things. Some drive trucks or lay bricks. Some keep records. Most use arithmetic. Some lift and carry things. Some keep places clean.

How Would You Learn It?

You could learn to be a mechanical worker by taking courses. You could also become an apprentice. **Apprentices** learn by working with a skilled worker. They get paid while they work. Also, they take classes to learn certain skills. It takes a few years to develop good mechanical skills.

Is the Work for You?

1. Do you like machines?
2. Do you like to use hand tools?
3. Have you taken a shop course? Did you like it?
4. Do you fix things at home?
5. Can you do hard work?
6. Have you ever worked on a car?
7. Can you do arithmetic?

Industrial

Many industrial jobs are like mechanical jobs. There is one main difference. **Industrial** jobs are jobs done in factories. Factories make things. Each factory makes just a few kinds of things. But it makes many of them. The workers do the same task over and over.

Industrial workers use their hands. They use tools. They work with machines. They must follow instructions. Some instructions are written or drawn. Some are spoken. The workers follow instructions exactly.

There are thousands of different jobs. Some workers set up machines. Others use the machines. Some put things together. They might put together big things, such as furniture. Or they might make small things, such as radios. Someone needs to check what they make. Some workers just do the checking. They are called **inspectors.**

Some workers get paid for each hour they work. Some get paid for each thing they make. Some work in the day. Others work at night.

How Would You Learn It?

Many of these jobs take little training. You can learn them on the job. Shop courses are useful. So is arithmetic.

Is the Work for You?

1. Have you ever visited a factory? Did you like it?
2. Do you like machines?
3. Have you ever put something together (such as a bicycle)?
4. Can you catch mistakes?
5. Do you like to do the same thing over and over?
6. Do you like to work with other people?

Business Detail

All companies have some office work that needs to be done. Office work includes answering the phone and keeping records. It may include handling money, sending out bills, or making reports.

An office worker in a small business may do many of these detail tasks. A worker in a large office may do only one or two. Some type or put records in files. Some copy records. Others use adding machines and calculators.

Detail workers need to get along because they depend on each other to get the job done. Some detail workers talk on the phone or in person. Some workers take money and make change.

Detail workers must work fast. But they should always be careful not to make mistakes. Sometimes they work with records that are secret. They must not talk about these records.

How Would You Learn It?

Some detail workers just learn on the job. Many take business courses. The courses are given in high schools, business schools, and vocational schools. Some important courses to take are English, math, typing, and record keeping.

Is the Work for You?

1. Have you ever written a letter to a business?
2. Have you ever balanced a checkbook?
3. Can you spot mistakes in words?
4. Do you like to work with forms?
5. Do you know how to find books in a library?
6. Have you ever kept records?

Selling

Selling is helping people decide to buy. It is not forcing them to buy. Most people buy only if they really want to. Salespeople tell what is good about what they sell. What they say often makes people decide to buy. Would you like to do this? If so, you might like selling.

Salespeople work in different places. Some work in stores. They study their products. Then they can talk about them easily. They can answer customers' questions. They show people the products. Sometimes they explain how to use the products. They also take money and make change.

Other salespeople go where customers live or work. They tell about the products they sell. They must like to talk with people.

Some salespeople work at fairs. They work at carts or stands. Some sell food. Others sell toys or hats. Some call to the customers.

All salespeople keep records. They write the date, item, and price of every sale. Sometimes they get paid just for what they sell. This makes them work hard to sell a lot.

How Would You Learn It?

Most salespeople learn on the job. Other workers teach them. A few jobs require college. Many require high school. It helps to have selling experience when you apply for a sales job. A high school distributive education course is one way to learn and get experience.

Is the Work for You?

1. Have you ever sold anything to make money? Did you like doing that?
2. Have you collected money for a charity? Did you keep records?
3. Do you talk with people easily? Could you make them want to buy?
4. Would you like to work in a store?

Accommodating

Accommodating means serving other people. Some workers help people on planes, trains, or buses. Others tell people where to find items in large stores. Guides show visitors through parks or factories. City bus drivers take riders where they want to go. There are many types of jobs in this area.

To do a good job, these workers must be friendly and helpful. They must listen well. They must talk to people and try to answer their questions. They must always be polite.

Some workers travel on the job. They may work indoors or outdoors. Many work at night and on holidays. Some are required to wear uniforms. Many workers in this area are self-employed.

How Would You Learn It?

Some workers learn on the job. People who know the work teach new workers. For other jobs, workers must go to special schools. Then they must pass tests. The length and type of training depends on the job.

Training in speaking clearly is offered in many high schools. Almost every worker in this area needs good speaking ability.

Is the Work for You?

1. Do you like to help others?
2. Do you make friends easily?
3. Do you like to talk?
4. Have you waited on people in a restaurant? Would you like to?
5. Do you follow directions well?
6. Can you give clear directions?

Humanitarian

Humanitarian workers take care of people. Some of the people they take care of have problems. They may be sick or unhappy. Some need special care. Other people may just need someone with them. They may be very young or very old. The workers help them do things they cannot do alone.

Some workers are nurse aides or orderlies. They assist nurses and doctors. They make beds and take temperatures. They help people bathe or eat. They lift people who cannot walk. Workers must stay calm and be kind and helpful. They must work fast in an emergency.

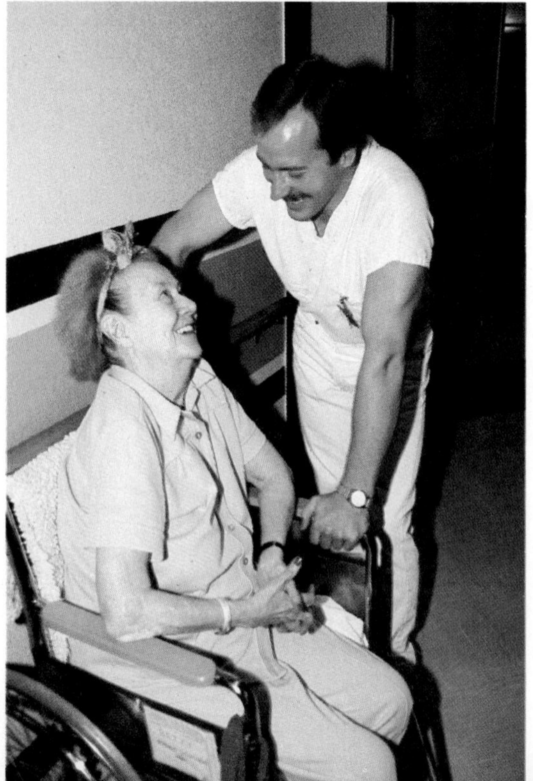

Some workers help people at home. The people may be old or sick. Workers help them cook or clean or exercise.

Other workers look after children. They may work in a day-care center. They watch the children. They try to keep them happy and safe.

The jobs may be during the day or at night. They may take hard work. Many workers enjoy humanitarian jobs because they feel good about helping people.

How Would You Learn It?

Many of the humanitarian jobs require high school. Some require a special license. Training may be in a hospital or school. It may take a year.

Is the Work for You?

1. Have you ever cared for a sick person? Would you want to again?
2. Can you stay calm when others are not?
3. Have you ever done work for a charity?
4. Would you like being around sick or helpless people?
5. Do you like old people? Do you like children?

Leading-Influencing

Influencing means making people want to do certain things. The leading-influencing group includes many different types of workers. Some workers deal with numbers to solve problems. Some teach. Some help businesses or agencies run smoothly. Others get lots of different types of information to people. Still others enforce laws.

There are many of these jobs in libraries. Some workers check out books, tapes, and films. Others check in and look for damage to these materials. Still others enforce library rules.

Government workers watch our country's borders. They make sure people entering the country have the right to do so. They also examine packages brought into this country. They report to police if rules are not obeyed.

There are many kinds of jobs for inspectors. Some make sure safety rules are obeyed. Others check on rules for care of animals. Workers who make sure that rules are obeyed help everyone.

How Would You Learn It?

Workers may learn on the job. Or they may get some training. Before being hired, they must show that they have good speaking and writing skills. Some need to have math and computer skills.

Is the Work for You?

1. Have you ever worked in a library? Did you like it?
2. Do you like to keep things in order?
3. Can you check people or things carefully?
4. Can you tell people about new things? Are you friendly?
5. Have you ever taught someone to do a new task?
6. Have you ever kept financial records?

Physical Performing

Physical performers do tricks or play sports games in front of audiences. They may work in sports arenas, stadiums, circuses, or gyms. This group includes baseball, soccer, and football players. It also includes jugglers, acrobats, and animal tamers. Many helpers are needed for these workers, too.

Physical performers do feats alone or with others. Some walk on high wires or lift very heavy things. Others play on a sports team. All performers must practice many hours every day to develop skills. They obey training rules and directions from their coaches.

Most performers travel. They entertain people in many places.

Helpers may take care of equipment. Some keep time and score records. Sometimes helpers take care of animals that do tricks or run races.

Some people teach sports. Others judge in sports events. They decide who are the best performers or teams.

How Would You Learn It?

Performers often learn as members of school teams. Coaches show them how to improve. Sometimes they learn by watching other performers. Practice is most important. Helpers need to know rules. They need to know how to take care of equipment.

Is the Work for You?

1. Do you often win at sports?
2. Can you remember rules of games?
3. Can you use a stopwatch?
4. Do you like to perform?
5. Do you like to travel?

Narrowing Your Choices

You now have a general idea of the twelve interest areas. Was it easy to drop some of them from your list of possible careers? Do one or two seem especially interesting to you? Which ones interest you? Write down their names on a sheet of paper.

On the following pages the interest areas are listed again. This time each interest area is broken down into small groups. Find the one or two areas that you chose. Read about the small groups within the area or areas you picked. You do not have to read all the others.

Now pick three or four of these small groups that seem most interesting. Write their names.

Look at the sample jobs in each of the small groups that you chose. Which ones might you like? Do you know of other jobs in these groups?

Choose three or four jobs. Write these job titles. In the next chapter, you will learn how to find out more about these jobs.

Once you narrow your career choices to just a few careers, you can learn more about these jobs. Then you will have enough information to make your career choice.

Artistic Interest Area

Visual Arts. Workers create original works of art. Some prepare commercial art. They may use techniques such as drawing, painting, and photography. Many workers are self-employed.

SAMPLE JOBS
• Photographer • Floral Designer • Screen Process Printer • Merchandise Displayer • Quick Sketch Artist

Performing Arts: Drama. Workers produce, direct, and perform in plays and shows. They also teach others to act and perform. Most are employed in motion pictures, television, and radio. Only those who are very good find work. There is much competition for jobs.

SAMPLE JOBS • Actor
• Announcer • Clown
• Disk Jockey • Magician
• Puppeteer

Performing Arts: Music. Workers sing songs or play instruments. Some arrange music. Others direct musicians. They work wherever music is recorded and musical entertainment provided. Many musicians are self-employed.

SAMPLE JOBS • Singer
• Accompanist
• Instrumental Musician
• Promptor

Performing Arts: Dance. Workers compose, perform, or teach dance routines and techniques. They are employed in nightclubs, theatres, and other places that provide entertainment. Most dancers must audition (try out) for jobs.

SAMPLE JOBS • Dancer
• Dance Instructor
• Choreographer

Craft Arts. Workers use tools and equipment to make things. They make them from stone, clay, metal, or gems. They work in many different kinds of businesses. Some are self-employed.

SAMPLE JOBS
• Sign Painter • Restorer
• Jewelry Maker • Airbrush Painter • Engraver • Gift Wrapper • Picture Framer

Amusement. Workers entertain people at carnivals, amusement parks, and fairs. They work with traveling carnivals or circuses. They also work at amusement parks. Some are self-employed. Job openings are limited. Highly specialized skills are needed.

SAMPLE JOBS
• Ringmaster
• Impersonator • Coach Driver • Weight Guesser

Modeling. Workers stand or walk in front of an audience or camera. They show clothes, jewelry, and hair styles. They often work for manufacturers and some retail businesses. Many are self-employed and get jobs through agencies. Most jobs are in large cities. Personal appearance is very important.

SAMPLE JOBS • Artist's Model • Fashion Model • Extra • Stand-In

Scientific Interest Area

Physical Sciences. Workers research some part of the earth. They also study the stars to learn about outer space. These are physical things, too. They try to find new ways to make materials and do things. They deal mostly with non-living things. Most jobs are in government agencies and large universities.

SAMPLE JOBS • Scientific Helper • Weather Observer • Lab Assistant • Water-Filter Cleaner

In the physical sciences, you would work with nonliving things, such as rocks, oil, or water. This worker is a lab assistant.

Life Sciences. Workers study and experiment to learn more about plants and animals. Most are employed in hospitals, government agencies, and universities.

SAMPLE JOBS • Animal Breeder • Fire Lookout • Biological Aide • Chick Grader • Feed Research Aide • Seed Cone Picker

Would you like to work with people, animals, or machines? Would you rather work indoors or outdoors?

Laboratory Technology. Workers perform tests in chemistry, biology, and physics. They keep records of their findings. Most work in such places as hospital and government agency labs.

SAMPLE JOBS
• Fingerprint Classifier
• Morgue Attendant • Yeast Culture Developer • Laboratory Assistant (Medical Services)

Plants and Animals Interest Area

Animal Training and Care. Workers feed, groom, and exercise animals. They train the animals to do many things. Workers are employed in such places as zoos, aquariums, and kennels.

SAMPLE JOBS • Horse Trainer • Dog Groomer
• Pet Store Worker
• Animal-Ride Attendant

General Work. Workers do active, heavy work. They usually work outdoors. They work on farms and fishing boats. They also work in forests, parks, and nurseries.

SAMPLE JOBS • Farm Worker • Groundskeeper
• Tree Trimmer
• Fish Hatchery Worker

Protective Interest Area

Safety and Law Enforcement. Workers watch out for people's safety. They make sure that people obey the laws. Most jobs are with government agencies, such as police and fire departments.

SAMPLE JOBS • Fire Fighters • School Bus Monitor • Fish and Game Warden • Deputy Sheriff

Security Services. Workers watch to see that people and property are safe. They guard against crimes, accidents, and other hazards. Many are hired by hotels, factories, and railroads. Others work on their own.

SAMPLE JOBS
- Bodyguard • Fire Ranger
- Airline Security Guard
- Jailer • Lifeguard

Mechanical Interest Area

Engineering Technology. Workers collect, record, and coordinate information. They do the technical detail work for engineers. Some work for manufacturing and construction companies.

SAMPLE JOBS
- Automobile-Lab Technician
- Drafter Assistant
- Surveyor's Helper
- Grade Checker

Craft Technology. Workers do highly skilled work with their hands and machines. Special techniques and experience is required. Most work is in manufacturing settings. Some own their own shops.

SAMPLE JOBS • Tool Grinder • Sign Erector • Musical Instrument Repairer • Cake Decorator • Bricklayer • Shoe Repairer • Welder

Land and Water Vehicle Operation. Workers drive vehicles to deliver and move products. They drive trucks, vans, locomotives, ambulances, and small boats. They work for many different kinds of companies.

SAMPLE JOBS • Tow-Truck Operator • Delivery Truck Driver • Tractor-Trailer Driver

Materials Control. Workers ship, receive, and store materials and products. They work in such places as factories, government agencies, and hospitals.

SAMPLE JOBS • Meter Reader • Stock Clerk • Checker

Crafts. Workers assemble, install, and repair products. They use their hands and hand tools. They work in such places as repair shops, garages, and hotels. The work is often learned on the job.

SAMPLE JOBS • Cook • Dry Wall Installer • Carpet Layer • Brake Repairer

General Work. Workers lift and carry materials, tools, and equipment. They also clean work areas and help skilled workers. They work in many different places.

SAMPLE JOBS • Janitor • Housekeeper • Jack Hammer Operator • Grip

Many workers in both the Mechanical and the Production areas do highly skilled work with their hands. These jobs require much training and experience.

Industrial Interest Area

Production Work. Workers do hand and machine work. This work requires special skills and training. Most work is found in factories. Many, many products are made by workers in this group. They probably would make one part of a product. Other workers would make other parts. Then workers would put them together.

SAMPLE JOBS • Drill Press Operator • Weaver • Butcher • Glass Cutter • Furnace Operator • Planer Operator

Quality Control. Workers inspect, test, weigh, and sort products and materials. Products are checked before they are sold. This work is done in factories. Workers match sizes, color, or shapes. To do this you would use your eyes, hands, and fingers with skill.

SAMPLE JOBS • Inspector • Grader • Lumber Sorter • Weigher • Color Matcher • Egg Candler

Do you like to do the same task over and over? If so, there are many jobs in the industrial area that you might enjoy.

General Work. Workers load and unload machines. They use simple hand tools. They perform routine tasks that require little training. They work in factory settings.

SAMPLE JOBS • Packager • Riveter • Feed Mixer • Assembler • Folding-Machine Operator • Brush Operator

Business Detail Interest Area

Oral Communications. Workers talk with people to give and receive information. They talk in person, by telephone, or by radio. They work in many different settings.

SAMPLE JOBS • Directory Assistance Operator • Service Clerk • Classified Ad Clerk • Police Aide

Records Keeping. Workers gather information, review data, and keep records. Almost all businesses, institutions, and governments need these workers.

SAMPLE JOBS • Mail Carrier • Bank Messenger • Coding Clerk

Business Routine. Workers file, sort, copy, or deliver information. Most large businesses and government agencies employ these workers. Little special training or skill is required.

SAMPLE JOBS • Coin Machine Collector • Copy Messenger • Teacher Aide • Page

It takes patience to make customers happy.

Selling Interest Area

General Sales. Workers sell many kinds of products or services. They also demonstrate and take orders for products and services. They work for many different kinds of companies. Many jobs require traveling.

SAMPLE JOBS • Sales Route Driver • Travel Agent • Auctioneer • Fund Raiser

Vending. Workers sell novelties and small items. They sell them wherever crowds gather. Many move from place to place to sell their items.

SAMPLE JOBS • Ice Cream Vendor • News Agent • Sports Event Vendor

Accommodating Interest Area

Hospitality Services. Workers plan and direct social events. They help people feel at home in new surroundings. They work for transportation companies, hotels, restaurants, museums, and retirement homes.

SAMPLE JOBS • Airline Flight Attendant • Butler • Host/Hostess • Tour Guide

Barber and Beauty Services. Workers provide many different barbering and beauty services. They take care of the hair, skin, and nails. They give haircuts, facial massages, and manicures. Many are self-employed.

SAMPLE JOBS • Barber • Cosmetologist

Passenger Services. Workers take people from one place to another. They do this in buses, taxis, limousines, and other vehicles. Taxi, bus, and railway companies hire most of these workers.

SAMPLE JOBS • Bus Driver • Taxi Driver

Customer Services. Workers provide customers with a variety of services. They deliver food and beverages, park cars, take orders, and much more. Many work in hotels, restaurants, and resorts.

SAMPLE JOBS • Waiter/Waitress • Parking Lot Attendant • Rental Clerk

Attendant Services. Workers make life easier and more comfortable for people. They do things such as open doors, deliver messages, and carry luggage. They work in such places as hotels, airports, and golf courses.

SAMPLE JOBS • Porter • Doorkeeper • Caddie • Usher

A "helper" is a word that best describes an accommodating worker.

Humanitarian Interest Area

Nursing and Therapy Services. Workers take care of people who are ill, injured, or handicapped. They work in hospitals, clinics, nursing homes, and rehabilitation centers.

SAMPLE JOBS • Nursing Aide • Ambulance Attendant • First Aide Attendant

Child and Adult Care. Workers tend to the physical needs and welfare of others. Workers help professionals treat the sick and injured. They work in schools, nurseries, and private homes.

SAMPLE JOBS • Child Monitor • Orderly • Companion • School Crossing Guard

Rules Enforcement. Workers enforce rules. These rules affect people's rights, health, safety, and finances. Most workers are employed by government agencies and health departments.

SAMPLE JOBS • Broadcast Checker • Sanitarian • Immigration Guard

Leading-Influencing Interest Area

Educational and Library Services. Workers teach, train, and advise others. They also do various kinds of library work. They give out books, tapes, records, or films. They are employed by schools, colleges, and libraries.

SAMPLE JOBS • Teacher Aide • Film Librarian • Library Assistant • Film Rental Clerk

Would you like a job that involves helping people with their problems or handicaps?

Physical Performing

Sports. Workers compete in athletic or sporting events. They also coach players and officiate games. Workers are employed by professional sports teams, ski resorts, and gyms.

SAMPLE JOBS • Car Racer • Professional Athlete • Scorer • Clocker • Dude Wrangler

Physical Feats. Workers perform unusual or daring acts to entertain people. These acts require physical strength or skill. They are employed by circuses, carnivals, and amusement parks.

SAMPLE JOBS • Juggler • Acrobat • Stunt Performer

A Desire to Succeed

Beating the Odds: Crawford Hall

Crawford Hall learned to ride a horse about the time he learned to walk.

After high school, Crawford studied business in college. But his first love was horses. So he took a job on a quarter horse ranch. Soon he was riding on the training track.

One morning in April, 1974, Crawford's life was changed. He was suddenly thrown from a running horse. He landed on the back of his head. He was paralyzed.

Doctors said he might live another five to ten years. There was no chance he could ever walk again. They said an operation might give him some use of his arms. After the operation, Crawford spent the next six months in the hospital.

Crawford had physical therapy every day. He began to move his arms. He gained strength.

One day a friend, Monty Roberts, visited him. Monty was building a horse farm. Crawford asked him if there was any hope he could ever train horses. Could he supervise the training from a wheelchair? Monty said yes.

Crawford had physical therapy for another nine months. In May, 1975, Monty called and asked him to visit his new horse farm. Monty wanted him to take over the training of all the race horses.

Crawford wanted to accept this new challenge. So three months later he returned as trainer.

For the past twelve years, Crawford has supervised the training at Flag Is Up Farm. He has had as many as 135 horses in his barns at one time. Most are thoroughbreds.

The most famous horse Crawford trained was Alleged. Alleged won the most important race in France twice. Another horse, Fighting Fit, won more than a million dollars.

Crawford Hall has overcome the handicap of being in a wheelchair because he is determined to succeed. He says, "We should not worry about the things we cannot do. Think about the things we can do when we try."

REVIEW

REMEMBER WHAT YOU LEARNED

The words

Listed below are the important new words that were used in this chapter. Next to each word is the page on which you will find the word in bold, black print. Turn back and read again the paragraph in which you find each word. Then write the word and its meaning on a sheet of paper. Also write a sentence of your own using each word.

1. accommodating (59)
2. apprentice (55)
3. humanitarian (60)
4. industrial (56)
5. influencing (61)
6. inspectors (56)
7. mechanical (55)
8. seasonal (53)
9. technician (52)

The facts

1. How can you find out what jobs people do?
2. What is a career interest area? How many are there?
3. Name two career interest areas. Describe the work in each.
4. How does grouping jobs into career interest areas help you choose a career?
5. Describe the kinds of jobs in the career area that appeal to you.
6. Name some skills that are important in many of the interest areas.
7. Name some skills that are especially important in the area you chose.
8. Tell how to narrow your career choices from all the jobs in the world to just a few.

What's right here?

ADD TO YOUR KNOWLEDGE AND SKILLS

Talk about your ideas

1. How do your interests, talents, values, and personality affect the final job choices you made in this chapter?

2. Does your first job choice fit in with the kind of lifestyle you want? Why, or why not?

3. Tell what you know about your first job choice. Do you know anyone who does this kind of work?

Do some activities

1. Talk with two adults about their occupations. Find out their job titles and the duties of their jobs. In which interest area is each job? In which small group is each job? Report to the class.

2. Time yourself for two minutes. Writing as fast as you can, write as many job titles as you can. How many could you list?

Improve Your Basic Skills

1. Read a book or magazine article that tells about a person's career.

2. Find a newspaper or magazine article that tells about an unusual job. Read it. Tell the class about the job.

1. In this chapter, find three new words that are not vocabulary words. Write them on a piece of paper. Find them in a dictionary. Write their meanings.

2. Select one of the three or four job choices you made in this chapter. Write a paragraph or two telling what you would do on this job.

1. Suppose there are 2,563 businesses listed in your local phone book. On the average, each business employs five people. How many jobs are available in your area?

2. You are comparing careers. You are interested in three different careers. How much would you earn a year in careers one and two?

- **Career One**--You will earn $6.25 per hour. You will work about 2,000 hours per year.
- **Career Two**--You will earn $300 per week. You will work 50 weeks per year. You will also be paid for two weeks of vacation.
- **Career Three**--You will earn $11,250 per year.

Suppose money is your main concern. Which career would you choose?

Chapter 4

Making Career Decisions

What's wrong here?

Words to learn and use

You will learn several new words in this chapter. The most important words are listed below. Do you know the meanings of these words?

personnel department
informational interview
card catalog
work experience program
short-term goals
long-term goals
on-the-job training
self-employment
trade school

Build on what you know

You already know. . .

- how to look at jobs based on the twelve career interest areas.
- how to narrow your career choices to just a few.
- that your skills, interests, values, and personality will help you choose the right career.
- that work experience is the best way to know if you like a job.

In this chapter you will learn. . .

- how to research jobs and careers.
- how to set your career goal.
- how to plan to reach your career goal.
- how to stay on a successful career path.

In Chapter 3 you picked some jobs that you might like to do someday. In this chapter you will learn how to find out more about these jobs. You will read about the work and talk to workers. You will also learn how to make career decisions and plans. You will even learn how to review your goals and plans. Working on your career is a job that is never done.

Research Your Job Choices

Do you have three or four jobs in mind that you think you might like? Good! Now it is time to find out more about these jobs. Learn as much as you can about each job. Then you will know if it is the right one for you.

What to Learn

There are certain things to look for in a job. As you research your job choices, find the answers to these questions:

- What will I do on this job? What are the duties? What will be expected of me? What will be my responsibilities?
- Where will I work? Will I be indoors or outdoors? Will I work by myself or with others? Is the workplace noisy or quiet? Is it dangerous? How will I dress and act in this workplace?
- When will I work? Are the hours long or short? Will I work all year long or just during busy seasons? Will I work during the day or nighttime hours? Will I work the same hours every week?
- What skills are needed for this job? Does it require physical strength? Math skills? Patience?
- What education and training are needed to do this job? Can I learn to do this job after I am hired? Will I need special schooling? College?
- What pay can I expect to earn? Will I get extra things working at this job? Things like travel, vacations, meals, or a retirement plan?
- Can a worker at this job expect to work up to a better job in the future? What kind of job could this one lead to?
- Will this job be available in the future? Is this a growing field? Are the jobs limited?

Picture yourself in different jobs, such as the one you see here. Imagine the tasks you would do. Think about where you would work. Would you like a job like this?

John was seventeen last week. He wanted to make a career choice this year. He liked art work. His art teacher told him he was good in sketching. John checked sketching jobs in the *Occupational Outlook Handbook*. He found that jobs in this work area are limited. The counselor at the area Job Service Center said there were only ten sketching jobs in the city. No job openings for sketching had been listed in two years.

As a second career choice, John chose sign painting. He was told there were many sign painting jobs in his community. John decided to apply for on-the-job training with a local company. He knew he could still do sketching as a hobby.

Check Up:✓✓ True or False?

1. It is not necessary to know about a job before you start work.
2. Understanding what training is needed will help you get ready for a job.

Where to Find Out

There is a great deal of information about jobs. You just have to know where to find it. Three ways to find information are

1. talk with people.
2. go to the library.
3. try jobs yourself.

Talk with people. Do you know someone who works at a job you chose? Ask if he or she will talk about the work. This is a good way to find out about the work.

Always talk politely. Do not ask embarrassing questions. Do not ask questions that are too personal, such as the worker's salary.

Suppose you do not know anyone who works at the job you are interested in. You may be able to talk with a worker anyway. Call a business or company that employs such workers. Make an appointment with the owner, the manager, or someone in the personnel department. People in the **personnel department** do the hiring.

Ask for an **informational interview.** This is a talk to learn about the type of work. Assume that you are not applying for a job right now. Explain that you want to learn more about a job to make a career decision. Ask if you can sit down with a person to talk about the job. Have your list of questions ready before you go in. Do not waste the interviewer's time.

Your teacher and your school counselor are good people to talk with. They can help you research your job choices. They may know people who can tell you more about your choices. Because they know you, they may have other helpful suggestions.

Go to the library. Your teacher and counselor may send you to the library to research careers. School and public libraries have career

A worker may be willing to show you what he or she does on the job. Ask questions to find out what the work is like.

information. The **card catalog** lists all the books in the library. Look in the card catalog for books about jobs. Check under the job title or area you are interested in. Ask the librarian if there is a career section at the library.

Magazines often have articles about jobs. Look for them in the *Reader's Guide.* Ask your librarian to show you.

Your library may even have career information on films, tapes, and cassettes. You may be able to find information on a computer at your library. Ask for help.

Try jobs yourself. The best way to find out if a job is for you is to try it. A part-time job now would give you good experience. It would help you find out if you would like this type of work. You could see if you have the right skills. You could find out whether or not you can learn the work.

The library has lots of information about careers.

A work experience program through your school is another good way to get job experience. A **work experience program** is one that helps you set career goals. It also helps you find part-time work. See if your school has one. You may be able to work at a job while you are going to school. On some jobs you would be paid.

A great many companies and organizations often use volunteer workers too. You could volunteer at your library, a local hospital, a nursing home, or a charity. You would not get paid for volunteer work, but you would gain experience. You would see if you like certain work settings. You would see if you like doing certain tasks.

Gather Your Information

Keeping a folder about the jobs you explore is a good idea. Write down what you learn at the library. Write down what workers tell you. Note your thoughts from job experiences you have.

Have you learned all you want to know about your job choices? Do you understand them?

Make a Decision

Once you have gathered all your job information, you need to think about your choices. Think of what you learned about yourself in Chapter 2. Think about each job. Think how you would fit into each job.

Then use this checklist for each job you have researched.

- Does this job fit my values and lifestyle?
- Does it still seem interesting to me?
- Would I like the hours, the workplace, the duties?
- Do I have the right skills? Can I learn to do this job well?
- Can I get the training or education I would need? Can I afford it?

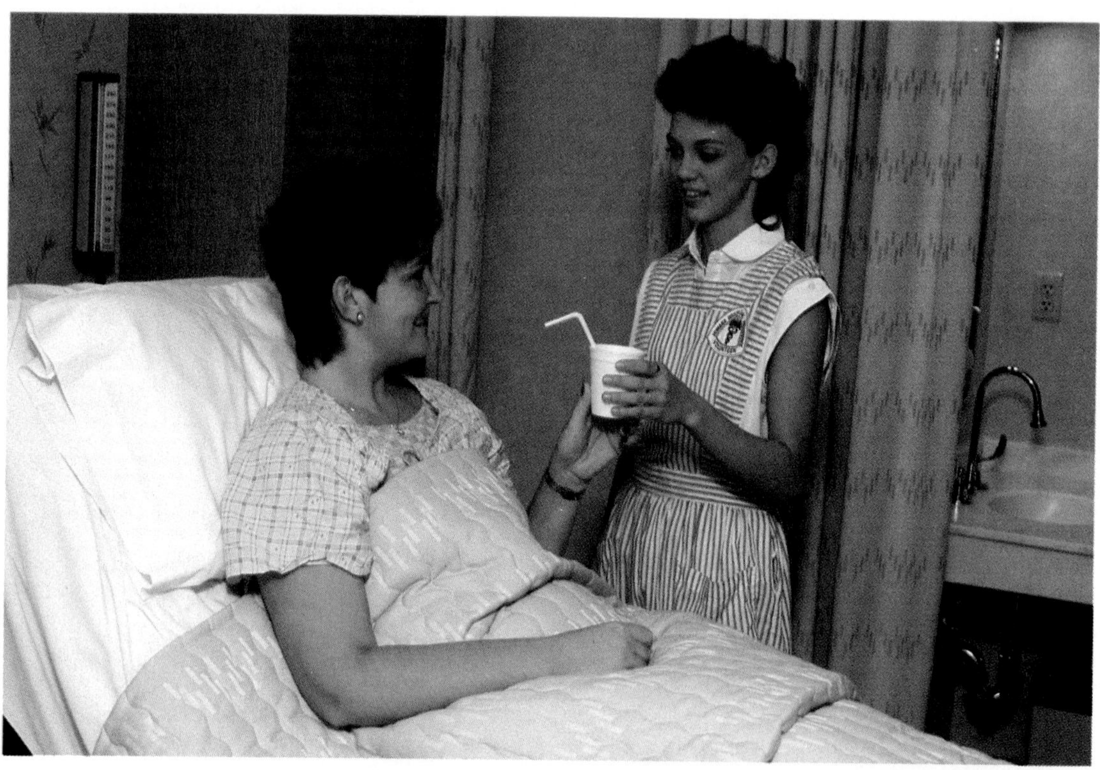

Every work experience you have will help you make your career decision. You may find you like certain tasks, but not others.

- Will I be happy with the salary?
- Will I be able to find a job?
- Will I be able to advance on the job? Can I do what it takes to advance on the job?

Now comes the hard part—making a career decision. Which job will you choose? Which career is the right one for you?

Choosing a career can be difficult. You may think you are not ready to decide. You may be afraid of making a wrong decision.

You know that your career will be a big part of your life. You know that it will affect your whole lifestyle. So it is important to make a career decision while you are still in high school.

But it is all right to change your decision later. Most people change jobs and careers several times during their lives. The important thing is to make a decision now and work toward your goals.

By working toward your career goal, you are learning many valuable things. If you stick with your first decision, you will be on your way toward your goal. If you change your mind, you still have learned valuable things. You may have learned skills that will help you in another job. You will at least have learned that there are some things you do *not* like. You will have narrowed your job choices through experience.

Working toward goals will also make you feel better about yourself. You will have something to work toward. You will know where you are going. You will be in control of your future.

Choosing a career goal now will get you started on a career path. Always have your goals in mind.

Plan to Reach Your Goal

Suppose you decide you would like to own your own auto repair shop. You think you would like the work. You have the aptitude to learn about engines. You have helped work on cars. You like keeping records of your work.

Are you ready to open your own shop the day you graduate from high school? Of course you are not. You will need to do many things before you reach your final goal. You will start by making a plan.

Your plan will begin with your career goal. It will include every step to reach that goal.

Plan the things you can be doing right now. These are your **short-term goals.** Then plan the steps you will take in the years to come. Those are your **long-term goals.**

To be a repair shop owner, you might make a plan like this:

1. Take shop courses in high school.
2. Get a part-time job in a garage.
3. Learn bookkeeping in high school or elsewhere.
4. Go to a two-year mechanic's school.
5. Get a full-time job in a garage.
6. Become manager of a garage.
7. Save enough money to open your own shop.
8. Buy your own shop.

Writing out your career plan will help you know what you need to do. It will help you to keep working toward your goal.

You can see that your plan must include both education and training. Each job requires different education and training. Sometimes there are several ways to prepare for the job you want. Find out what the education requirements are. Find out what training you need. Is there more than one way to learn the job?

Education

Education is becoming more important in today's work world. More education usually leads to better, higher paying jobs. Most employers want to hire workers who have *at least* a high school education.

Some jobs require a college education. Two-year courses are offered in community colleges.

Another way to learn in the classroom is to take some adult education classes. These classes are usually offered through city high schools. You may learn about business methods. You could learn to type. You might even learn another language.

You can usually work during the day. Then take a class or two in the evening. That way you will be earning money and improving your skills at the same time.

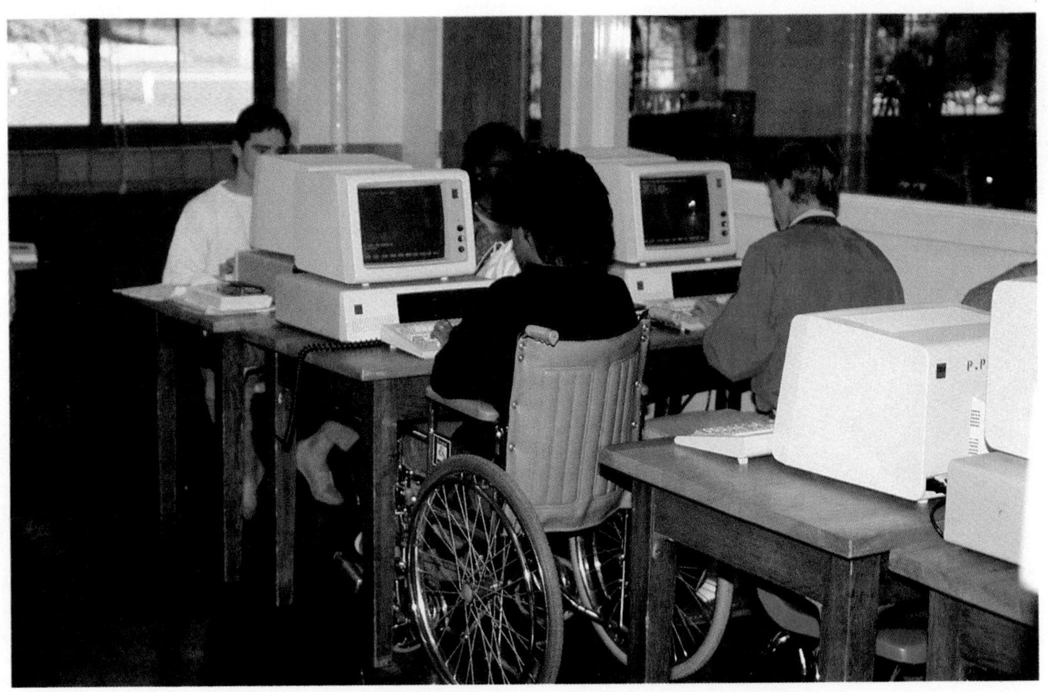

You can learn many job skills in the classroom.

Training

There are many ways to get training for the job you want. One way is to learn while you work. This is called **on-the-job training.** You may be hired to do a job. Then your boss or co-workers will show you what to do. Sometimes the pay is low while you are being trained. The pay may increase after you learn the skills and become a valuable worker.

Working as an apprentice is another way to gain experience. An apprentice is a person who works alongside a skilled worker. Would you like this? You would learn skills by watching and working. Are you interested in plumbing, carpentry, painting, or sheet metal work? You can learn these jobs and any of four hundred others as an apprentice.

On-the-job training gives you a chance to learn job skills plus earn a salary at the same time.

Trade and vocational schools give you the opportunity to learn valuable job skills.

A **trade school** is a school where you learn and practice skills for certain types of jobs. Some of the trades you could learn are auto mechanics, carpentry, and welding. Ask your counselor if there is a trade school near you. One may have a program that will help you reach your career goal.

Joining the military service is another way to get job training. You could learn a trade in the armed services. You would get job training for free. Then when you got out, you might find a job in your field. An Army, Navy, Air Force, or Marine recruiter can explain the programs to you.

Check Up:✓✓ True or False?

1. Once you make a career decision, you should never change it.

2. Your career plan should include education and training.

3. A high school education is not important in preparing for a job.

A Desire to Succeed

Living with Deafness: Marlee Matlin

Marlee Matlin could hear perfectly when she was born. Then, at eighteen months, she caught roseola, a childhood illness. She had a high fever.

The roseola made Marlee totally deaf in one ear. It made her nearly deaf in the other ear.

Marlee was angry that she was deaf. She did not accept her deafness until she was nearly twenty years old.

As a child, Marlee acted at the Children's Theater for the Deaf in Des Plaines, Illinois. By the time she was eight, she was getting big parts. She played the lead in *The Wizard of Oz*, *Peter Pan*, and *Mary Poppins*.

Marlee decided she wanted to be a police officer. She went to William Rainey Harper College. She studied criminal justice. Then she learned that being deaf would limit her jobs. She would not be able to go out as a patrol officer. Or be a detective. She would have to work in a police station. She did not want to do that. So she quit college.

At eighteen she tried out for a small part in the Chicago stage production. It was called *Children of a Lesser God*. She got the part. Then Paramount Pictures wanted to make a movie of that play. William Hurt would play the male lead. The studio was looking for a young woman to play the female lead.

Marlee went to New York for an audition. Then she went to California for a screen test. She got the part of Sarah Norman. Sarah was a stubborn young woman, bitter about being deaf.

The movie became a success. In the spring of 1987, Marlee won an Academy Award. She was voted Best Actress for her part as Sarah Norman.

Marlee thinks her success will help others who are deaf get started in acting careers.

She plans to play more parts in plays, movies, or TV shows. She thinks maybe she will start a children's theater for the deaf in New York.

Self-Employment

Self-employment means being your own boss. Would you want to run your own business? Many young people do. They start a small business and it grows. Some have good earnings. A few make lots of money.

It takes hard work to run a business. Self-satisfaction and a feeling of independence are the rewards. If you are interested, you can get help in planning. You may be able to borrow to start your business. Many people work at a job and save money to start a company.

What kind of a small business would you like to start? It should be something you know about. You need some skill in doing the work. Your business might be furniture finishing or upholstery. It could be clothing alterations. Car washing and polishing is a popular small business. You might buy a truck and start a delivery service.

You might start a business on a part-time plan. Then, when the business grows, you could work full-time. Sometimes a small business becomes a big company. Sometimes a person operates the same small business as a life-time career.

To plan and run a small business, you need all the training possible. You need to learn how to do your work. You also must learn to keep records. You need skills in working with people, in managing your business, and possibly in hiring workers.

Most training does not cost much money. Some small business owners learn how to manage a business in high school work experience programs. Others are paid by the government to learn a trade. Some take adult education courses or a few college classes. Training and plans for a small business should start early.

Doug always liked driving a car. When he was eighteen, he started to work as a truck driver. He drove a delivery truck for City Furniture. He saved his money for two years so he could buy a truck. With the help of a loan, he bought a tractor truck. Now he is pulling a large trailer for a big trucking company. He likes the work and is making a lot more money. Doug is proud to be in business for himself.

Review Your Plan and Goals

An important thing to remember about setting career goals is that they are never final. You may change your mind. Something could go wrong. Your plans may not work out. A good opportunity to do something else may come up.

Review your goals and your plan often. Ask yourself, "Do I want to keep the same goals?" If the answer is "Yes," ask yourself another question, "Am I following my plan?" If that answer is "Yes," keep up the good work. If the answer is "No," decide what you need to do to follow your plan. Read over the steps to career success on the next page. You may need to go back to step 7.

You may decide that your goals are not right for you. Perhaps you tried a job and found that you did not like the work after all. Maybe the education or training was too hard for you. Maybe you have your eye on another job that you think you would like better. That is all right.

In this case, revise your plan. Do not just quit. You may need to go back to Step 6. Decide new goals for yourself. Then make a new plan.

You may need to go all the way back to Steps 3 and 4. You can take another look at the job market. You can choose another career interest area or at least a different job group. Reviewing your plan often will keep you on the right track. It will also keep you moving toward your goal.

Get Started

You have your career goal in mind. You also have a plan for reaching your goal. Now you need to get busy. What steps should you be doing right now?

Whatever they are, start doing them. Sign up for courses that will help you. Look for a part-time job. Volunteer your time at a job that you might like to pursue. Talk with people about their jobs. Do not wait until tomorrow or next week. Get started today.

Check Up:✓✓ True or False?

1. You should start to work on your career goals after high school or after trade school.
2. If you change your career goal, just stick with your first plan.
3. Once you make your career plan, you are done with it.

Steps to Career Success

1. Understand the world of work.
   Know how important work is.
   Understand how work fits together with your total lifestyle.
2. Understand yourself.
   Know your interests, values, talents, and personality.
   Know what kind of lifestyle you want.
3. Know what jobs there are.
   Know there are thousands of different jobs to choose from.
   Understand that jobs can be broken down into twelve interest areas and many smaller groups.
4. Narrow your choices.
   Rule out the job groups that are not interesting to you.
   Pick a few jobs to research.
5. Research your choices.
   Read about your job choices.
   Talk with other people about their jobs.
   Try some jobs you think you might like.
6. Make your decision and set your goals.
   Decide on a career goal.
   Know that you may change your plan later.
7. Plan how to achieve your goal.
   Study the research you have done.
   Make a plan, outlining the steps you will take. Start with things you can do right now.
8. Review often.
   Look at your goals and plan regularly.
   If you no longer like your goals, change them. Back up on this list of steps and start over.
   Be sure your plan is working. If not, plan new steps.

The words

Listed below are important new words that were used in this chapter. Next to each word is the page on which you will find the word in bold, black print. Turn back and read again the paragraph in which you find each word. Then write the word and its meaning on a sheet of paper. Also write a sentence of your own using each word.

1. card catalog (81)
2. informational interview (80)
3. long-term goals (84)
4. on-the-job training (86)
5. personnel department (80)
6. self-employment (89)
7. short-term goals (84)
8. trade school (87)
9. work experience program (81)

The facts

1. Why would you research a job? What do you want to find out from your research?
2. Name three sources of job information.
3. Name three guides found at the library that contain career information. What other sources are available at the library?
4. After you have researched a job, how can you decide if it is a good choice for you?
5. Why is it important to make a career decision now?
6. Name some short-term career goals. Some long-term career goals.
7. List six ways to learn job skills.
8. What are some good reasons for changing your career goal?
9. What should you do if you change your career goal?
10. What are the eight steps to career success?

What's right here?

ADD TO YOUR KNOWLEDGE AND SKILLS

Talk about your ideas

1. Suppose you research a job. You find that there will be few job openings in the coming years. Should you plan to work in that field? Should you pick another job? Why?

2. What work experience have you had? Do not forget jobs that did not pay a wage. What did you learn from each that will help you with your career decision?

Do some activities

1. Choose a job to study in the *Occupational Outlook Handbook.* Is the job outlook good? Visit a Job Service Center near you. Ask about the outlook for that job. Report your findings.

2. Decide on a job you might want. Make a collage of all the tools, equipment, and other things you would use. Show your collage to the class. See if your classmates can guess what your job choice is.

3. Keep a notebook or folder of job information. Collect as much information as you can about your top three job choices.

Improve your basic skills

1. Using the *Reader's Guide,* try to find at least two magazine articles about one of your job choices. Read them. Be prepared to tell what you learned.

2. See if the career center in your school library has pamphlets about your job choices or your career interest area. Read several.

1. Write a thank you letter to someone who has helped you with the job research.

2. Make a list of all of your experiences that will help you on the job of your choice. Include basic things such as reading books, writing reports, and belonging to clubs.

1. In 1985 there were 115 million people in the U.S. civilian labor force. Of this total, 107 million had jobs. How many people did *not* have jobs? Can you find out the unemployment rate? (Clue: Divide the number unemployed by the total number in the labor force.)

PART TWO

GETTING THE JOB YOU WANT

In Part One you made some career decisions. You set some goals. Your next step is one of action.

First, you must seek out the job you want. Employers are not going to come to you. You may have many skills employers need. Still, it is unlikely that employers will come looking for you. It is up to you to find the available jobs.

Second, you must convince employers that you will be a good worker. Many others will be looking for jobs. Their skills may be as good as—or better than—yours. You must know what to say and how to act. This can make the difference between being overlooked and being hired.

Part Two tells you how to look for job openings. It explains the *right* way to land the job you want.

Chapter 5

Finding Job Openings

What's wrong here?

Words to learn and use

You will learn several new words in this chapter. The most important words are listed below. Do you know the meanings of these words?

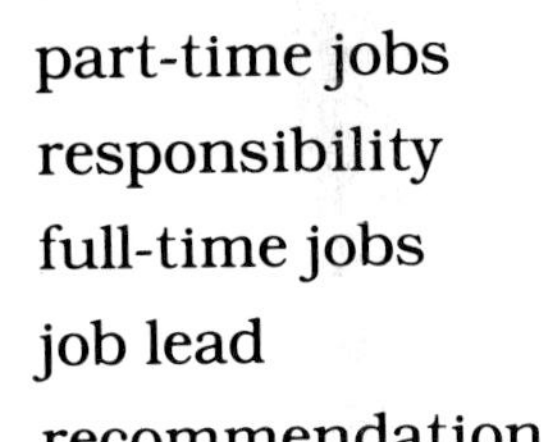

part-time jobs
responsibility
full-time jobs
job lead
recommendation
employment agencies
work permit
Social Security card
reference

Build on what you know

You already know. . .

- that there are a number of jobs you could do and would like.
- that setting goals is important in getting the right job.
- that there are many places to look for a job.

In this chapter you will learn. . .

- a good plan for finding the right job.
- sources of job leads.
- how to use job lead cards.
- what you need to have before you apply for a job.

In Chapter 1, you learned about work and lifestyles. In Chapter 2, you learned how to understand yourself better. Then, in Chapters 3 and 4, you evaluated some possible jobs and set some goals for your future. In this chapter, you will learn to find job openings. You will learn what you need to have before you apply for a job. You will develop a plan to help you get just the right job.

Getting Started

Finding a job is a job itself. It is not always easy. Having a plan, being prepared, and being organized will help. Your first job may be quite different from jobs you will have later. But the way you go about getting each job is much the same.

Part-Time Jobs

While you are in school, you may want a part-time job. **Part-time jobs** are jobs in which you work less than the full forty hours per week. You may already have one.

Most part-time jobs are after school or weekend jobs. You may not earn a lot of money on a part-time job. But you will gain more than money. You can learn how to succeed on a job. For example, you can learn

1. to get along with other workers on the job.
2. to accept responsibility.
3. to spend money wisely.

Those who lose their jobs are most often fired because they do not get along at work. A part-time job helps you learn to work well with others. Most people are pleasant on the job. But some are hard to work with. Working can help you learn how to get along with *all* kinds of people.

A part-time job will help you learn to take responsibility. Taking **responsibility** means doing the things you should do. It includes being on time for work. It includes calling your boss when you are too ill to go to work. It includes doing what you are told and doing your fair share of the work, too.

Spending money may seem easy. It is not easy, though, to get your money's worth. A part-time job gives you a chance to learn to handle your own money.

A part-time job also lets you try out a job. This will help you decide what type of work you want to do when you finish school.

Another advantage of part-time work is that you gain experience. Employers are more likely to hire you if you have experience. They are less likely to hire someone who has never worked before.

Full-Time Jobs

Most adults have **full-time jobs.** These are jobs in which people work about forty hours a week the year round. You will probably not get your first full-time job until you finish school. You will probably have several part-time jobs before you accept your first full-time job.

Summer Jobs

Employers know students can work during the summer. They often plan their work so they can hire students. There are many summer jobs. Many students want to work, too. If you want a summer job, look for it *early*. Late winter or early spring is a good time. By the time school is out, most summer jobs are taken.

Think of the jobs you *know* you can do and those you *think* you can do.

Making a Plan

In Chapters 3 and 4 you set some goals for yourself. You now know several types of jobs that you would like. You know what jobs you have the talent for. And you know when you can work.

Now you need a plan for finding a job that you will like, and can do well. You can use the same plan to find a part-time or a full-time job.

Here is a good plan for finding the right job for you.

1. Find as many job leads as possible.
2. Keep a file of job leads.
3. Get the necessary papers to be hired.
4. Gather together your personal information.
5. Follow through on your job leads.

Check Up:✓✓ True or False?

1. Finding a part-time job is different from finding a full-time job.
2. A part-time job teaches you how to succeed on the job.
3. Early summer is a good time to start looking for a summer job.

Finding Job Leads

Some people go looking for a job without knowing where the jobs are. That is the hard way. It is like fishing in a lake that has only one fish. If you follow a plan, you will know where job openings are.

Information about a job opening is called a **job lead.** The more job leads you have, the better your chance of getting a good job. Some sources of job leads are

- your family and friends.
- your school.
- newspaper ads.
- employment agencies.
- government agencies.

Your Family and Friends

One of the best places to get job leads is in your own home! A good time to talk about job leads is during the evening meal. Talk with your parents. Talk with your older brothers and sisters or aunts and uncles. They may know of job openings where they work. Or they may know that someone will quit soon. They can tell you about an opening before it is advertised. If you are the first to apply, you have a good chance of being hired.

Do you have friends who work? Ask your friends about job leads for you. Talking with them in person is probably better than talking on the phone. They may not know of any jobs right now. Ask them again in a week or two.

Sometimes a job has been filled by the time you get to the employer. If so, you may get a job anyway. The employer may know of another job you would like.

Keep a list of people who may help you with job leads. Start with your own family. Add names of friends of your family who work. One of them may have a job for you. Or they may know of others who are looking for workers. Add names of school friends. The father or mother of a friend may work where there is a job for someone with your skills.

Simply talking at the dinner table may give you some good job leads.

Some young people do not want to get a job through a friend or relative. They think it is unfair. There is nothing wrong with getting a job through your family or a friend. Of course, you must have the skill to do the job. Many jobs are never advertised. They are filled through friends.

Your School

Your school may be able to help you in several ways. Your school may have a work placement office. If it does, someone there can help you look for job leads. Some schools have work experience programs. Such programs can help you plan your career. They may help you locate a job. Some schools have bulletin boards with lists of jobs. If yours does, check it every day while you are looking for a job.

Other people in your school can help you, too. Talk with your counselor and your teachers. Talk about the types of jobs you think you would like. Ask if they know of any jobs that are available. Ask if they would be willing to give you a good recommendation for an opening. A **recommendation** is a statement to an employer that you can do a job. It often helps an employer decide to hire you.

Schools may send three or four students to try for each job. You must show the employer that you can do the job better. You cannot just sit back and wait for your school to find a job for you! However, your school is a good place to find job leads.

Teachers and school counselors often hear of job openings. Tell them you are looking for a job.

Check Up:✓✓ True or False?

1. Having a number of job leads increases your chances of getting a job.
2. You should never ask a friend for a job lead.
3. Your teachers and counselor may be able to tell you about job openings.

Newspaper Ads

Do you read the help wanted ads in your newspaper? If so, you can learn a lot about the jobs that are open. You can learn how much different kinds of jobs pay. You can also find out what skills are needed for different jobs.

Make it a habit to read these ads daily. Call or write to find out about the jobs that interest you. You must be careful, though. Some ads ask you to send some money. These are often not jobs at all. Someone may just be trying to sell something by making it look like a job.

Abbreviations are shortened forms of words. Ads often use abbreviations to save space. Some often used abbreviations are shown below. Read them. They will help you understand ads for jobs in the newspaper.

Then read the ads on the next page. They were taken from several newspapers. When you are home tonight, look through your own newspaper. If you have questions about the ads, talk about them with your teacher or your family.

Abbreviations Often Used in Newspaper Ads

a.m. = morning
appl. = applicant
appt. = appointment
asst. = assistant
ATTN = attention
ben. = benefits
co. = company
c/o = in care of
dept. = department
EOE = equal opportunity employer
etc. = and so on
exc. = excellent
exp. = experience
FT = full time
gd = good
hr. = hour
hrs+ = at least that many hours
immed. = immediate
incl. = included
info = information
lic. = license or licensed
M-F (Mon.-Fri.) = Monday through Friday
mfg. = manufacturing
mgr. = manager
min. = minimum
nec. = necessary
ofc. = office
oppor. (oppty.) = opportunity
PC = personal computer
pd. = paid
ph. = phone
p.m. = afternoon or evening
pos. = position
pref. = preferred
PT = part time
qual. = qualified or qualifications
ref. = reference
rep. = representative
req. = required
sal. = salary
sec. = secretary
w/ = with
wk. = week
WP = word processing
wpm = words per minute
yrs. = years

Understanding the abbreviations to the left can help you read the want ads more easily.

400—Help Wanted

Housekeeper wanted. Need someone to do housecleaning, laundry on Thursdays or Fridays. If you are dependable & pay attention to detail, call 778-9378. (keep trying). Student inquiries welcome, but needs to be available summers.

COMMERCIAL ACCOUNT MGR.
(Customer service rep.) in a large, independent insurance agency. Duties will include all aspects of servicing a commercial insurance account. Excellent clerical and communication skills a must. For a personal interview, call 398-4444.
EOE.

Legal Secretary to start April 15. Shorthand required. Experience preferred. Send resume, salary requirements, and references to: PO Box 218 Urbana, IL 61801.

OFFICE ASSISTANT
Part time to full time Office Assistant for rental property. Typing, public relations, and bookkeeping skills desired. Apply to Box #89 c/o News-Gazette, 15 Main, Champaign, IL 61820.

RECEPTIONIST
Full time experienced receptionist. We need a reliable person that can handle phones for busy real estate office while performing varied clerical duties. Excellent typing and pleasing personality a must. Some light housekeeping. $5/hr. Send a thorough but brief resume to COLDWELL BANKER MILLER & MILLER, 1712 S. Benson, Champaign, IL 61821. ATTN., Martie Smith.

WE WANT YOU!
...if you can type 60-70 wpm, have superior word processing skills, substantial transcription experience and a good command of the English language. We are a growing marketing communications agency that will offer you a competitive salary, a part time position with the potential of becoming full time, varied responsibilities and pleasant working conditions. Call Heather at 749-2400. Equal Opportunity Employer.

AUTOMOTIVE SALES PEOPLE—Needed. Apply in person at: A-1 Used Cars, 1100 S. Main, Bloomington.

AUTOMOTIVE SALES PERSON
Experience desirable but not required. Benefits available. Reply to: W-12-M, News-Gazette.

CONSTRUCTION HELP WANTED

CALL 367-8396

400—Help Wanted

Activity Aide, experienced, full-time. Greenbrier Nursing Center, 1915 S. Mattis, Champaign.

Alterations person needed. Dress making skills necessary. Apply in person. Ducky's Formal Wear.

EXCELLENT WAGES
For spare time assembly work; electronics, crafts.
Others.
Additional Information, call 504-641-00091 ext. 4125. 7 days.
CALL NOW!

Black & Co. Hardware is now accepting applications for full & part-time help. Apply in person. 709 W. Green, Champaign.

BONANZA NOW HIRING!
Apply in person,
1201 N. Mattis, Champaign.

BUS PERSONS
Part time positions available day and evening shifts including weekends. Experience desired, must be 19 years of age. Apply in person at the University Inn / Chancellor Hotel Personnel Office, 302 W. Kirby, C. Monday-Friday, 9-4pm.
EOE.

Ace Hardware is accepting applications for full-time and part-time Sales, Stock, and Cashiers. Apply in person to Ace Hardware 107 W. Springfield, Champaign between 1pm-4pm.
Equal Opportunity Employer.

Pest control route position available. Permanent job; benefits, promotion possible. Set your own working hours. Experience preferred but not necessary. Mature individuals, call Terminix for an interview, **442-2404. EOE.**

COLLINS OIL
Full and part time attendants. Apply at 106 E. Main, Urbana.

ARBY'S IN CHAMPAIGN is accepting applications for part time help. Apply in person after 2pm.

400—Help Wanted

ADMINISTRATIVE ASSISTANT—To chief financial officer. Degree preferred. Accounting or bookkeeping experience with secretarial skills. Fee negotiable.
CAPITAL EMPLOYMENT Agency
Ph. 827-3333

ACCOUNT REPRESENTATIVE
National company seeks person to call on commercial accounts in Bloomington, IL $21,000 base plus liberal commissions. FEE PAID. Ph. Andy, 663-0482, Snelling & Snelling, 2401 E. Washington, a private agency.

★EXECUTIVE SECRETARY★
Not just typing all day! Lots of vendor contact. Advancement. Benefits include profit sharing. $12,000, FEE PAID! Ph. Jean, 663-0482, Snelling & Snelling, 2401 E. Washington, a private agency.

MANAGER TRAINEE
Corporation experiencing strong growth seeks individuals for their operations. $14,500 while training. Earn mid-twenties as manager. FEE PAID. Ph. Andy, 663-0482, Snelling & Snelling, 2401 E. Washington, a private agency.

MAINTENANCE PERSON
Experienced, excellent benefit package. Apply in person at Bloomington Nursing and Rehabilitation Center, 1509 N. Calhoun, Bloomington, IL.
Equal Opportunity Employer.

INTERIOR DESIGNER
Experienced only—for expanding drapery and interior design firm. Must be highly motivated, self-starter. Call Barb at Knight Interiors Mon.-Thurs., 9-12, 748-9823

JANITOR—Experience in hard floor care needed for third shift. Part-time and 1 full-time position available. Send resume in confidence to:
P.O. Box 1611, Bloomington

The United States Coast Guard offers guaranteed job benefits to young men & women between the ages of 17 & 28.
Training, 30 days paid vacation, college aid, and much more.
Ask about our summer job program or two year enlistment. Call "COLLECT" 314-425-7107

DAIRY QUEEN BRAZIER
Now accepting applications for Full-time employment for days and nights. Inquiries can be made between 2-4pm. Monday-Friday. No phone calls please. 911 W. University, U.

Read this sample page from the "Help Wanted" section of the newspaper. Do you understand each ad?

Employment Agencies

Employment agencies find workers for employers. Many employers call these agencies to find workers. So employment agencies often have lists of many types of jobs. People wanting work may go to an employment agency. So the agency also has lists of people who want jobs. Then the agency matches workers with jobs.

There are two types of employment agencies. One is *public.* The other is *private.* Public agencies do not charge a fee. Private agencies charge the worker or the employer a fee for filling the job. Most cities have both public and private agencies.

Public employment agencies are run by the government. They do not charge a fee. Instead, taxes pay for the service. These public agencies are called by the name of the state, such as *Texas State Employment Service.* You can find the phone number and address in the telephone book. Look under *employment* in the yellow pages.

Many jobs are listed with this public agency. Go to the public employment agency near you and fill out an application form. Someone there will ask you some questions. This is just to find out what you can do best and what you like to do. He or she will try to find you a job. When the right job comes along, you will be called.

Private employment agencies do not get tax money to run their business. They charge a fee if they help you get a job. This is how they earn their money.

You must sign an agreement before they will help you. It says that you will pay a fee if they send you for a job where you are hired. The fee is often part of the first few months' wages. For some jobs the employer will pay the fee. You can ask the agency which ones do. Getting a job through a private agency may cost you some money. But it may be the way to find just the right job.

If an agency sends you to see an employer, you will be given a card with the employer's name and address. Make sure you know where to go before you leave the agency.

Workers in employment agencies find jobs for people. Private agencies may charge you a fee. Public agencies do not.

Government Agencies

Federal, state, county, and city governments hire many workers. Together, they hire more workers than any other kind of employer. They hire thousands of new workers every year.

State and federal agencies offer civil service jobs. To get a civil service job, you must pass a test. The test covers the work you will do if you are hired.

Workers on civil service jobs have many good benefits. They cannot be fired without a good reason. They get medical insurance and regular raises in pay.

All cities have city government agencies that hire workers. Most have county, state, and federal agencies, too. These agencies hire workers to do hundreds of different types of jobs.

You may be surprised by all the workers an agency needs. You know that schools need teachers. But they also hire many other workers. These include cooks, kitchen helpers, office workers, bus drivers, crossing guards, and mechanics.

Think of the variety of jobs in each agency. These jobs usually offer good pay and good working conditions.

Are you interested in a job with the government? If you are, look up the address in the phone book. Federal agencies are listed under *UNITED STATES GOVERNMENT.* State agencies are listed under the name of the state. An example is *CALIFORNIA, STATE OF.* County and city agencies are listed under the name of the county or city. Here are some examples: *SANTA BARBARA, COUNTY OF* and *SANTA MARIA, CITY OF.*

Government agencies hire many different types of workers.

Check Up: ✓✓ True or False?

1. To find a government employment agency, look under "Employment" in the telephone book's yellow pages.
2. Private employment agencies may charge a fee to find you a job.
3. Government agencies hire very few workers.

Being Organized

You will probably be talking with many people about job openings. Write a list of people to talk with. The more leads you have, the better your chance of getting a good job. It is important to remember all the details about each job lead. Keep a record of each lead on a 3" x 5" index card. When you hear about a job, write down

- the name of the business.
- the address and phone number.
- the name of the person to see.
- where you learned about the job.
- the type of job.

Write just one job lead on each card. Look at the card samples on the next page. The name of the person to see is written in the middle of the card. If you know the person's job title, write that down, too. Next are the name, address, and phone number of the business. Where you learned about the job is in the lower left corner. After you call for an appointment, write the day and time in the upper right corner.

Sometimes you may need to apply for a job without a lead. If so, you do not have to call ahead to fill out an application form. Simply use the telephone book. The yellow pages list most businesses. Read through the sections that sound interesting. Write down the names and addresses of businesses where you might like to work. Then go to these companies and ask to fill out a job application.

Now turn the card over. Use the back to write what you know about the job. Notes about the company can also be helpful. Look for its listing in the yellow pages of your local telephone book. Also notice newspaper ads or stories about the company. Talk to people who work there. Call your local Chamber of Commerce. Write down what you learn.

Keep your list of people to talk with and your job lead cards together. You may want to get a folder to keep them in. You will be preparing other papers for job hunting, too. Add these to your folder.

Check Up:✓✓ True or False?

1. You should never apply for a job without a lead.

2. Writing job lead cards will help you remember details about the company and the job.

3. You should keep your job hunting materials all together in a folder.

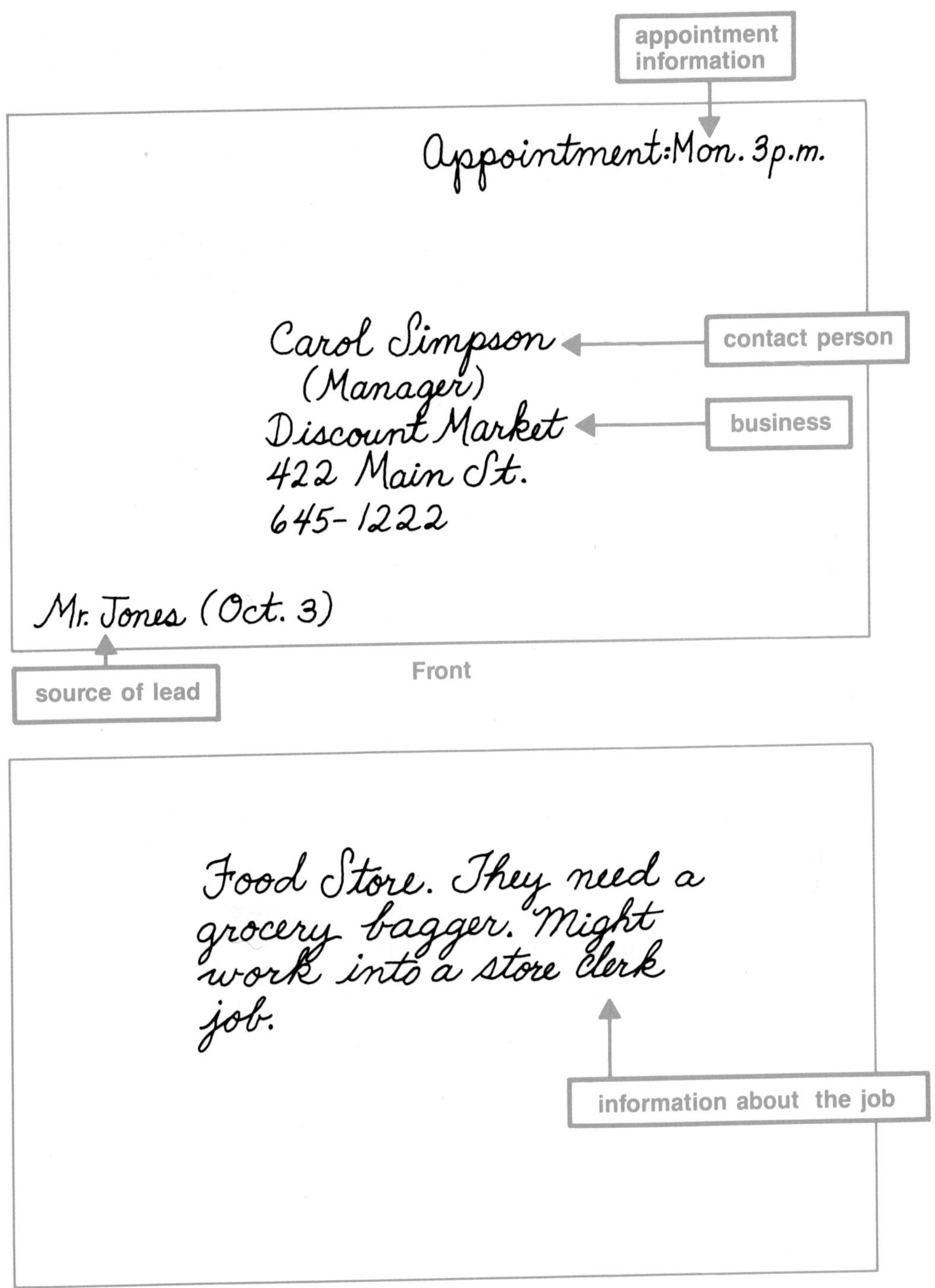

Job lead cards help you remember important information and keep track of your appointments.

A Desire to Succeed

Changing Her Life: Jill Kinmont

"It was a beautiful morning and the snow was like velvet." That was how Jill Kinmont describes the day of the big ski race. It was 1954, just before the Olympic tryouts.

As she skied down the mountain that Sunday morning, Jill went too fast. She started her jump just a little too late. She crashed into the snow, and tumbled down the slope.

When she came to a stop, Jill could not feel anything. She could move her head, but she could not move her body.

Jill had surgery on her back. Doctors drilled two shallow holes in her head. They put steel tongs into the holes to keep her from moving her head. They tied her to a big metal frame. Jill had to stay this way for many weeks. She felt no pain.

Jill was paralyzed from the neck down. She would never be able to walk again. She would certainly never be able to ski again.

In a few months Jill could sit up most of the time. Her doctor found that a few of her muscles could still work. She exercised those muscles so she could improve them.

It took Jill a long time to be able to do simple things again. She learned to feed herself. She used a hand brace to hold a pen so she could write.

Then Jill learned to use a wheelchair. She could get around by herself that way.

Jill decided that she wanted to start college. Her friends helped her and she studied hard.

Jill decided to become a teacher. At first many people told her that she was handicapped. She could not teach. Then she found a school that would hire her. Now she teaches children to read.

A book was written about Jill Kinmont's life. A movie was made from her story. Both are called *The Other Side of the Mountain.*

Many people look to Jill for inspiration. Her first love, skiing, was made impossible for her by an accident. But Jill did not quit. She learned to live as a paralyzed person. She learned to achieve new goals.

Other Things You Will Need

Before you are ready to contact an employer, you will need several things.

1. A work permit
2. Social security card
3. A fact sheet

A Work Permit

A **work permit** is a form saying that it is all right for you to work. In many states, it is against the law for someone under eighteen to work without a **work permit.** There are several kinds of work permits. Some are good on any job that is not too dangerous. Other permits are good for only one job. Some permits allow you to work only during the hours written on your permit. Ask your teacher or counselor if you need one. If so, you can get a work permit at your school.

If you need a work permit, you will likely need your family's permission, too. You may need to get your parent to sign an application for a work permit.

A Social Security Card

A **social security card** is a card issued by the U.S. government. You may already have one. If you do not, you will need one before you start work. You will not be paid without one.

To get your social security card, fill out an application form. An example is shown on the next page. You can get this form at your Social Security Office or U.S. Post Office. Your school placement office or work experience office may have these forms.

Fill out the form carefully. Print or use a typewriter. Some students have trouble with line 9. It asks for your mother's maiden name. That was her last name before she was ever married.

Your social security card will come to you by mail. It may take six weeks or longer to get your card. Your social security card has a number on it. You will be the only one with your number.

When you work on most jobs, a small part of your pay is taken out for social security. Your number helps keep track of that money. Your employer puts in the same amount of money as you do. Then, when you retire in your later years or are not able to work, you will get a check each month. This is how the government helps you have some money when you no longer work.

DEPARTMENT OF HEALTH AND HUMAN SERVICES
SOCIAL SECURITY ADMINISTRATION

Form Approved
OMB No. 0960-0066

FORM SS-5 – APPLICATION FOR A SOCIAL SECURITY NUMBER CARD (Original, Replacement or Correction)

Unless the requested information is provided, we may not be able to issue a Social Security Number (20 CFR 422-103(b))

INSTRUCTIONS TO APPLICANT ▶ **Before completing this form, please read the instructions on the opposite page. Type or print, using pen with dark blue or black ink. Do not use pencil. SEE PAGE 1 FOR REQUIRED EVIDENCE.**

NAA NAME TO BE SHOWN ON CARD — First | Middle | Last

NAB FULL NAME AT BIRTH (IF OTHER THAN ABOVE) — First | Middle | Last

1

ONA OTHER NAME(S) USED

STT **2** MAILING ADDRESS (Street/Apt. No., P.O. Box, Rural Route No.)

CTY CITY (Do not abbreviate) | **STE** STATE | **ZIP** ZIP CODE

CSP **3** CITIZENSHIP (Check one only)
- ☐ a. U.S. citizen
- ☐ b. Legal alien allowed to work
- ☐ c. Legal alien not allowed to work
- ☐ d. Other (See instructions on Page 2)

SEX **4** SEX
- ☐ MALE
- ☐ FEMALE

ETB **5** RACE/ETHNIC DESCRIPTION (Check one only) (Voluntary)
- ☐ a. Asian, Asian-American or Pacific Islander (Includes persons of Chinese, Filipino, Japanese, Korean, Samoan, etc., ancestry or descent)
- ☐ b. Hispanic (Includes persons of Chicano, Cuban, Mexican or Mexican-American, Puerto Rican, South or Central American, or other Spanish ancestry or descent)
- ☐ c. Negro or Black (not Hispanic)
- ☐ d. Northern American Indian or Alaskan Native
- ☐ e. White (not Hispanic)

DOB **6** DATE OF BIRTH ▶ MONTH | DAY | YEAR — **AGE** **7** PRESENT AGE — **PLB** **8** PLACE OF BIRTH ▶ CITY (Do not abbreviate) | STATE OR FOREIGN COUNTRY (Do not abbreviate) | **FCI** ☐

MNA **9** MOTHER'S NAME AT HER BIRTH — First | Middle | Last (Her maiden name)

FNA FATHER'S NAME — First | Middle | Last

PNO **10** a. Has a Social Security number card ever been requested for the person listed in item 1? ☐ YES(2) ☐ NO(1) ☐ Don't know(1)

b. Was a card received for the person listed in item 1? ☐ YES(3) ☐ NO(1) ☐ Don't know(1)

▶ **IF YOU CHECKED YES TO A OR B, COMPLETE ITEMS C THROUGH E; OTHERWISE GO TO ITEM 11.**

SSN c. Enter the Social Security number assigned to the person listed in item 1. ☐☐☐–☐☐–☐☐☐☐

NLC d. Enter the name shown on the most recent Social Security card issued for the person listed in item 1.

PDB e. Date of birth correction (See Instruction 10 on page 2) ▶ MONTH | DAY | YEAR

DON **11** TODAY'S DATE ▶ MONTH | DAY | YEAR

12 Telephone number where we can reach you during the day. Please include the area code. ▶ HOME | OTHER

ASD **WARNING: Deliberately furnishing (or causing to be furnished) false information on this application is a crime punishable by fine or imprisonment, or both.**

IMPORTANT REMINDER: WE CANNOT PROCESS THIS APPLICATION WITHOUT THE REQUIRED EVIDENCE. SEE PAGE 1

13 YOUR SIGNATURE

14 YOUR RELATIONSHIP TO PERSON IN ITEM 1 ☐ Self ☐ Other (Specify) ______

WITNESS (Needed only if signed by mark "X") | WITNESS (Needed only if signed by mark "X")

DO NOT WRITE BELOW THIS LINE (FOR SSA USE ONLY)

DTC (SSA RECEIPT DATE) | NPN | DOC

NTC | CAN | BIC | IDN | ITV | ☐ MANDATORY IN PERSON INTERVIEW CONDUCTED

TYPE(S) OF EVIDENCE SUBMITTED

SIGNATURE AND TITLE OF EMPLOYEE(S) REVIEWING EVIDENCE AND/OR CONDUCTING INTERVIEW

DATE

DCL | DATE

Form SS-5 (11-86)
5/84, 1/85 and 8/85 editions may be used until supply is exhausted

3

This is a social security card application. Always fill out an application carefully and read it over to check for errors.

A Fact Sheet

When you apply for a job, the employer will want to know some things about you. Be prepared to answer some questions about yourself. The best way is to write out a fact sheet about yourself.

Prepare your fact sheet carefully. Keep it in your job folder. Take it with you when you apply for a job.

Most employers want to know

- some personal facts.
- some facts about your family.
- where you lived in the past.
- where you live now.
- your personal limitations.
- work you have done.
- work you would like to do.
- personal references.
- your school attendance.
- if your health is good.

Personal Facts. Employers will want to know your name and where you go to school. They will also need to know if you are old enough to get a work permit. Some may ask about hobbies. Be ready to say how you use your free time.

Facts About Your Family. Employers may want to know some things about your family, too. They may ask where your parents work. An employer needs to know this to call them in an emergency. Some may ask about brothers or sisters who could give you a ride to work.

Where You Lived in the Past. Some employers may ask where you have lived in the past. Know the addresses and dates of when you lived at each place.

Where You Live Now. Most employers will ask where you live now. They will want to know how you will get to work. Employers like to hire workers who are always on time for work. Getting to work is not often a problem for workers

- who live close enough to walk to and from work.
- who live on a bus line.
- who have a car or bicycle.

Employers would rather not hire a person who must depend on getting a ride with a friend. Your friend may be dependable, but how will you get to work if your friend is sick? Of course, this may be the only way you can get to work. If so, you must convince the employer that you will always be on time.

Personal Limitations. Every person has limitations. Do you have a handicap or a condition that might keep you from doing certain tasks? Maybe you cannot lift heavy things. Maybe you do not see well enough to drive at night. If the employer knows these things, it is easier to decide which job you can do best. An employer must not refuse to hire you just because of a handicap if you can do the job. This is the law. If an employer asks about these limitations, be honest.

Work You Have Done. If you have worked before, you have experience. Employers like to know what type of work you have done. Have you ever worked on a job like the one you are applying for? If you have, it will not take you long to learn the new job. Workers with experience are more valuable employees right away.

Work You Would Like to Do. Employers need to know the type of work you want. This helps them put you on a job you can do well and will like. Some students do not know what type of job they want. They say they will do anything. Employers do not like to hear that. They may even ask you what you want to be doing in five years! They want to know if you would like to work for them in the future on a better job.

Personal References. Some of the employers often ask for references. A **reference** is a person who can tell your employer that you will do a good job. Your references should be adults who know you well. Adult friends of your family, teachers, and counselors who like you make good references. Do not list relatives or students.

Your employer may call these people to ask them about you. Be sure to pick references who have a good opinion of you and will say nice things about you.

School Attendance. Most of the employers you contact will be interested in your school record. They think that if you go to school every day, you will go to work every day, too. If you miss a lot of school, you may miss a lot of work. Some employers check with the school on the attendance of students who apply for work.

Your Health. Employers know that when you feel good you work better. Your work is easier and more fun. Some people are careless about their health. They do not eat the right foods or get enough sleep. They may get by with poor habits for a while. But then these poor habits begin to affect their work. Some employers will ask about health habits.

Check Up:✓✓ True or False?

1. A fact sheet lists personal information about yourself that you will need when applying for a job.

2. Do not tell an employer about your handicaps. You may not get the job.

3. Select people who know you well and like you as references.

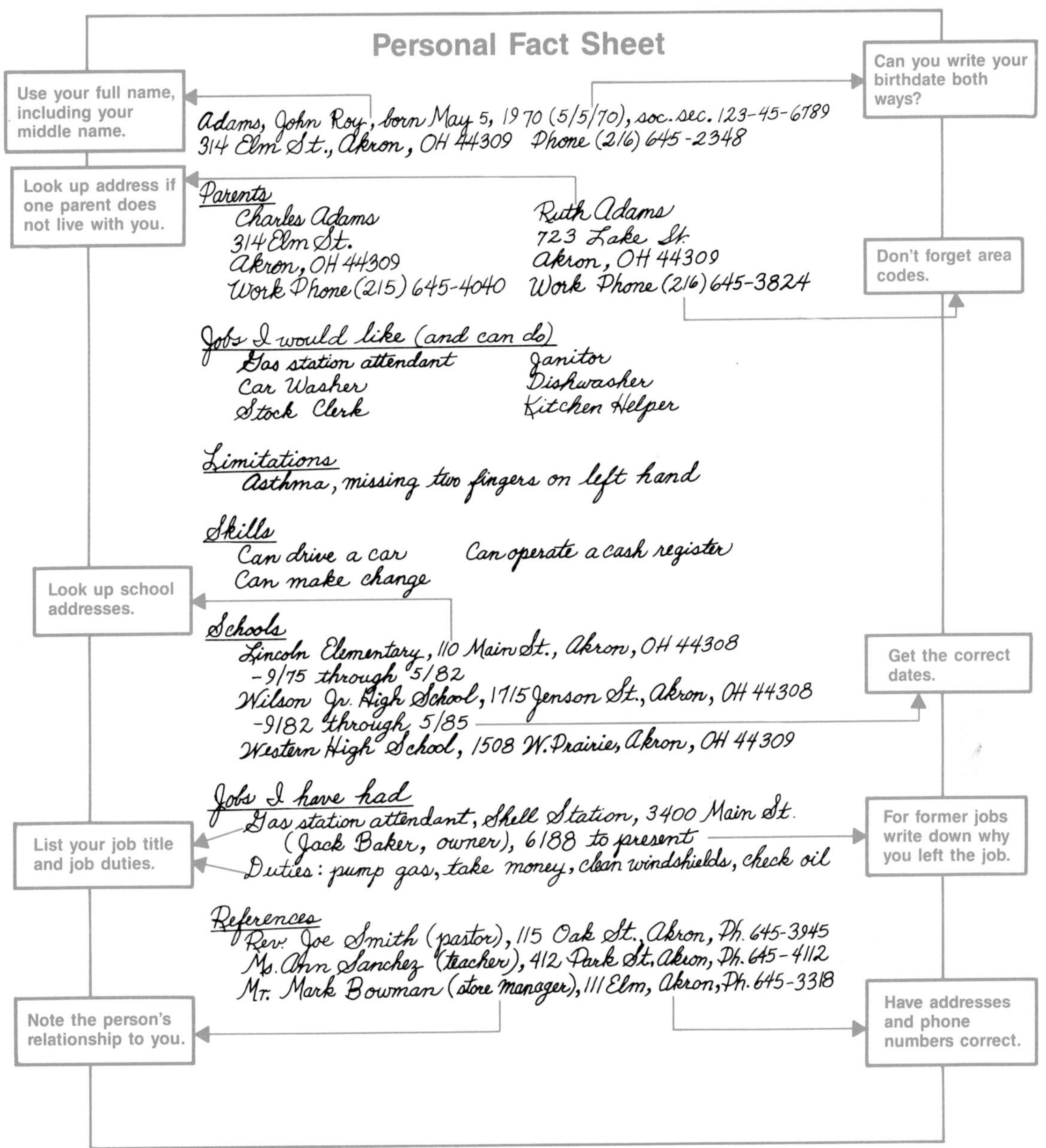

Personal Fact Sheet

Adams, John Roy, born May 5, 1970 (5/5/70), soc. sec. 123-45-6789
314 Elm St., Akron, OH 44309 Phone (216) 645-2348

Parents
Charles Adams
314 Elm St.
Akron, OH 44309
Work Phone (215) 645-4040

Ruth Adams
723 Lake St.
Akron, OH 44309
Work Phone (216) 645-3824

Jobs I would like (and can do)
Gas station attendant
Car Washer
Stock Clerk
Janitor
Dishwasher
Kitchen Helper

Limitations
Asthma, missing two fingers on left hand

Skills
Can drive a car
Can make change
Can operate a cash register

Schools
Lincoln Elementary, 110 Main St., Akron, OH 44308
-9/75 through 5/82
Wilson Jr. High School, 1715 Jenson St., Akron, OH 44308
-9/82 through 5/85
Western High School, 1508 W. Prairie, Akron, OH 44309

Jobs I have had
Gas station attendant, Shell Station, 3400 Main St.
(Jack Baker, owner), 6/88 to present
Duties: pump gas, take money, clean windshields, check oil

References
Rev. Joe Smith (pastor), 115 Oak St., Akron, Ph. 645-3945
Ms. Ann Sanchez (teacher), 412 Park St., Akron, Ph. 645-4112
Mr. Mark Bowman (store manager), 111 Elm, Akron, Ph. 645-3318

Be sure to have a personal fact sheet with you when you apply for a job. This will help you remember details and keep dates straight.

The words

Listed below are important new words that were used in this chapter. Next to each word is the page on which you will find the word in bold, black print. Turn back and read again the paragraph in which you find each word. Then write the word and its meaning on a sheet of paper. Also write a sentence of your own using each word.

1. employment agencies (104)
2. full-time jobs (98)
3. job lead (100)
4. part-time jobs (98)
5. reference (112)
6. recommendation (101)
7. responsibility (98)
8. social security card (109)
9. work permit (109)

The facts

1. What are three things you can learn from working part-time?
2. What's the difference between a part-time job and a summer job?
3. When is the best time of year to look for a summer job?
4. Name four places to get job leads.
5. How can your school help you find a job?
6. What is the difference between a state employment agency and a private employment agency?
7. What should you write on your job lead cards?
8. What are the yellow pages? How can they help you find job leads?
9. Name six things an employer may want to know about you.
10. What three things will you need before you apply for a job?

What's right here?

ADD TO YOUR KNOWLEDGE AND SKILLS

Talk about your ideas

1. Have you had a part-time job? If so, what did you do?

2. When or what hours would you like to work? Why?

Do some activities

1. If you do not have a social security card, get an application. Then fill it out and send it in.

2. Buy some 3 x 5 cards. Then ask your parents, friends, and teachers about job leads. Try to fill out at least ten job lead cards.

Improve your basic skills

1. Read "Help Wanted" columns in your local newspaper. Look for jobs you would like to do someday. Circle the ads in red. Then look for jobs you can do when you finish high school. Circle these ads in blue. Now look for jobs you are able to do now. Circle these in black.

Be ready to discuss your choices with the class. Tell why you are interested in jobs that you are not able to do now.

1. Prepare a fact sheet for yourself. Include at least three references. Look up their addresses and phone numbers to be sure you write them correctly. Keep this fact sheet and refer to it each time you apply for a job.

2. Write a half page on the most important things to remember about finding job openings.

3. Suppose that you would like to apply for some jobs. But you do not have any leads. Look through the yellow pages in your phone book. Find listings of places you would like to work. Then make a list of the names, addresses, and phone numbers. Save the list for future use.

5×7=?

1. Carmen has a lead for a job she would like. She could earn about $75 a week. But the job is twenty miles from her school. Carmen would have to borrow her mother's car and pay for the gas. If she gets twenty miles per gallon, how much gas will Carmen use each day? (Do not forget to include the mileage both to and from work.)

2. How much does gas cost per gallon in your area? Multiply the cost per gallon times the gallons per week. How much will it cost Carmen to drive to and from work each week?

Chapter 6

Applying for the Job

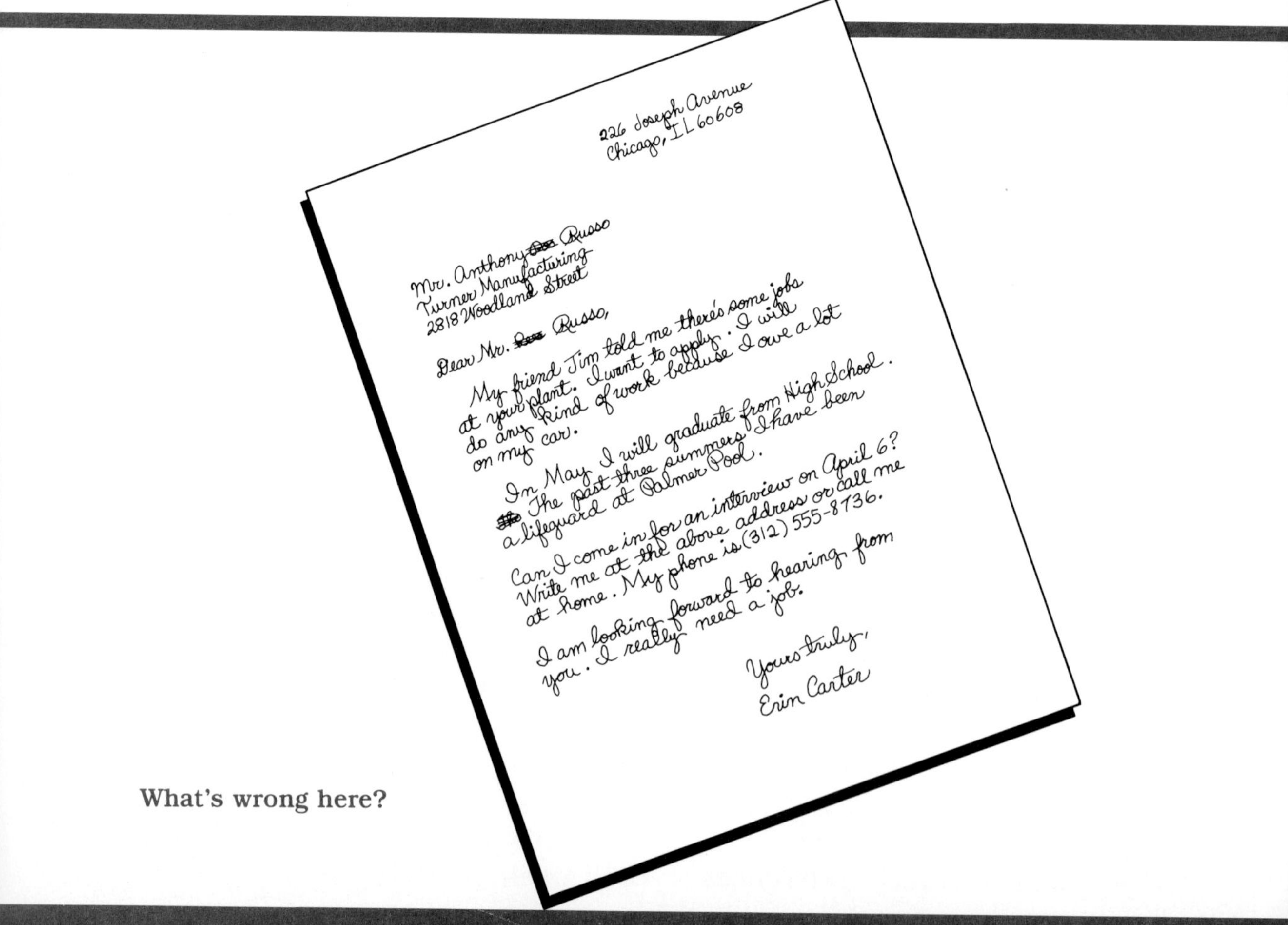

226 Joseph Avenue
Chicago, IL 60608

Mr. Anthony Russo
Turner Manufacturing
2818 Woodland Street

Dear Mr. Russo,

My friend Jim told me there's some jobs at your plant. I want to apply. I will do any kind of work because I owe a lot on my car.

In May I will graduate from High School. The past three summers I have been a lifeguard at Palmer Pool.

Can I come in for an interview on April 6? Write me at the above address or call me at home. My phone is (312) 555-8736.

I am looking forward to hearing from you. I really need a job.

Yours truly,
Erin Carter

What's wrong here?

Words to learn and use

You will learn several new words in this chapter. The most important words are listed below. Do you know the meanings of these words?

interview	negative
applicant	first impression
application form	resume
letter of application	dependable
positive	performance test

Build on What You Know

You already know . . .

- what jobs you are suited for and how to get job leads.
- how to use the phone properly and politely.
- how to write a letter.
- how to fill out a form.

In this chapter you will learn . . .

- three things to say when calling about a job.
- what to write in a letter of application.
- how to fill out an application form.
- how to write a resume.

In Chapter 5 you learned how to find job openings. You also discovered what employers will want to know about you.

In this chapter, you will learn how to apply for a job and the importance of an interview. Most employers use application forms. So you will learn how to fill out application forms. For some jobs you must write a letter of application. You will learn how to do this in six easy steps.

You will also learn what a resume is. You will learn how you can use one to help you get a job.

Contacting Employers

You now have your work permit, social security card, fact sheet, and job lead cards. You are ready to contact employers. Your goal in contacting employers is to get an interview.

An **interview** is a talk with an employer about a job. Employers will usually interview several applicants for each job. An **applicant** is a person applying for a job. Employers will ask each applicant many questions. Then they will select the person they want to hire.

Your first contact with an employer is very important. It is your first chance to make a good impression. It is your chance to get an interview. If you do not do well in your first contact with an employer, you may not get an interview. Without an interview, you cannot get the job.

There are three ways to contact employers.

1. Call on the telephone.
2. Write a letter.
3. Go in person.

Your first contact with an employer—whether it be by phone, mail, or in person—should make a good impression.

Calling on the Telephone

Calling on the telephone is often the easiest and best way to contact an employer. Call if you have a job lead from a relative, friend, or someone at school. If a newspaper ad gives a phone number, call to make your contact. An employment agency may tell you to call an employer.

Remember your telephone manners when you call.

- Speak clearly.
- Speak loudly enough to be heard, but not too loudly.
- Speak at a medium speed, not too fast and not too slow.
- Use proper English.
- Be polite.
- Know what you are going to say before you call. (Make notes ahead of time if you need to.)
- Be brief.

When you call, say these things.

1. Give your name. Simply say, "Hello. This is. . . . "
2. Say you are interested in a job. Tell the name of the job and how you heard about the job.
3. Ask when you may come in to apply.

Have you used the phone to call an employer? If not, practice with a friend. Have your friend play the part of the employer. Practice each call before you make it.

At the end of the call, be sure you understand what you are to do next. The employer may ask you to write a letter of application. He or she may ask you to fill out an application. He or she may ask you to fill out an application form or to be interviewed. Take notes so you do not forget. Get the details correct. Then do what you were asked to do.

When you contact an employer by phone, be sure you understand how you are to apply for the job. Write down the instructions.

Writing a Letter

Sometimes it is better to write the employer a letter than to call. In some cases you may have to write rather than call. For example, you may not have the phone number or be able to get it. In such a case you would have to write a letter or go in person. You will also find that some newspaper ads ask that you write a letter.

There are two kinds of letters that you may want to write.

1. A letter asking for an application form
2. A letter of application

The first kind of letter is very short. You just write that you are interested in a job and ask for an application form. An **application form** is a printed sheet with lots of blanks. You will write information about yourself in the blanks provided. You will learn how to fill in application forms later in this chapter.

A sample of a short letter asking for an application form is shown on the next page. Notice that the letter is written neatly. It has straight, wide margins. It is centered on the page. Of course it would make an even better impression if it were typed. When you get the application form, fill it out to apply for the job.

A letter of application is a longer letter. It takes the place of an application form. Letters of application will be discussed later in this chapter.

Going in Person

If you do not have a job lead, go in person. If a newspaper ad gives an address and no phone number, you can apply in person. An employment agency may ask you to apply in person. This means you will walk into the business and do these things.

1. Give your name.
2. Say you are interested in working on a certain kind of job.
3. Ask for an application form.

You may be told that there are no jobs available. Or the position may have already been filled. If this happens, ask for a job lead. Someone may know of an available job that you would enjoy. If you do get a lead, be sure to thank the person.

Check Up:✓✓ True or False?

1. You can contact an employer by phone, by letter, or in person.
2. When you call an employer on the phone, talk as long as you can.
3. It is okay to walk into a business and ask for an application form.

800 Main Street
White Plains, IL 63105
March 14, 1988

Joe's Steak House
815 Garden Street
Jonesville, IL. 67890

Dear Sir or Madam:

When I graduate from White Plains High School in May, I plan to move to Jonesville.

I have worked part time as a waitress and would like to work at Joe's Steak House. Please send me an application form.

Yours truly,

Linda Hill

You can ask for an application form in a letter.

The Application Form

Most employers require you to fill out an application form. Some employers ask you to fill out the form at the place of work. Others let you take it with you. If they will let you take the form with you, do so. Then you can take your time with it. Also, you can get help if you need it. A teacher or someone at home may help you. The better job you do filling out the application form, the better your chance of being hired. Those who do a poor job on the form will not be called for an interview.

If you fill out the form at the place of work, do it carefully. Take your time. Read the directions.

You must fill out the form yourself. You may not understand some questions on the form. If not, it is all right to ask the person who gave it to you to explain it. But do not ask for help filling out the form.

Be prepared to fill out an application form when you go to the place of business. Have a pen with you. Take your personal fact sheet along. Most businesses have their own application forms. They are all different. But they all ask about the same questions. Your fact sheet will have most of the answers for you.

Practice filling out some application forms before you apply for a job. Study the form on the next page. Ask your teacher for some practice forms. Here are some hints to help you fill out application forms:

1. Use a pen.
2. Most forms ask you to print. If so, do not use cursive writing with letters connected.

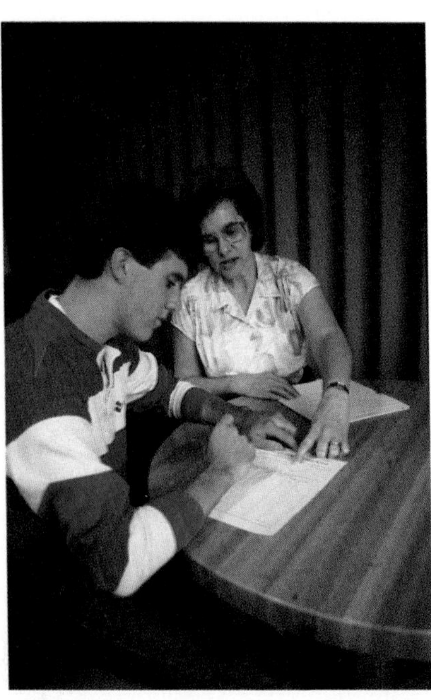

If you take an application form home, you can have a parent or guardian check it over for you.

3. Notice if the form asks for your last name first. Most of them do.
4. Answer every question. Do not leave any blanks. If a question does not apply to you, draw a short line in the space. This shows that you did not skip over it.
5. Give your complete address. List your street number and name, your city and state, and your zip code.
6. Spell correctly. Refer to your personal fact sheet. If you are not sure how to spell a word, use a dictionary. If you do not have one, use another word with the same meaning.

Say "Thank you," as you turn in the application form. Ask when you can expect to hear about the job. Ask if you should call back about the job.

7. There may be a question on "job preference" or "job for which you are applying." Answer this question with the name of the job you want. DO NOT just write the word "anything." Employers expect you to know what you can do.
8. There may be a question about your special skills. If so, write down all the things you can do that might help you on a job with that company. If you apply at a car wash, a helpful skill would be knowing how to drive. If you apply for an office job, typing 40 words a minute is a helpful skill.
9. When you sign your name on the form, use your correct name. Do not use any nicknames. Write your name in cursive writing. Your signature is never printed.
10. Be very neat. Tell the truth.

Check Up:✓✓ True or False?

1. Fill out an application form in pencil so you can correct your mistakes.

2. Application forms are all different but most of them ask for the same information.

3. Do not leave any blanks when you fill out an application form.

APPLICATION FORM

Joe's Steak House **815 Garden Street** **Jonesville 67890**

PLEASE TYPE OF PRINT CLEARLY

Hill	Linda	Ann	123-46-6789
Last Name	**First**	**Middle**	**Social Security Number**

800 Main St.,	White Plains,	IL	36105	(609) 963-1421
Address	**City**	**State**	**Zip**	**(Area Code) Home Phone**

In case of an emergency, whom should be called? Louis Hill (Name) (609) 963-8486 (Telephone Number)

What job or jobs are you applying for? Waitress (part-time)

What special skills do you have? Get along well with people

Education: Circle Highest Grade Completed. 1 2 3 4 5 6 7 8 9 10 11 12 13 14 15 16 17 +

List schools you have attended:

Grade School (last attended)

Name of School	Address	Dates You Attended	
Adams	100 Oak St., Ventura, CA	Sept., 1977-June, 1983	

Junior High School (last attended)

Name of School	Address	Dates You Attended	Did You Graduate?
Lakeview	530 4th St., White Plains, IL	Sept., 1983- June, 1986	Yes

High School (last attended)

Name of School	Address	Dates You Attended	Did you Graduate?
White Plains	700 Mill St., White Plains, IL	Sept., 1986-present	will graduate 5/89

Colleges or Trade Schools Attended

Name of School	Address	Dates You Attended	Did you Graduate?
—	—	—	
—	—	—	

Employment History (list most recent job first):

Employer	Address	Date of Employment	Salary or Wage
Chicken Betty's	White Plains, IL	Oct., 1986-Sept., 1987	3.75 hr.
7-11 Store	900 State, Marion, IL	June, 1985-Sept., 1986	3.50 hr.

References (not related to you):

Name	Address	Telephone
Mr. Harold Sims	3741 Carol St., Santa Barbara, CA	(805) 259-3414
Ms. June Taylor	1601 Menor, White Plains, IL	(609) 684-1439
Ms. Ann Thach	412 L St. Marion, IL	(609) 687-1341

Signed Linda Ann Hill

Your personal fact sheet should help you fill out an application form. Don't leave any spaces blank.

Letters of Application

Sometimes the only way to get an interview is to write a letter of application. A **letter of application** is a letter that asks for a job. In it you try to convince the employer to hire you. You may need to write a letter of application when

- you apply for a job out of town.
- you want to be interviewed by a business friend of your family.
- you answer a newspaper ad that asks you to apply by mail.
- an employer asks for your letter of application. A few employers want to see how well you use written English. Some do not have application forms printed.

Writing an Application Letter

A letter of application is a sales letter. In it, you sell yourself to the employer. The employer must feel that hiring you will make money for the business. That is the only reason you will be hired.

Explain your skills. Tell what experience you have had that will help you with this job. Do so in a **positive** manner. That is, tell good things about yourself. You might say,

> "I had straight As in my shop classes. I have changed tires and replaced spark plugs. I have also repaired brakes on my job at the gas station."

Do not say that you had bad grades in another subject. Do not say that you really need a job. Stress positive things you have done. Do not mention **negative** (bad) things.

As in any sales letter, you must make a good **first impression.** A first impression is the first feeling people have about you. They may like you. Or they may not like you at first. But first impressions often last a long time. You can make a good first impression in your letter by being very neat.

You may write your letter by hand or type it. If you write by hand, take your time. Write neatly. If you type well, you should type your letter. If you are applying for an office job, this letter is a chance to show how neatly you can type. For any job, a neatly typed letter with all words spelled correctly is impressive.

Letter Writing Checklist

Here is how to write a letter that will get attention.

1. In the first sentence, write where you learned of the job. You might begin, "Miss Smith asked me to write to you about the job as mail clerk in your office." The employer should know the person who told you of the job. If not, you must say who he or she is. You could begin, "Miss Smith, my math teacher, said you will need a mail clerk in your office. She suggested that I write to you." When answering a newspaper ad, you might begin, "Your advertisement in the TIMES for an assembler interests me."
2. In the second sentence, say you are applying for the job. You can say, "I would like to apply for this job."
3. Write about your education and work experience in the second paragraph. If you have not worked, do not say so. Write about the classes you have had and skills you have learned that can help you on the job. You may have had a lot of helpful classes and worked, too. If so, write the second paragraph on your education. Then write the third paragraph on your experience.
4. If you include references in your letter, write these in the next paragraph. Get permission from people to use their names.
5. In the last paragraph, ask for an interview at the employer's convenience. Write when you can be reached by phone and give your number. Thank the person for considering you.
6. Now read your letter and make changes to improve it. Make sure it is in the proper form. See the examples on pages 127 and 129. Then, rewrite your letter. Make sure the grammar and spelling are correct. Your teacher or a friend in business can help you. Read it one more time to be sure everything is right.

Interviews are given to those whose letters show they can do the job. Write one really good letter. Then you can use it as a guide when you write other letters. Of course, you will have to change the first paragraph. But the rest of the letter will be about the same.

A good, neat letter of application will help you get an interview.

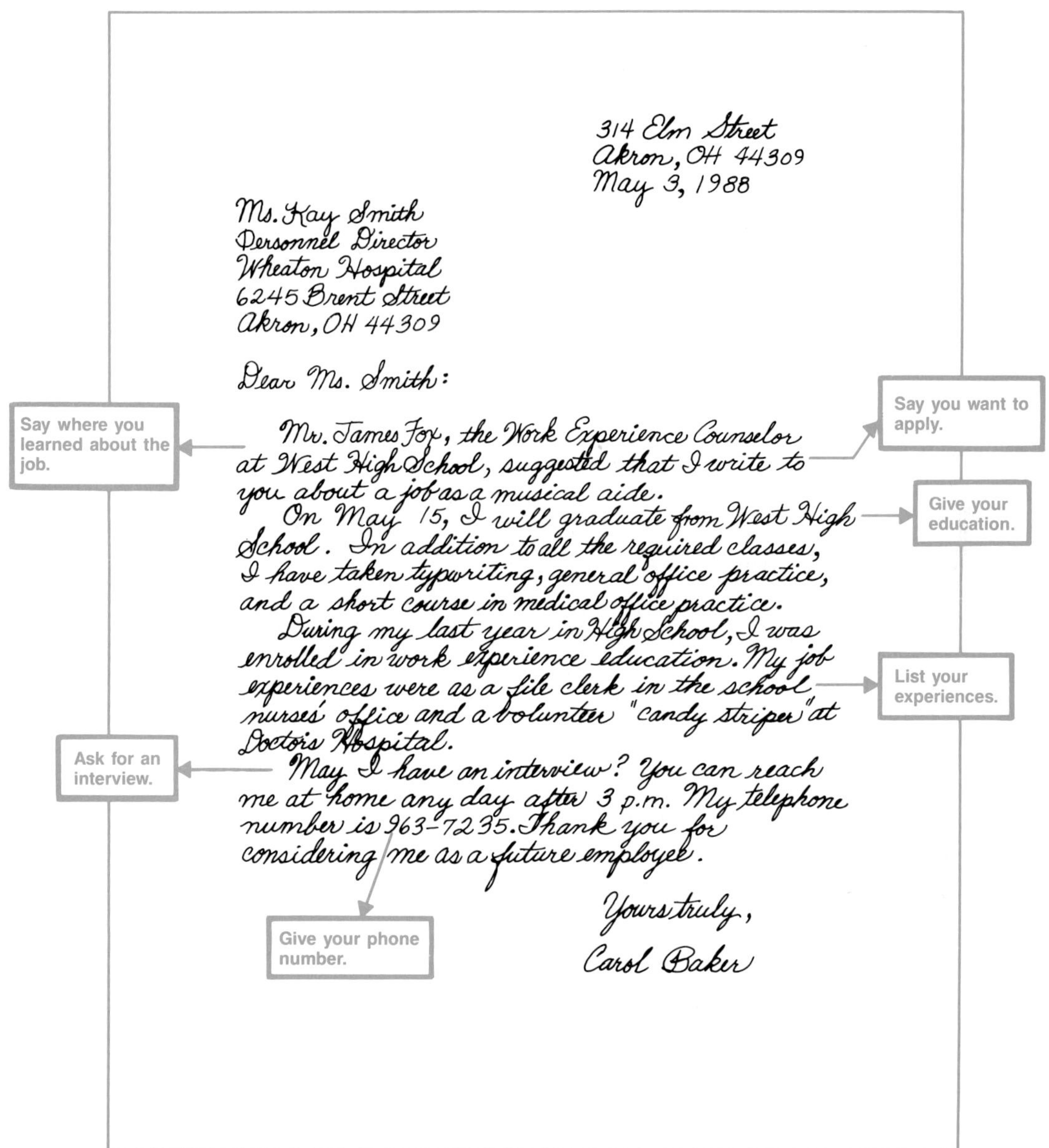

314 Elm Street
Akron, OH 44309
May 3, 1988

Ms. Kay Smith
Personnel Director
Wheaton Hospital
6245 Brent Street
Akron, OH 44309

Dear Ms. Smith:

Mr. James Fox, the Work Experience Counselor at West High School, suggested that I write to you about a job as a musical aide.

On May 15, I will graduate from West High School. In addition to all the required classes, I have taken typwriting, general office practice, and a short course in medical office practice.

During my last year in High School, I was enrolled in work experience education. My job experiences were as a file clerk in the school nurses' office and a volunteer "candy striper" at Doctor's Hospital.

May I have an interview? You can reach me at home any day after 3 p.m. My telephone number is 963-7235. Thank you for considering me as a future employee.

Yours truly,

Carol Baker

A letter of application should tell what job you want and something about yourself. It should also ask for an interview.

Typing an Application Letter

A neatly typed letter is easy to read. You may have a better chance of being hired if you type your letter. If you type, these hints will be helpful:

1. Place a sheet of typing paper, 8½ by 11 inch size, in your typewriter. Set both margins 1½ inches from the paper edge.
2. Type your street address 2 inches down from the top of the sheet. Look at the sample letter on the next page. The address should end even with the right margin. On the line below your street address, type your city, state, and zip code. On the next line, type the date.
3. Begin the employer's name and address 1½ inches down from the date line at the left margin. Check the spelling of the name of the person and business. Be sure that the address is correct.
4. If you are addressing your letter to a person, the greeting should look like this:

   Dear Mr. Dale:
   or
   Dear Ms. Hall:

   When you do not know the name of the person who will read your letter, use a greeting like this:

   Dear Sir or Madam:

   The greeting should be followed by a colon (:) as shown.
5. Type your letter carefully. One or two corrections are all right.
6. Your closing should be typed two (2) spaces down from the last sentence. It should be like this:

   Yours truly,
   or
   Yours very truly,

   Only the first word of the closing is capitalized. The closing is followed by a comma (,) as shown.
7. After the closing, space down four (4) spaces and type your name.
8. Before you take your letter from the typewriter, read it. Check for mistakes. It is easier to correct them while the letter is still in the typewriter.
9. Sign your name with a pen above your typewritten name.

Check Up:✓✓ True or False?

1. The purpose of a letter of application is to ask for an application form.
2. In a letter of application you should tell all the bad things about yourself.
3. Typing your application letter may help you get a job.
4. If you make errors typing your letter, just leave them. An employer will not notice them.

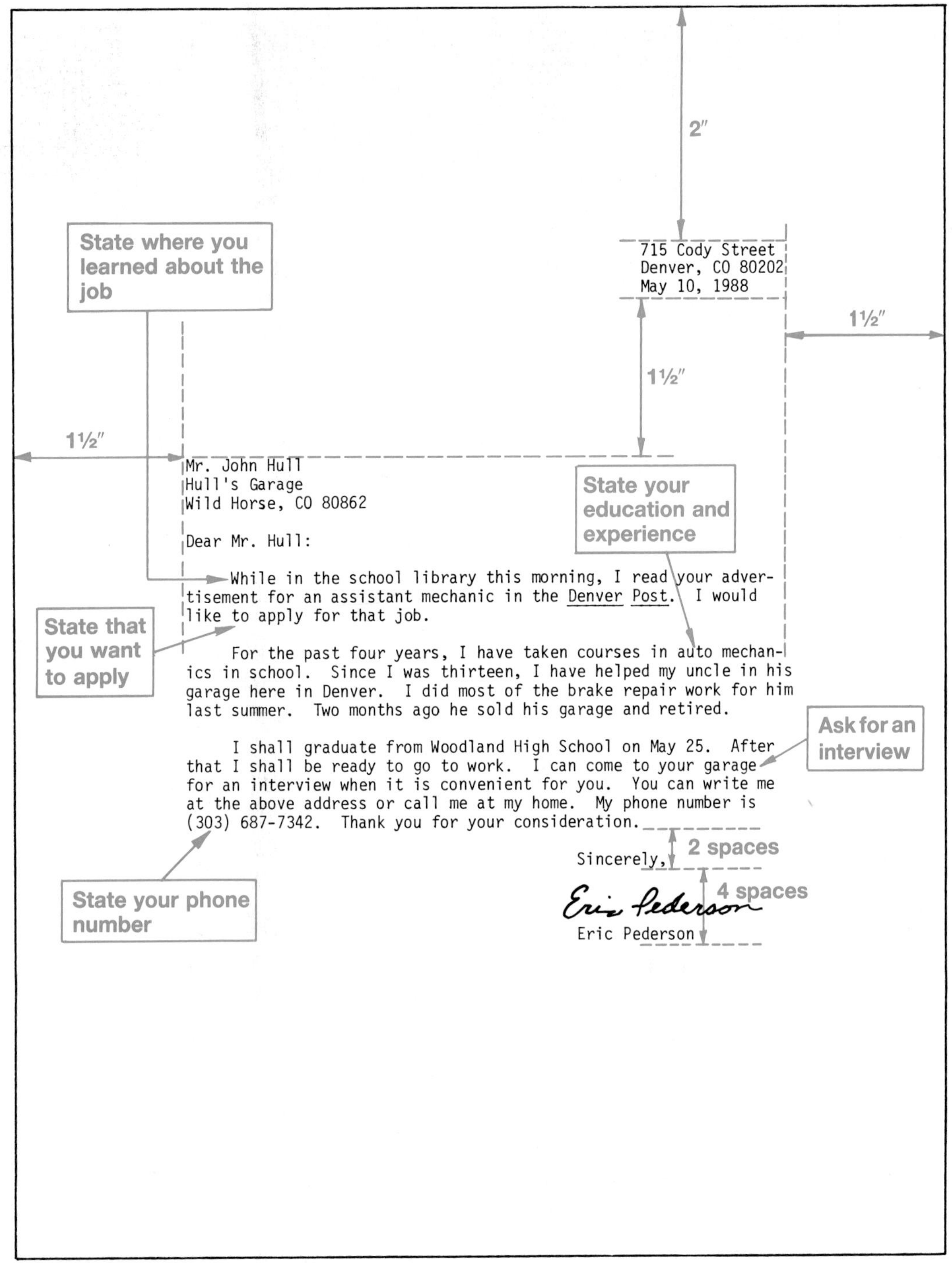

715 Cody Street
Denver, CO 80202
May 10, 1988

Mr. John Hull
Hull's Garage
Wild Horse, CO 80862

Dear Mr. Hull:

While in the school library this morning, I read your advertisement for an assistant mechanic in the Denver Post. I would like to apply for that job.

For the past four years, I have taken courses in auto mechanics in school. Since I was thirteen, I have helped my uncle in his garage here in Denver. I did most of the brake repair work for him last summer. Two months ago he sold his garage and retired.

I shall graduate from Woodland High School on May 25. After that I shall be ready to go to work. I can come to your garage for an interview when it is convenient for you. You can write me at the above address or call me at my home. My phone number is (303) 687-7342. Thank you for your consideration.

Sincerely,

Eric Pederson

Eric Pederson

A letter of application should be typed neatly just like any other important business letter.

Resumes

You know how to fill out an application form. You know how to write a letter of application. These skills can help you get an interview. But a lot of other young people can do these things, too. What else can you do to help yourself get an interview and be hired? You can make up a very neat resume.

"Resume" is a French word, pronounced rez-oo-may. A **resume** is a summary of facts about you that might be of interest to an employer.

Most resumes include seven parts.

1. Your name, address, and phone number.
2. The type of job you want.
3. Your skills. Include such skills as typing, filing, and using a calculator. List all skills that apply to the job you want.
4. Your education. List vocational classes. List other classes that might help you on the job.
5. Your work experience. List all the jobs you have had. Include the name and address of each employer. List your jobs in reverse order. That is, write down your most recent job first. Then write your next most recent job. Your first job will be listed last. Even short-term jobs like baby-sitting and gardening can show that you are **dependable.** Being dependable means that others can count on you.
6. Personal information. Include your date of birth and hobbies. Then list your best personal traits. For example, you might write "dependable, good at following directions, and take pride in my work."
7. References. List three or four adults who know you and will give you a recommendation. Again, do not list relatives.

Write the first copy of your resume. Use the example on page 131 as a guide. Then make corrections. Rewrite it. Then correct it again. Then type it very neatly. If you do not type, have someone type it for you.

Make a dozen copies of your resume. Send a copy with each letter of application. Hand a copy to each employer where you fill out an application form, too.

Check Up: ✓✓ True or False?

1. You should list your skills on your resume.
2. A resume should be typed.

KAY ANDERSON
314 Mission Drive
Wichita, Kansas 67213

(316) 369-2305

JOB OBJECTIVE

Waitress or Hostess

SKILLS

Follow directions well
Have good handwriting
Type 40 words a minute

Get along well with others
Operate a cash register
Have good calculator skills

EDUCATION

Will graduate from Wichita West High School in May, 1989. My courses include:

Home Economics	3 years
English	3 years
Math	3 years
Typing	1 year

WORK EXPERIENCE

Cashier, Northside Hardware Store, 2400 W. Douglas Street, Wichita, KS (May, 1987 to present)

Desk Clerk, Western Motel, 320 Hydraulic, Wichita, KS (May, 1986 to September, 1986)

PERSONAL INFORMATION

Date of birth:	September 16, 1970
Interests:	Photography, swimming, reading
Transportation:	Drive my own car to school and work
Traits:	Dependable, good at following directions, always on time
Limitations:	Limited vision in right eye

REFERENCES

Mrs. Arleen Jacobs
Wichita Electric Co.
444 Camden Street
Wichita, KS 67213
(913) 762-1438

Dr. Louise Fisher
Snyder Medical Clinic
510 West Redford
Wichita, KS 67213
(913) 762-7827

Mr. Arnold Smith
Marion High School
Marion, KS 66861
(913) 828-1640

Miss Lynne Morrison
720 Newton Avenue
Newton, KS 67114
(913) 438-1492

On a resume you can add personal traits and skills that you might not write on an application form.

A Desire to Succeed

Learning to Learn: Ervin Carpenter

Ervin Carpenter is a person with a handicap. His is not a handicap you can see. Ervin's handicap is a learning disability. It is called *dyslexia*. This handicap makes reading very difficult.

Ervin grew up not knowing that he had dyslexia. He saw letters and numbers upside down and backwards. To Ervin, *b* was *d* and *g* was *p*. He saw *from* instead of *form*, *was* instead of *saw*.

Ervin failed first grade. By the time he was in high school, he was far behind the others. So at sixteen, Ervin dropped out of school to go to work.

Getting a job was not easy. He could not read job application forms. He became a laborer and earned the minimum wage.

Ervin worked until he was seventeen. Then he joined the Army. While in the Army, Ervin studied hard and finished high school. It took him twelve years!

In the Army, Ervin was in the airborne infantry. He jumped out of airplanes. Several times he was injured. After his last injury, in 1982, he was given medical retirement.

Retired from the Army at thirty two, Ervin was frightened. He did not know how he would earn a living. By then he had a wife and four children. With his medical handicap, he could not do physical labor.

Ervin's wife, Kim, wanted him to go to college. Ervin never thought he could do that. But he told Kim he would try.

At the University of Wisconsin in Oshkosh, Ervin learned that he had dyslexia. With special help, there was a good chance that he could learn to read.

At the university, a group called Project Success helped him. He learned to read, spell, write, and do math. They also made him feel good about himself.

After five years, Ervin graduated from the university. He is now a special education teacher. He is happy helping others who have a hard time learning—especially learning to read.

Employment Tests

Employers may ask you to take some tests when you apply. These tests help them learn who will be best for the job. There are several different kinds of employment tests.

If you apply for skilled work, you may be asked to show your skill. You will take a performance test. A **performance test** is doing some of the work you will do if hired. It is a "try out."

The kind of test you take depends on the job you want. For a typing job, you will take a typing test. For a welding job, you may do some welding. For a job as a carpenter, you may do some carpentry work. These tests let you show that you can do the work.

Some employers give aptitude tests. These tests show how easy it will be for you to learn some things. Here is an example. Suppose you applied for a job as an assembler. As an assembler you would put parts together with your hands. The parts must be put together very fast. But the work must be done right, too. An aptitude test can show how well you can learn to do this.

A performance test will help the employer decide if you have the necessary skills for the job.

REVIEW

REMEMBER WHAT YOU LEARNED

The words

Listed below are the important new words that were used in this chapter. Next to each word is the page on which you will find the word in bold, black print. Turn back and read again the paragraph in which you find each word. Then write the word and its meaning on a sheet of paper. Also write a sentence of your own using each word.

1. applicant (118)
2. application form (120)
3. dependable (130)
4. first impression (125)
5. interview (118)
6. letter of application (125)
7. negative (125)
8. performance test (133)
9. positive (125)
10. resume (130)

What's right here?

The facts

1. Name three ways to contact an employer.
2. What are three things you should say when you call an employer about a job?
3. What two kinds of letters are often written to employers?
4. When you walk into a business without a job lead, what three things should you say?
5. When might you write a letter of application?
6. What should you write in the first sentence of your letter of application?
7. What should you write in the second paragraph of a letter of application?
8. What should you stress in a letter of application?
9. How can your personal fact sheet help you fill out an application form?
10. What three things should you write first in your resume?

ADD TO YOUR KNOWLEDGE AND SKILLS

Talk about your ideas

1. Would you rather fill out an application at the place of work or take it with you? Why?
2. Should you always tell the truth on an application? Why?
3. How can you make your letter of application sound positive?

Do some activities

1. Ask your teacher for sample application forms. Fill in the forms. Then give them to your teacher. Ask you teacher to help you correct any mistakes.
2. Go to three local businesses and ask for application forms. Fill out the forms. Then ask your teacher to check them. Once you have filled them out correctly, return the forms to businesses where you would like to work.

Improve your basic skills

1. Read again the letters on pages 127 and 129. Make notes on which are the best parts of each letter. Also, note whether some parts are not so good. How could these letters be changed to make a better first impression? Discuss your ideas about these letters with the class.

1. Check the "Help Wanted" columns. Find a job that you would like. Write a "first copy" of a letter of application. Refer to pages 125-129. Show your teacher your letter. Then make changes to improve it. Rewrite the letter. You may use it as a guide for other letters.
2. Prepare the first copy of a resume. Write it out by hand. Then show your resume to your teacher. Ask for help to correct any mistakes you may have made.
3. Prepare a file of sample forms that you can refer to later. Include the following:
- personal fact sheet
- a sample job application, neatly filled out
- a sample letter of application, neatly typed
- a sample resume, neatly typed

5×7=?

1. Suppose you mail 12 letters of application along with your resume. How much will stamps cost if they are 22 cents each?
2. Suppose you make a long-distance phone call to apply for a job. The rate is $1.35 for the first minute and 60¢ for each additional minute. You talk for four minutes. How much will the call cost?

Chapter 7

Interviewing for the Job

What's wrong here?

Words to learn and use

You will learn several new words in this chapter. The most important words are listed below. Do you know the meanings of these words?

reputation	letter of thanks
appearance	follow up
appropriate	attitude
standard English	empathy
qualifications	

Build on what you know

You already know. . .

- how to contact employers.
- how to fill out application forms.
- how to write a letter of application.
- how to write a resume.

In this chapter you will learn. . .

- how to prepare for a job interview.
- how to act at an interview.
- how to answer interview questions.
- how to write a thank you letter after the interview.

In the last two chapters, you learned how to find job leads and how to apply for a job. These are the things that will get you an interview.

In this chapter, you will learn to prepare for a job interview. You will learn what clothing to wear and what to take with you. You will then learn what questions the interviewer may ask. You will also learn what questions to ask the interviewer. Finally, you will learn how to write a letter of thanks for the interviewer's time.

Before the Interview

When employers are ready to hire a new employee, they read the application forms they have received. They pick several people they think might be right for the job. Then they call each of these people in for an interview.

The interview is a chance to show the employer that *you* are the right person for the job. The employer will ask you many questions. He or she will want to find out about you. Can you do the job? Can you get along with others? Can you talk well?

After the interview, the employer will make a decision. He or she will decide who will make the best new employee. That person will get the job. So doing well at the interview is very important.

When you are offered an interview, write down the time of the interview. Also write the address and the name of the person you are to see. Ask for the spelling of the interviewer's name and how to pronounce it. This can all be written on a job lead card.

Take some time to get ready for an interview. Look over your personal information sheet. Make a list of classes you have had in school. If you have worked, be ready to talk about your jobs. Try to find out something about the company. Know what products it makes or what services it gives. Know how big it is. Know its **reputation,** that is, what people think of it. Make notes about the company so you will remember.

Here are some things you will want to take to the interview.

- A pen and pencil (You may need to fill out some forms.)
- Your social security card
- A work permit, if required
- Your personal information sheet
- Notes about the company

Being prepared for the interview will help you relax and do a good job.

Check Your Appearance

When you go to the interview, the employer's first impression of you will be based on your **appearance,** or how you look. So give some care to your grooming and clothes. You should, of course, take a bath before you dress for an interview. Some people forget to do this. Their body odor may end any chance of being hired. The smell of cigarettes loses jobs, too. This odor is annoying to people who do not smoke.

Your hair must be clean and neat. Fingernails must be clean and trimmed. Boys, shave before the interview. Girls, use only a little makeup.

Remember you are looking for a job, not going to a party.

Carefully select what you will wear to the interview. Choose clothes that are **appropriate,** or proper, for the job. Boys who apply for a job as salesclerk will wear a suit or sports coat and slacks. Girls will wear a dress or skirt and blouse. Do not wear a lot of jewelry.

Leather dress shoes look better than tennis shoes in an interview. Well shined shoes make a good impression. The employer will look at you as one who will represent the business.

If you apply for an outdoor job, such as working in a horse stable, casual clothes are okay. You could wear jeans and tennis shoes. Whatever you wear, be sure it is clean and pressed.

Your skills may be about the same as those of others who apply. If so, the employer will hire the one who makes the best impression. Do not lose a job because of sloppy or improper dress.

Check Up:✓✓ True or False?

1. An employer usually interviews several people for the job before deciding whom to hire.
2. You do not need to take anything with you to the interview.
3. It does not matter what you wear to an interview. The boss just wants to hear what you have to say.

Going for the Interview

A few days before the interview, find out how to get to the business. Have you been in that part of town before? If not, you may want someone to go with you. A friend, your teacher, or a parent may go along. But only as far as the front door! From there, you are on your own. The only exception is if your teacher or parent knows the employer and plans to introduce you.

One boy took his friend with him to the interview. The employer liked his friend better and hired the friend. A girl took her mother in for the interview. The girl was not hired. Neither was her mother. Employers seldom hire those who need help in the interview.

Plan to arrive for the interview about five minutes early. If you are driving, allow some extra time in case traffic slows you up. If you are even one minute late, it makes a bad impression. But do not be too early. Five minutes early is about right. When you arrive, you may ask other workers for directions to the employer's office. Be very pleasant to them. After you leave, the employer may ask them how they liked you.

Rushing in at the last minute makes a bad impression.

At the Interview

During the interview, the employer will try to learn more about you. How you look, how you speak, and how you act will affect your chances for the job. Do your best to make a good impression.

Use Standard English

When you apply for a job, use standard English in everything you say and write. **Standard English** is the use of words that mean the same thing to everyone. It means using proper grammar and spelling words correctly. This is the kind of English you have learned in school.

Not everyone uses standard English. Some people use much slang. Slang is all right around home or with friends. But it is not all right during an interview or on the job. If you use slang, you may not be understood. Using clear, standard English shows that you can communicate clearly.

Check Up:✓✓ True or False?

1. It is all right to be a few minutes late for a job interview.
2. You should not take a friend with you for an interview.
3. Always use standard English during a job interview.

Mrs. Jones is interviewing Karen and George.

Interview I

MRS. JONES: The person on this job will also answer the phones. Can you handle the typing and the phones, too?

KAREN: My typing teacher says I do real good. And I got tons of experience talking on the phone.

MRS. JONES: I see. How would you get to work, Karen?

KAREN: Well, I don't got a car. So to apply, you know, for this job I come with Mary. She got a car.

Interview II

MRS. JONES: If you are hired, you will also answer the phones. Can you handle the typing and the phones, too?

GEORGE: Yes, I'm sure I can. I type 60 words a minute. My teacher says he will recommend me. I have not answered a business phone, but I know I can learn how.

MRS. JONES: Good. If you are hired, how will you get to work?

GEORGE: I don't have a car, but I can ride the bus and be here by three.

Which person do you think Mrs. Jones hired? Why?

A Desire to Succeed

Living with Deformity: Charles Steinmetz

Charles Steinmetz was born in Germany in 1865. He was born deformed. He never grew to be very tall. His head was oversized. His arms and legs were twisted. In fact, it sometimes hurt him to walk.

At first, Steinmetz did not like school. But he knew that school was his chance to learn about things that made him curious.

He graduated at seventeen. He was the only one in his class who did not have to take the oral exam. This was an honor because he had done so well in his studies.

Then Steinmetz went to college. He was outstanding in math. He joined the math society. There he made many friends who were interested in the same things he was.

When he was a young man, a friend was going to the United States to find work. He invited Steinmetz to go with him. His friend paid his way.

The officials in New York almost did not let him stay. He had no money. He had no job. He could not yet speak English. He was deformed. His friend talked them into letting him into the country.

In two weeks, he found a job. He used his math skills to design new motors. He developed a famous theory about magnetism.

Later he went to work for the General Electric Company. He improved transformers by using alternating current. He figured out how to calculate alternating current.

Steinmetz was elected president of the American Institute of Electrical Engineers. He was made Master of Arts by Harvard University. He taught electrical engineering at Union College in New York.

It is said that Steinmetz had a good sense of humor. He gave to charity. He was a friend of many famous people—Albert Einstein, Marconi, and Thomas Edison, to name a few. He gave speeches. He was quite famous himself.

Steinmetz had this to say about work. "To succeed is to make a living at work which interests you. Because your work interests you, it is not work at all."

Be Polite and Businesslike

Part of acting correctly in an interview is using good manners. Another part is being able to carry on a good conversation. Here are some tips on how to act at an interview.

Introduce yourself. The employer may know you and call you by name. If not, another worker may introduce you. Sometimes you must introduce yourself. You might say, "I am Lynn Fisher. I am interested in a job as a waitress."

Speak clearly and loudly enough to be heard. Smile, and stand up straight. Do not offer to shake hands until the interviewer does. When the interviewer does offer to shake hands, grasp his or her hand firmly. A limp handshake makes a bad impression. However, do not try to show how strong you are by squeezing too hard!

Stand until the interviewer asks you to sit. If you are not asked to sit down, then stand for the interview. When you do sit, sit up straight. Do not slouch. You may feel nervous at the start. But you will relax some after the interview begins. Look the interviewer in the eye most of the time. Some people do not trust a person who cannot look them in the eye.

Start the interview by introducing yourself and giving a firm handshake.

Show that you respect the interviewer. If you have a book or purse with you, keep it in your lap or on the floor. Never place anything on the interviewer's desk. Do not lean on the desk or read papers on it. Keep your hands in your lap. Do not chew gum or smoke.

Be ready to talk about you. There are two ways to interview. The interviewer may ask you to tell about yourself. If so, you must do most of the talking. You must tell why you think you can do the job.

You can show your respect for the interviewer by not leaning on the desk or placing any of your belongings on it.

The other way an interviewer finds out about you is by asking questions. This is what most interviewers do.

In your first interview you will probably be a little nervous. Every person is. The interview can be easier if you know some of the questions that will be asked.

Look at the list of interview questions on page 146. Be ready to answer them all. You may want to practice answering them with a friend before the interview.

Be totally honest during the interview. If you do not know an answer, say you do not know. Most interviewers can tell if you are not honest.

There are two questions that cause problems for some young people.

1. What kind of work do you want?
2. How much pay per hour do you expect?

Think about these questions before your interview. How will you answer the first question? Some young people just say, "anything." This upsets many employers. They want to put you on the job you can do best. Be ready to say what jobs you would like and could do.

How will you answer the other question, about money? It is best not to state an exact amount. It may be too low. Then you may earn less than others doing the same work. If you say too high an amount, you may not be hired at all. What you can say is, "I am sure you know more about what is fair pay than I do. What do you pay for this type of work?"

If pressed for an answer, say an amount you know others earn for this work. The employer may not mention money. Then it is all right to ask what you will be paid. However, do not bring it up too soon. It would sound as if you only care about the money.

If you are applying for a permanent, full-time job, you may ask about vacations. But wait until the interview is almost over. Most part-time workers do not get vacations.

Talking at the Interview

A big part of doing well at an interview is being able to talk well. When an interviewer asks a question, answer it pleasantly, honestly, and thoroughly. Be enthusiastic. Try to sell yourself. Here are some questions that Mr. Brown asked job applicants. Which answers are good answers? Which answers are poor ones?

____

MR. BROWN: Jane, why do you want to work for this company?
JANE: I'm interested in working with the computers. And this company has a good reputation. I think your products are among the best. I also understand that workers here are treated very well.

____

MR. BROWN: Ann, why do you think you should be hired for this job?
ANN: Because I'm behind on my car payments. And I need to buy some new clothes. I owe my parents money, too. If I don't get a job soon, I don't know what I'll do.

____

MR. BROWN: Bill, what job are you interested in?
BILL: Anything.
MR.BROWN: I see. Well, what job would you most like?
BILL: Anything.

____

MR. BROWN: Jack, what subjects did you like best in school?
JACK: I enjoyed most of them. But I think I liked math best.

____

MR. BROWN: Carol, what do you want to be doing in five years?
CAROL: Who knows. I can't plan that far ahead.

Questions Often Asked in an Interview

The interview is an exchange of information. It is helpful both to the employer and to you. The employer tries to learn what you are really like. You have a chance to see if you really want the job. In most cases, the employer asks you questions. You can also ask questions.

Questions the Employer Might Ask

1. Why would you like to work for this company?
2. Do you want a permanent or temporary job?
3. What job would you most like?
4. What do you want to be doing in five years?
5. What **qualifications** do you have for this job? (This just means what skills and experience you have that will help on this job.)
6. What subjects in school did you like best? Least?
7. Do you prefer working alone or with others?
8. How do you use your free time?
9. What can you do best? What can you not do?
10. What jobs have you had? Why did you leave?
11. What pay do you expect?
12. Have you had any serious illnesses?
13. Do you smoke?
14. How many days of school did you miss last year?
15. What grades did you get in your schoolwork?
16. What hours can you work?
17. How will you get to work?
18. Do you take part in sports at school? Are you on a team? (Some employers think if you are on a team you will not have time to work.)
19. Are you willing to work overtime when needed?
20. What questions would you like to ask me?

Questions You Might Ask

1. What are the duties on this job?
2. What are the hours?
3. Would I be working with someone else?
4. If I need help, whom can I ask?
5. What is the pay?

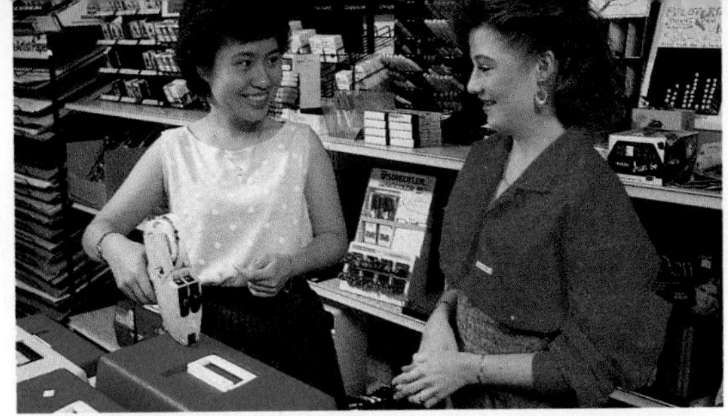

The interview is a good time to find out more about what you will be doing on the job. It's also a good time to give information about yourself.

Show interest in the company. Most interviewers are pleased if you also say why you want to work for the company. This is one reason to check on the company before the interview.

Ask some questions about the company, too. Does it make a product? If so, ask where it sells its products. Think about what you want to know about the company before the interview.

Be prepared to be interviewed twice. You may have two interviews for the same job. The interviewer may ask you to talk with someone else in the company. This person may be a supervisor or someone you will be working with if hired. This may mean that the interviewer thinks you can do the job. Your chances are good!

When the interviewer is over, go! If you have told why you think you can do the job and have answered all the questions, the interview is over. At the close of the interview, one of these things may happen.

1. You are offered the job.
2. You are told they will let you know in a few days.
3. You are asked to call them in a few days.
4. You are told they cannot use you.

If you are offered the job, you will have to decide whether to take it. You may say yes and start work right away. You may turn it down. Or you can say, "May I let you know in a day or two?"

This is a good idea if you have other interviews lined up. Some employers will not want to wait. If this is the case, you will have to say yes or no when the job is offered.

The interviewer may not tell you whether you got the job. Then you can ask one of these questions.

1. "Will I be called when you make a decision?"
2. "May I call in a few days for your decision?"

Then say "thank you," and go.

Check Up:✓✓ True or False?

1. Using good manners and acting businesslike are important at a job interview.
2. You will give better answers at an interview if you do not know what questions to expect.
3. Never ask the interviewer any questions. That would not be polite.

After the Interview

When the interview is over, you have several things to do. You will want to think about the interview so you can learn from your experience. You will want to thank the interviewer. You will want to follow up on the interview.

Think About It

After each interview, take time to think about it. How did it go?

- Were you properly dressed?
- Did you arrive on time?
- Did you answer all of the interviewer's questions?
- How did you handle the question about pay?
- Do you still want the job?
- Were you offered the job?
- What can you do better next time?

After the interview, take time to think about how well you did. Then write the employer a thank you letter.

Write a Thank You Letter

Write a **letter of thanks** for the interview. This shows you are still interested. It shows you care enough to make time to write a letter of thanks. Most people do not do this. However, it impresses employers! It increases the chances of being hired. Do it the very next day after the interview.

Your letter may be typed, handwritten, or printed. But it must look neat. A sample thank you letter is shown on the next page.

Follow Up

Finally, do not forget to follow up on the interview. To **follow up** means to finish or to do the next step.

If you are told to call in a few days, wait two or three days. Then call. If you are told that you will be called, wait about a week. Then call to say that you are still interested.

Check Up:✓✓ True or False?

1. After the interview, your work is done. Just wait for a call.
2. You gain experience with each interview.
3. A letter of thanks may impress your employer.

142 Circle Drive
Brockton, MA 20403
May 14, 1988

Mr. Charles North
276 Mill Street
Brockton, MA 20403

Dear Mr. North:

I want to thank you for interviewing me yesterday afternoon.

The job interests me very much, and I believe I can do a good job for you. Even if I don't get the job, though, I appreciate the opportunity to be interviewed.

Sincerely yours,

Rebecca Cole

A letter of thanks like the one above helps make a good impression on the employer.

Reasons People Are Not Hired

You will not be offered a job every time you are interviewed. Nobody is. When you are not hired, you will want to know why. A survey was made to find out the main reasons people are not hired. The most important reasons are listed first.

1. Poor appearance
2. Poor attitude
3. Poor use of English
4. No career goals
5. Lack of interest in the job
6. Not sure of the kind of work wanted
7. Wanted too much money
8. Poor school record
9. Made excuses
10. Poor work record
11. Lacked experience
12. Criticized past employer
13. Not tactful
14. Not courteous
15. Disliked school
16. Did not look interviewer in the eye
17. Limp handshake
18. Could not answer questions
19. Did not get along well with parents
20. Sloppy application form
21. Did not seem serious about working
22. Only wanted to work a short time
23. No interest in the company
24. Critical of others
25. Does not know right from wrong
26. Does not always try to do what is right
27. Lazy
28. Could not take criticism
29. Late to interview without good reason
30. Did not say "thank you" for the interviewer's time
31. Did not ask questions about the job

"I just can't understand why we wasn't hired."

An Employer's Point of View

When you start looking for a job, it may help to know what employers think is important. The following letter was written by an employer to a teenager who was not hired. Read the letter. Then think about how your attitude compares to Frank's.

Dear Frank:

Today you asked me for a job. From the way you walked in, I suspect you have been turned down before. Maybe you think you will never find work.

But I hired a teenager today. You saw him. He was the one wearing polished shoes and a necktie. What was so special about him? Not experience. Neither of you had any. It was his **attitude,** his outlook on life, that put him on the payroll instead of you. Yes, attitude. He wanted that job enough to get a haircut. He looked in the phone book to find out what this company makes. He did his best to impress me.

Some young people think they are *entitled* to a job! That is, they think we owe them a job even if they are not qualified. But those of us who hire do not feel we owe anybody a living. Maybe that makes us old fashioned. But our checks are good. If you want one, try to please us.

Ever hear of *empathy?* **Empathy** means seeing the other person's side of things. You said you were behind on your car payments. That was no reason for me to hire you. What I needed was someone who would work for me like he would work for himself. If you have ANY idea of what I am trying to say, let it show the next time you apply for a job. You will be way ahead of others who apply.

All around you, employers are looking for willing, eager young men and women. When they find them, they are happy to hire them. For all our sakes, try to become a willing worker. Try to improve your attitude.

Carol Simpson

REVIEW

REMEMBER WHAT YOU LEARNED

The words

Listed below are the important new words that you learned in this chapter. Next to each word is the page on which you will find the word in bold, black print. Turn back and read again the paragraph in which you find the word. Then write each word and its meaning on a sheet of paper. Also write a sentence of your own using each word.

1. appearance (139)
2. appropriate (139)
3. attitude (151)
4. empathy (151)
5. follow up (148)
6. letter of thanks (148)
7. qualifications (146)
8. reputation (138)
9. standard English (141)

The facts

1. Why is a job interview so important?
2. What five things will you want to take with you to the interview?
3. How should you dress for a job interview at an insurance company? At a summer camp?
4. Should you take someone with you to the interview? Why, or why not?
5. Should you arrive early for your interview? How early?
6. Should you use slang at the interview? Why, or why not?
7. What are three examples of good manners you should use at an interview?
8. Name two ways an employer may interview you.
9. Name five questions an employer might ask on an interview. Name three things you might want to ask an employer.
10. What three things should you do after the interview?

What's right here?

ADD TO YOUR KNOWLEDGE AND SKILLS

Talk about your ideas

1. How have you dressed for job interviews? Will you dress the same way next time? Explain.
2. If you must introduce yourself to employers, what will you say?

Do some activities

1. Follow your teacher's directions. The class will be divided into two groups, "employers" and "applicants." The employers will conduct interviews with applicants. Applicants may choose the type of job to apply for. Employers may use the questions on page 146 or make up their own questions. After the first interview, employers and applicants will change places. Your teacher may set up an "office" for the interviews.
2. Write down five questions from page 146 that you think are easy to answer. Then write down five questions that you think are hard. Help others with questions you can answer. Ask for help to answer your hard ones.
3. Write down which reasons, from page 150, that you think are "good" reasons for a person not to be hired. Then write down the ones that you think are *not* good reasons. Explain your choices.

Improve your basic skills

1. Find a book about manners or business etiquette in your school or local library. Read parts of it. Decide what parts could be used to help you make a good impression at an interview. Report your findings to the class.

1. Write the name of a job you might apply for. You may use one that you found in the want ads when you studied Chapter 5. Write a paragraph explaining to the employer why you would be good for that job.
2. Write a letter of thanks for an interview. Make up the name of the company and interviewer.

5×7=?

1. Suppose you have an interview at 4:30. It is a twenty minute drive from home to your interview. But it is raining. So it may take an extra five minutes. You want to be five minutes early. What time should you leave home?
2. Suppose you need new shoes for your next interview. You find a pair for "half off" the regular price. Sales tax is 6%. How much will you pay for shoes regularly priced at $40?

PART THREE

YOU ON THE JOB

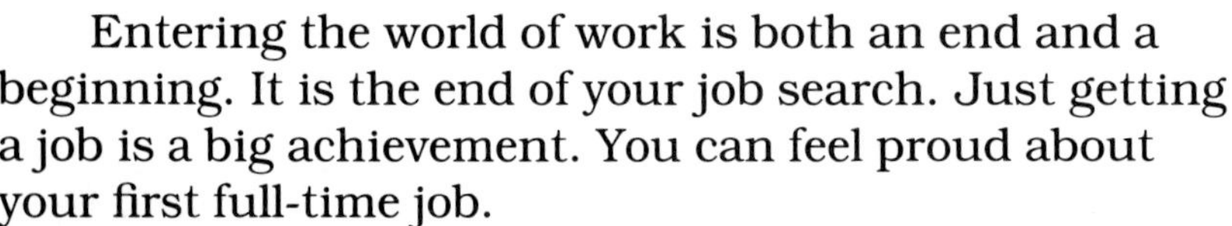

Entering the world of work is both an end and a beginning. It is the end of your job search. Just getting a job is a big achievement. You can feel proud about your first full-time job.

Starting a job is also a beginning. You have new people to meet. You have new things to learn. And you will probably be a little nervous.

Knowing what to expect on a new job can help. You will be more confident and know the right way to act. You will get started on the right foot. You will be a better worker.

Part Three gives you lots of information. It is all about your first days on the job. It tells what it means to be a good worker. You want to do things right from the very beginning. This will help you reach your career goals much faster.

Chapter 8

Your First Days on the Job

What's wrong here?

Words to learn and use

You will learn several new words in this chapter. The most important words are listed below. Do you know the meanings of these words?

Employee's Withholding Allowance Certificate (Form W-4)
fringe benefits
pension
unions
collective bargaining
labor contract
right-to-work laws
union steward
body language
good grooming

Build on what you know

You already know. . .

- how to get along with classmates and teachers.
- how to decide what job you want.
- how to apply for a job.
- how to interview for a job.

In this chapter you will learn. . .

- what decisions you will make during your first days on the job.
- how to make a good first impression on your boss and co-workers.
- how to learn to do you new job well.
- what to learn about the company you work for.

In Part 2 of this book you learned how to get the job you want. Now it is time to start your new job. There are many things to learn and remember. There are decisions to make.

In this chapter you will learn about some decisions you need to make. You will learn how to meet and make a good impression on your co-workers. You will also learn about your new job and the company you work for.

Getting Started

During your first days on the job, you will be expected to learn and to do many things. You may work for a large company. If so, you will receive booklets and other written material about the company. Take them home and read them carefully.

You may work for a small company. Then your boss may just explain things about the company. Listen carefully. Ask questions about information you do not understand.

The W-4 Form

An **Employee's Withholding Allowance Certificate** is a written statement. It gives your boss information that will affect your income taxes. It is often called a **W-4 form.**

All new employees must fill out a W-4 form. Your boss will ask you to fill out one when you start work.

Each time you are paid, your employer will keep a small part of your wages. Then this money will be used to pay your taxes. The W-4 will help your boss know how much to keep for your taxes.

As a young, single person your W-4 will probably be easy to complete. Write in your name, address, and social security number. Check the box marked "single." On line 4, the form asks for "total number of allowances you are claiming." Enter "1." Sign and date the form at the bottom. See the example below.

Lower income workers may have no tax money held back at all. Ask your boss if this might be true for you. If so, fill in the boxes on line 6.

Are you married? Do you have more than one job? Do you have other income? In these cases ask if you should fill out a W-4 worksheet.

Cut here and give the certificate to your employer. Keep the top portion for your records.

Form **W-4A** Department of the Treasury Internal Revenue Service

Employee's Withholding Allowance Certificate

▶ For Privacy Act and Paperwork Reduction Act Notice, see reverse.

OMB No. 1545-0010 **1987**

1 Type or print your full name: Tamara June Wilson

2 Your social security number: 408-10-1452

Home address (number and street or rural route): 111 Timberlane Dr.

City or town, state, and ZIP code: Mooresville, NY. 11000

3 Marital Status: ☒ Single ☐ Married ☐ Married, but withhold at higher Single rate

Note: *If married, but legally separated, or spouse is a nonresident alien, check the Single box.*

4 Total number of allowances you are claiming (from line G above, or from the Worksheets on back if they apply) . . . 4 | 1

5 Additional amount, if any, you want deducted from each pay . . . 5 | $

6 I claim exemption from withholding because (check boxes below that apply):

a ☐ Last year I did not owe any Federal income tax and had a right to a full refund of **ALL** income tax withheld, **AND**

b ☐ This year I do not expect to owe any Federal income tax and expect to have a right to a full refund of **ALL** income tax withheld. If both **a** and **b** apply, enter the year effective and "EXEMPT" here . . . ▶ Year 19

c Are you a full-time student? . . . ☐ Yes ☐ No

Under penalties of perjury, I certify that I am entitled to the number of withholding allowances claimed on this certificate or, if claiming exemption from withholding, that I am entitled to claim the exempt status.

Employee's signature ▶ Tamara June Wilson **Date ▶** March 2, 1988

7 Employer's name and address **(Employer: Complete 7, 8, and 9 only if sending to IRS)** | 8 Office code | 9 Employer identification number

A Desire to Succeed

Driving for Independence: Paul Ceriale

Paul Ceriale lives in Santa Barbara, California. He is the youngest of six children. Paul has a learning handicap. Reading, math, and motor skills are hard for him. At San Marcos High School, Paul took classes for special needs students.

Most of Paul's friends got their driver's license when they were sixteen or seventeen. But not Paul. Paul could not read. So he failed the driver's education class. Then he could not take driver's training.

Paul was not happy about that. Driving, he thought, would help make him independent.

But Paul is a determined young man. He had learned responsibility on part-time jobs. He began his first job when he was in ninth grade. He helped keep his school campus clean. Later he worked part-time in a print shop.

Paul had learned to stick with a job until it was done, and done right.

Paul had learned the benefit of working hard in sports, too. His motor-skill problem made running, jumping, and throwing difficult. But he worked very hard and overcame this problem. He won the 400-yard race in the South Coast Special Olympics. He also won the mile race and set a new record. In the State Special Olympics, he won a silver medal in the mile race. He was named Athlete of the Year for the South Coast.

Paul continued to study for the driver's test. At nineteen he passed. Getting his license was a big step for Paul.

After graduation from high school, Paul took a job at the Biltmore Hotel. His boss says that he is very successful on his job. Of course, he drives his car to work every day.

Paul still gets excited about sports. He also enjoys flying model airplanes. Sometimes he just takes off in his car to enjoy the drive.

Paul is not a quitter. He continues to study and to learn. Despite his disability, he is becoming an independent person.

Fringe Benefits

When you are hired for a job, you agree to work for a certain wage. You will receive a paycheck every payday. Some companies give special pay or services to their full-time workers, too. These extras are called **fringe benefits.** At first you may receive only a few of these benefits. After you have worked awhile, you may receive others.

Not every company gives all or the same benefits. You will be told about your company's fringe benefits. You may be asked to make some decisions about certain benefits.

Paid holidays. Most companies give holiday benefits. Several days each year are holidays. Workers are paid without working on these days. Your boss should tell you which days are paid holidays.

Vacations. Most employers give vacation time, too. You may get a day or two vacation time for each month of work time. Suppose you get a day of vacation for each month you work. After you have worked for a year, you can take a twelve-day vacation. You will be paid for the time you are gone from work.

Some employers let their workers take vacation a day or two at a time. Always plan your vacation ahead of time. Talk with your boss about taking vacation time.

Most companies give their workers some paid vacation time each year.

Sick leave. Some companies give workers paid time off if they are sick. You may be allowed a day or two a month. Your boss will explain the company's sick leave policy.

Profit sharing. Companies with good profits may give a part of this money to workers. This is called a profit sharing program.

You may be able to buy stock in the company. When you buy stock shares, your company may give you some shares, too. This is a good way to make and to save money. It can also help you feel more a part of the company.

Insurance. Some companies offer health insurance to their workers. Some offer life insurance, too. Workers often pay part of their insurance costs. The company pays the rest of the cost. Your employer will ask you if you want to buy the insurance they offer. Buying insurance on your own is very expensive. Buying insurance through your work is usually cheaper.

Retirement benefits. Older workers may get a **pension** when they quit work. A pension is like a salary you receive after you retire. You must work for the company a number of years to get a pension. You can usually sign up for a retirement plan after you have worked awhile.

Leisure activities. Quite a few companies have leisure activities for their workers. They may have a tennis court or a swimming pool. Employees may play on ball teams or be invited to social activities.

Education. Many companies pay part of the cost of classes taken by a worker. These classes may help you learn to do your job better.

Legal help. A few companies give legal assistance. If workers have tax or credit problems, they may get help.

Discounts. Some retail stores allow their employees to buy their products at less cost. This is called a **discount.**

Baby-sitting. A few companies provide child care for workers' children. There may be a day care center in the building where you work or nearby.

Retirement benefits give older people an income after they retire.

Check Up:✓✓ True or False?

1. You will fill out a W-4 form at the end of each year.
2. All companies give their workers many fringe benefits.
3. Sick leave is time off work with pay while you are sick.

Unions

In the early days of industry, most people worked twelve hours a day. They worked for very low wages. Working conditions were often dangerous. Those who complained were fired.

Then workers on some types of jobs formed groups. These groups were called **unions.** Workers in a union stuck together. The union leaders spoke for all the workers, so employers listened.

Today, many factory workers belong to unions. Many in skilled trades, like carpenters and plumbers, belong to unions. There are unions for many other types of work, too.

Now most people work only eight hours a day. There are minimum wage laws. So you will likely be paid well. If you are under eighteen, you will not have to do dangerous work.

Still, employers and workers disagree sometimes. Workers may want more money. They may want to work fewer hours. Or they may want better conditions. Union leaders and company managers try to settle the problems.

They sit down and talk. Each side has to give a little. This is **collective bargaining.** When they agree, they sign a **labor contract.** It covers wages, hours of work, and working conditions.

Find out if the workers in your company belong to a union. If so, find out if all workers must join or if you have a choice.

Union workers sometimes strike to get the benefits they want. Workers are not paid by the company while they are on strike.

John had an interview with a trailer manufacturing company. He was happy when he was hired. His job was to assemble cabinets for trailers. John liked his first job very much.

It was the second week at work. John was invited to join the union. He did not know what to do. Then a friend told him that he did not have to become a union member. Their state had a *right-to-work* law.

So John decided to wait. Later he would know more about the factory. Then he could decide what was best for him.

Some states have laws about workplaces that have union contracts. These laws require all workers to belong to the union if their place of work has a union contract. If you work there, you must become a union member.

Twenty states have passed **right-to-work laws.** These laws allow you a choice. So you may choose whether you want to join a union.

Most unions give workers a copy of the contract. As a new worker, you should read it carefully. It tells about workers' pay, promotions, and work times. It lists times you may be absent, tardy, or work overtime. It describes working conditions. It tells how to report times when these rules are not obeyed.

Under a union contract, the boss represents the employer. A **union steward** represents the workers. The steward is elected by union members. A new worker should meet the steward soon after starting to work. The steward tries to help you if the contract is not followed. Most union members also help new workers.

It will cost you money to belong to a union. It may cost over $100 just to join. then you must pay dues every month. Monthly dues are usually at least $20. And they may run more than $100.

Unions can give you good benefits. But they can cost you a lot, too. If you have a choice, ask questions. Make your decision carefully.

Check Up:✓✓ True or False?

1. Right-to-work laws let you choose whether or not to join a union.
2. If you join a union, you should read the union contract so you will know the rules.
3. Unions are free.

Meeting People

The first days on the job you will meet some of the people in the company. You will be working together. So you will want to make a good impression on them. You want to *relate* well.

Relating means getting along. It means understanding others. It also means making others understand you. Here are some hints that will help you relate well with people.

- Smile.
- Meet people pleasantly.
- Introduce yourself.
- Show an interest in other people.
- Show a positive attitude.
- Do not get too chummy.

Smile

Notice the expression on the faces of students as they walk to class. Some will be smiling. Some will look sad. Others may have no expression at all.

The expression on a person's face says a lot. Have you known anyone who wore a frown most of the time? Such people are not easy to like. But the person who smiles easily and often is easy to like. When you smile, it is like saying, "I like you." When you smile at others, they smile back.

Meet People Pleasantly

On many jobs, the boss will introduce you to the other workers. If the boss does not introduce you, sometimes one of the other workers will.

When you are introduced, you should say, "How do you do," and repeat the person's name. If you are introduced to Joe, you should say

"How do you do, Joe."

A less formal greeting that is acceptable to most people is simply

"Hello, Joe."

If Joe Green's last name is given, you should say

"How do you do, Mr. Green."

Many people also shake hands. If you do, use a firm grip—but not too firm.

When you are introduced to a co-worker, say hello. Use the person's name. Repeating the name will help you remember it.

Introduce Yourself

Sometimes no one makes the introductions. Be prepared, then, to introduce yourself. Some people do this easily. However, many workers are shy. Sometimes people do not know what to say.

Some people are not good at introductions. It is awkward working with people when you do not know their names. Someone needs to make the introduction. It might as well be you.

An easy way to introduce yourself to another person is to smile and say hello. Then give your name. If your name is Ann, you would say

"Hello. My name is Ann."

The other person will almost always give his or her name. If not, you can ask

"What is your name?"

After you exchange names, it is courteous to make some "small talk." You can ask about the other person's job. You can say you are happy to be working with that person. You can say something nice about the company. Once you start talking, you will feel more at ease.

Show Interest in Other People

On most jobs, people work together. It is fun to work with people who like you. The best way to get people to like you is to be interested in them.

Show your interest by asking about things that interest them. Talk about their hobbies. Listen to them. Many people do not listen well. Some interrupt others to talk about their personal interests. Interrupting is bad. You will not make many friends by talking about yourself and your interests. You can make friends by talking about their interests.

Body language is another way to show your interest. **Body language** is what your body tells others. And it tells a lot! You show how you feel by how you sit, stand, or move. Body language tells a person how interested you are in what he or she is saying.

People who are bored may show it by tapping a foot or staring blankly. People who are interested often show it by looking in the eyes of the person talking. They also sit on the edge of a chair and lean toward the person talking.

Check Up:✓✓ True or False?

1. If your boss does not introduce you to your co-workers, you should introduce yourself.
2. Smiling is one way to show people you are friendly and willing to get along.

Show a Positive Attitude

Your attitude is your outlook on life. You show it in your behavior. Your attitude forms over the years, beginning when you are a small child.

A good attitude is sometimes called a positive attitude. A poor attitude is negative. If you always look for the good things, you have a positive attitude.

If you look only at the bad side of things, you may have a negative attitude. Those with negative attitudes often feel they are treated unfairly. They may not like people much. If this is you, you can change! You can do a lot to become the person you want to be.

The chart below lists the behavior of those who have positive and negative attitudes. Practice being positive. Do this while you are young. The longer you wait, the harder it is to change.

Having a positive attitude will help you get along well with your co-workers, your boss, and others. Getting along with people is very important. In fact, the main reason young workers lose their jobs is that they do not get along with people.

Work Attitudes

Most people have some positive and some negative traits. Practice these positive traits. Try to get rid of the negative ones.

Positive Attitude	Negative Attitude
• Smiles easily	• Rarely smiles
• Is willing to change ideas and behavior	• Is unwilling to change
• Can see another person's point of view	• Cannot see another person's point of view
• Rarely complains	• Complains about everything constantly
• Accepts responsibility for their mistakes	• Blames others for their own mistakes
• Seldom criticizes others	• Is very critical of others
• Is considerate of others	• Thinks only of self
• Looks other people in the eyes when talking with them	• Does not look other people in the eyes
• Respects the opinions of others	• Forces own opinions on others
• Never makes excuses	• Often makes excuses
• Has a variety of interests	• Has few interests

Do Not Get Too Chummy

In Chapter 1 you learned that one reason for working is social contact. You can meet new people on the job. You may develop friendships at work.

But remember, your workplace is not a social club! Employers are in business to make money. You must help make money for the company.

How friendly should you be at work? You should always be pleasant. Try to be friendly with everyone. But do not get too "chummy" too soon. Take your time making close friends.

Do not spend too much time with one or two people. You might pick the wrong people for friends. They may turn out to be troublemakers. Then others may think that you are a troublemaker, too. Learn about everyone before you pick your best friends.

In some workplaces people use only first names. In other companies, beginning workers call older workers by their last names. If you are not sure, use a person's last name. Say "Mr.," "Mrs.," or "Miss." Then say the person's last name. Some women prefer "Ms." (pronounced *miz*). When you do not know if a woman is married, use "Ms." You might say

"Good morning, Ms. Jones."

or

"Hello, Mr. Smith."

Some workers, when you are first introduced, may ask you to call them by their first names. Then, of course, you would do so. But if they do not ask you to call them by their first names, begin by using their last names.

Finally, do not try to be too chummy with the boss. Other workers may not like you if you do. Do not try to be the boss's "favorite." The boss may think you are not showing him or her respect.

Last month Carol began her first full-time job. She is a typist in an insurance office. Ann is another typist in the same office. Ann is very friendly, so Carol spends all her coffee breaks with her. Ann tells Carol all the office gossip. Now Carol has noticed that some of the other workers do not like to talk with her. Since Ann is a gossip, they think Carol is one, too.

George began working at the ABC Auto Shop last month. He helps the mechanics. Larry is one of the mechanics. He is very friendly. So George eats lunch with Larry. They have gone bowling together several times. George is more helpful to Larry than to the other mechanics. One of them has told the boss that George is not a very good worker.

Learning Your Job

Employers only hire workers when a job needs to be done. If you are hired, it is because your employer thinks you can do the job. It is important that you do the job well. You may want to keep it for a long time.

If you do quit, you may need a *recommendation*. This is a letter from your employer saying that you are a good worker. So do your very best. Start by learning how to do each task properly.

Follow Directions

Your boss will tell you what to do. He or she will tell you how to do it. Listen carefully. If you do not understand something, ask about it.

What to do and how to do it are directions. Follow them exactly. You may not understand why something is done. But as a beginner, just do it. After you have worked for a while, you may make some suggestions. But be careful! Some employers do not like new workers to suggest ways of doing things. On the next page is a test on following directions. It is just for fun.

Ask for Help When You Need It

Your boss or another worker will show you how to do your job. There are times when you will need help. If you do not know what to do, ask someone. If you do not know how to do something, ask for help.

Most often, when you need help, you should ask your boss. Your boss may be called a *supervisor*. Sometimes the boss is called a *foreman*. At times, your boss may not be around. Other workers are often glad to help a beginner.

After you know how to do your job, do it yourself. Do not depend on others. They have their own work to do.

Your boss or co-workers will be glad to show you how to do your job correctly. Listen carefully so you can soon do it on your own.

Five-Minute Timed Test on Following Directions

How well do you follow directions? Follow the directions and you should finish this in five minutes. Your teacher will time you. Close your book when you finish.

Wait until your teacher says "go." Then follow the directions exactly. You will need one sheet of paper.

1. Read all directions before doing anything.
2. On a sheet of paper, write your name in the upper right corner.
3. Number from 1 to 6. Leave three blank lines between each number.
4. Put an "X" by number 1.
5. Count the number of pages in Chapter Four of this book. Write the answer by number 2.
6. Write today's date by number 3.
7. Say your name out loud.
8. Count the number of persons in the room. Write the answer by number 4.
9. Say, "I have reached number 9. I am following directions carefully."
10. Now that you have finished reading, do only what is said in numbers 1 and 2.

Becoming a "Team" Worker

On some jobs, you may work alone. You may not even see anyone else. But on most jobs you will work with others.

Companies are in business to make money. When you work, you must help the company make money. If the company does not make money, it "goes broke." Then there is no money to pay you. The company goes out of business.

So, working well with others is even more than "getting along" with them. It means doing your part to help the company make money.

It is like being on a team. Everyone must do his or her job. Have you played baseball? Each player has a job to do. When the ball is hit, the other team tries to get the batter out. One way is to quickly throw the ball to first base. It must be thrown fast to beat the runner. It must be thrown straight so the player at first base can catch it. The player who always throws fast and straight is a good team "worker."

Playing on a team can help you learn to work with others. Being a good "team worker" on the job is even more important than on a baseball team. No one worker can do everything. Each must do his or her job. Each is part of the team. Get that team spirit in your work.

All members of a team must pull together to win the race. This idea is also important in the world of work.

Working on a job is like being a member of a team. Everyone does a fair share of the work to get the job done right.

Work Fast, but Do a Good Job

You know that you must do enough work to help the company make money. You must make more money for the company than you are paid in wages. You cannot work too slowly. You must get the job done without taking too much time. However, do not try for just speed. If you try to do things too fast, you may make mistakes. The work may be sloppy. Work as fast as you can to do a good job.

Work as fast as you can, but do a good job. Mistakes are costly to the company.

Do More Than You Are Asked to Do

As a new worker, do exactly what you are told to do. Learn your job well. Then look around where you work. You may see things that need to be done. Ask your boss if you should do them. Soon you will know which things you can do. If you can do it, do it. Employers like this. It saves them time and makes them money. Some of this money may be used to give you a raise!

Finish Each Job

Some people are always starting something new. They never finish anything. Have you known anyone like this? On the job, you must finish what you start. Of course, you may have to leave one task for a while to do something else more important. But always come back and finish what you started. Sometimes this is hard, but always do your best.

Check Up✓✓ True or False?

1. It is important to make a best friend or two during your first week on the job.
2. You can learn to do your job well by following directions and asking questions.
3. A good team worker works well with co-workers.

Starting on the Right Foot

When you start a new job, your boss and your co-workers may watch you very carefully. They watch new workers for many reasons. They want to know if you are doing a good job. They watch to see if you need help. They watch to see that you are following company rules. They want to know if you are using your work time fairly. They want to see if you are a team worker and whether you fit into the workplace.

You will want to find out company rules right away when you start a new job. Then keep your eyes and ears open. Look for ways that you can become a good company team member.

Use Your Employer's Time Fairly

Find out what time you are to be at work each day. Learn when quitting time is. Always be on time for work. Never leave early or quit working early.

Also learn when lunch and break times are. Do not stretch your breaks into longer time periods than they are supposed to be.

Never leave work to run errands of your own. Work hard while you are on the job. Not working at your job during your work hours is stealing from your employer. It will make your co-workers dislike you. It is also a good way to lose your job.

Use your company's time fairly. When you are at work, do your job.

Lunchtime can be a good time to get to know your co-workers. Be sure to follow company rules, however, as to when and where you eat your lunch.

Follow Other Rules

There may be other things you should learn about during your first few days. For example, if you drive to work, find out where to park your car. If you ride the bus, find out where the nearest bus stop is.

See if there are company rules about things such as where you eat your lunch. Do most of your co-workers bring a sack lunch to work? If so, you may want to also. Does your company have a lunch room? You may want to eat lunch at a restaurant. If so, be sure that it is all right with your boss. Then be sure that you are back to work on time.

You may work in an office. If so, you may be allowed to have food or beverages at your desk. Notice if other workers do. There may be a soft drink machine or a coffee pot in the building. Do not eat or drink at your workplace if you are not supposed to.

Check Up: ✓✓ True or False?

1. You can learn a lot about company rules by noticing how other workers act.
2. Not working hard while you are on the job is cheating your employer.
3. Your boss cannot fire you just because you are often late for work.

Always Show a Good Appearance

You know that appearance is important in an interview. You must show a good appearance on the job, too. It is a way to show respect for those around you. Remember, they see more of you than you do! You only see yourself when you look in the mirror.

The clothes you wear will depend on the type of job you have. Look around to see what other workers are wearing. A suit may be proper for the office. Jeans and a sweatshirt may be correct for a factory job. Always dress correctly.

Be sure your clothes are clean and neat. Many employers feel that sloppy looking workers will do sloppy work.

A good appearance includes **good grooming,** too. This means being clean, neat, and showing good taste in hairstyle and clothing.

For example, women may want to wear some makeup and a little perfume. Too much of either may prevent a woman from being well groomed.

Men need to shave as often as necessary. Those with beards should keep them well trimmed.

Which of these two workers would you hire? Why?

Grooming Checklist

Good grooming is being clean, neat, and showing good taste in hairstyle and clothing. How do you rate yourself?

	Good	Poor
BODY	☐ Daily bath or shower ☐ Use deodorant ☐ Underarms dry and clean	☐ Body odor ☐ Needs shaving ☐ Dirty skin
HAIR	☐ Clean ☐ Neat	☐ Dirty ☐ Needs trimming
FACE	☐ Clean ☐ Fresh, natural looking	☐ Dirty ☐ Beard stubble ☐ Too much makeup
TEETH	☐ Clean, brushed often ☐ Fresh breath	☐ Not brushed today ☐ Bad breath
HANDS	☐ Clean ☐ Nails trimmed	☐ Dirty or stained ☐ Nails too long ☐ Nails chewed off
POSTURE	☐ Stand and sit straight	☐ Stoop or slouch
CLOTHES	☐ Correct for work ☐ Clean ☐ Look pressed ☐ Fit well	☐ Not correct for work ☐ Dirty or stained ☐ Wrinkled ☐ Fit poorly
SHOES	☐ Correct for work ☐ Clean, polished	☐ Not correct for work ☐ Dirty or scuffed

The words

Listed below are the important new words that were used in this chapter. Next to each word is the page on which you will find the word in bold, black print. Turn back and read again the paragraph in which you find the word. Then write each word and its meaning on a sheet of paper. Also write a sentence of your own using each word.

1. body language (165)
2. collective bargaining (162)
3. Employee's Withholding Allowance Certificate Form (W-4) (158)
4. fringe benefits (160)
5. good grooming (174)
6. labor contract (162)
7. pension (161)
8. right-to work laws (163)
9. unions (162)
10. union steward (163)

The facts

1. What is a W-4 form? When will you get one?
2. Name six fringe benefits that you may get from your employer.
3. How can being a union member help you? What is a disadvantage to being a member?
4. What are right-to-work laws?
5. What are five rules you should follow when meeting your co-workers?
6. How can you show a positive attitude? How can you overcome a negative one?
7. Name two rules for learning to do your job well.
8. What does it mean to be a team worker? How can you become a good team worker?
9. Name at least three ways to use your employer's time fairly.
10. What does it mean to show a good appearance at work?

What's right here?

ADD TO YOUR KNOWLEDGE AND SKILLS

Talk about your ideas

1. Which do you think is more important—a good salary or many fringe benefits? Why?
2. Think of someone who seems to care about others. How does that person show his or her interest? Can you show others that you are interested in them? Why, or why not?
3. What are some ways people show what they think or feel through body language? What does each action tell you about that person?

Do some activities

1. Divide into small groups. Have one person be the boss, one a new worker, and the others co-workers. Practice making introductions. Trade roles and practice again.
2. Talk to a worker in a large company and one in a small company. Find out what fringe benefits their companies offer.
3. Talk with someone who is a member of a union. Talk with someone who is the boss of union members. Ask them about the good and bad points of unions. Do they have different ideas about unions?

Improve your basic skills

1. Find a newspaper or magazine article about body language or labor unions. Read the article and tell the class what you learned.
2. Read a book or article about two of the following:
   - how to act at work.
   - dressing for success.
   - good grooming.

Tell the class what you learned.

1. Write a paragraph about what you can do to develop a more positive attitude.

5×7=?

1. You decide you would like a cup of coffee each morning at work. The cost is 15 cents a cup. Suppose you work twenty days each month. How much will you spend each month for coffee?
2. You decide to treat your co-workers to doughnuts. They are $3 a dozen. You buy eighteen doughnuts. What is the cost before adding tax?
3. You and two friends go out to lunch. The waiter brings a bill for $15. You decide to add 10% for a tip. Then you each pay one-third of the total. How much will each person pay?

Chapter 9

Safety on the Job

What wrong here?

Words to learn and use

You will learn several new words in this chapter. The most important words are listed below. Do you know the meanings of these words?

OSHA
ground
high voltage
fire extinguisher
flammable
ventilated
vapors

Build on what you know

You already know . . .

- safety rules for your home.
- safety rules for your school.
- some traffic safety regulations.

In this chapter you will learn . . .

- personal habits that will keep you safe and healthy on the job.
- how to use tools and machines safely.
- how to prevent fires and what to do in case of fire.
- what to do in case of illness or injury on the job.

In Part Three you are learning about being on the job. Chapter 8 gave you suggestions for your first days. You read tips to help you make a good impression. Now you will learn another tip. This important tip is to "Practice safety on the job."

How do you practice good safety on the job? You can dress right and act right. You can learn to handle tools and machines safely. You can learn how to handle dangerous materials and prevent fires. You can learn what to do if someone becomes ill or injured at work. You will learn about all of these things in Chapter 9.

Safety Is Important

Can you imagine how much money a million dollars is? It is certainly a very large sum. It can buy a lot of things. It would be a shame to waste that much money. Yet every year accidents on the job cost many millions of dollars.

Who pays for the cost of accidents? You do. Everyone does.

If you are the one who is injured, you have two kinds of costs. One, you may suffer pain from a cut, a burn, or a broken bone. Two, an injury can cost you money. You may have to pay for medical care that your insurance does not cover. You may miss work and not get paid for a while. You may never be able to work again.

Even if you are not the one hurt in a work accident, you still pay part of the cost. Suppose an accident happens in a shoe factory. The shoe company has to pay for the medical help for the injured workers. It has to pay them sick leave. It must hire temporary workers to make the shoes while the injured people are off the job.

All of these costs are figured into the cost of the shoes the company sells. So when you buy a pair of shoes, you pay part of the cost of that accident.

It is no wonder that employers like to hire safe workers. Safe workers prevent accidents and save money. Other people like to work with safe workers. Safety helps you, your employer, your co-workers—everyone.

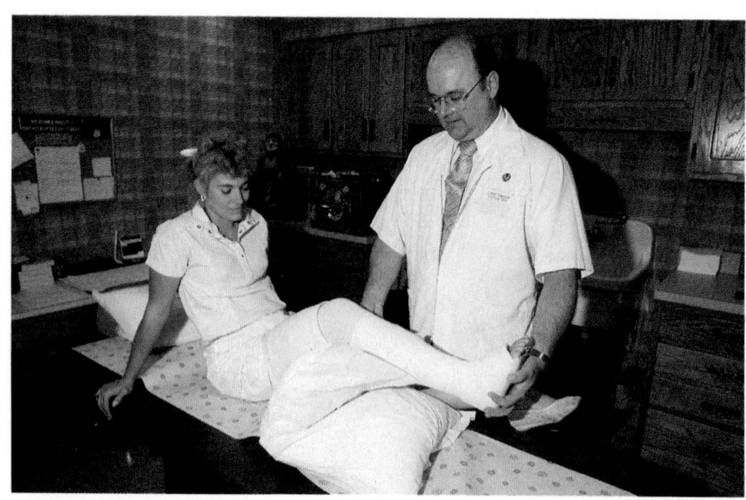

Accidents cost—both in pain and money. Don't let this happen to you.

OSHA

There are fewer accidents now than in the past. Today workers are better trained. Places of work are safer and more healthful.

One reason is that there is now a federal law to help prevent accidents. It is the **O**ccupational **S**afety and **H**ealth **A**dministration, **OSHA** for short. This law must be obeyed. Employers must follow seven rules:

1. Provide leadership for workers in health and safety.
2. Make workers responsible for safety.
3. Find and control dangers at the place of work.
4. Train all workers before they start to work.
5. Keep records of all accidents.
6. Give workers first aid and medical care.
7. Keep workers thinking about safety and acting safely.

Almost all jobs have danger of some kind. Each place of work has different dangers. Dangers in a cafe are different from those in a garage. Dangers on a farm are different from those in a factory.

Some places have dangerous machines. Other places have fire danger. Dust may be a danger when working with wood. Falling is a danger in construction.

Your boss will show you the dangers of your job. Know what they are. Then learn to work safely.

OSHA wants everyone to be responsible for health and safety. Do your part by being a safe worker. Prevent accidents.

Working safely affects you, those around you, and your employer.

Check Up:✓✓ True or False?

1. Everyone pays for accidents on the job.
2. OSHA is a federal law that promotes safety on the job.

Safety Begins with You

You are the one who can make your job healthful and safe. Start by understanding safety. Know what to wear and how to act on the job.

How You Think about Safety

No matter what kind of work you do, follow these guidelines, or general rules.

- Know safety rules.
- Know what you are able to do.
- Think safety.

Know Safety Rules. You probably already know many safety guidelines. Listed below are some examples.

- Keep your work area clean and orderly.
- Keep your equipment in good repair.
- Do not climb, stand, or sit on unsteady surfaces.
- Handle tools carefully.
- Do not clown around on the job.
- Never use alcohol or drugs on the job.

In addition, your workplace and your job may have other safety rules. Your boss should explain all of them to you. Be sure you understand. If you operate a machine, a nearby poster may give you some safety rules. Read it carefully. Follow the rules.

If you do not understand the safe way to do something, ask someone who does. There is a proper way of doing the simplest chore. See page 188 for the correct way to use a ladder.

Know What You Are Able to Do. All workers cannot do the same things. Some can lift more than others. Some can see and hear better. Some have better balance. Some can reach farther. Find out what you can and cannot do.

Be sure you are suited to the tasks you are given. Trying to do a task you cannot handle may cause injury to yourself and others.

Think Safety. Thinking safety includes having a good attitude toward safety. Realize that safety is important and be serious about maintaining safety.

Thinking safety also includes remembering safety rules at all times. Stop when you see an unsafe action about to happen. Learn safe habits. Never say, "It will not matter just this one time." That may be the time an accident will happen.

A Desire to Succeed

Setting Goals: Mike Singletary

When he was a little boy, Mike Singletary was a sickly child. He had pneumonia and high blood pressure. He was in the hospital a lot.

Other bad things happened to Mike. His brother Dale died in a home accident. Mike's father did not stay close to his family. He finally moved out of the house. Later he divorced Mike's mother.

Mike's older brother Grady became like a father to Mike. Then Grady was killed in a car accident by a drunk driver.

In spite of all these hardships, Mike was helped by his mother and his grandparents. Mike decided that his strongest desire in life was being the best at whatever he did.

When he was in the seventh grade, Mike tried out for football. He was five feet, two inches tall and weighed 130 pounds. He was the smallest one on the team.

Mike loved to read, especially about football. His high school football coach made him work hard on the field. The coach also made him take hard classes. He always pushed Mike to get better grades.

Mike got a scholarship to Baylor University. During his freshman year, he made the starting team and won awards.

Playing football was not easy for Mike. He had some breathing problems. As a result, he learned to work hard at practice.

Mike Singletary went on to play pro football. He became captain of the Chicago Bears' defensive team. He was the NFL Defensive Player of the Year.

Mike continues to work out. He wants to earn the Most Valuable Player award. He wants people to think of athletes as humans, not just "dumb jocks." He works with children. He often speaks about preventing drug abuse.

Mike had several physical handicaps. He also suffered great sadness over the loss of his family members. But he worked hard to overcome all of this.

Today he sets goals to be the best he can be. He accepts encouragement and advice from people around him.

What You Wear on the Job

Wearing proper clothes on the job can prevent accidents. For example, you may work near a machine or an open flame. If so, do not wear loose clothes or a tie. On some jobs you will not want to wear a watch or other jewelry. If you work around food or near a machine, cover or tie your hair back.

Always keep your clothes clean and in good repair. Oil spots on clothes can easily catch fire. Chemicals on clothing can burn your skin. Torn clothing can be caught in a machine.

If you work outside, wear light protective clothing to protect your skin. Wear a hat to protect your face. Apply skin cream to block out the sun's rays.

Some jobs require special protective clothing or equipment. Hard hats must be used on a construction site. Workers at an airport wear head sets to protect their ears from loud engine noises.

When using some machines, you must wear safety glasses, goggles, or a face shield. Use them for dangerous jobs like welding, or hammering metal, too.

Face masks help protect you from chemicals and vapors that can cause cancer. Special gloves and steel-toed shoes can prevent injuries to hands and feet.

If your job requires safety clothing, learn how to wear it. Be sure it fits. Get in the habit of wearing these protective items. If you do not follow the rules, you may have an accident or lose your job.

Can you see three types of safety equipment being worn by this airport worker?

How You Act on the Job

You know that cleanliness is important. Wash your hands with soap and water. Wash after you use the bathroom and right before you eat. Never eat your lunch in a place that is not clean.

Sometimes people must change their clothes before they eat. For example, farm workers may spray chemicals to kill weeds or insects. They must change clothes before handling food.

Smoking is dangerous to your health anytime. But it can be even more dangerous on some jobs. Avoid smoking around engine exhaust, gas, and dust.

What is this worker doing wrong?

Why should you not eat in these places?

You may be required to drive on your job. Know the traffic laws and obey them. Be a defensive driver and know how to drive safely in bad weather.

Every car, truck, or van is different. Know where all the controls are before you start the engine. Then you can keep your eyes on the road while driving.

Check Up:✓✓ True or False?

1. You should find out the safe way to do even simple tasks.
2. Cleanliness and safe driving procedures are important on and off the job.

Use Tools Safely

On any job you will have to work with some types of tools and machines. A store clerk may use a cash register. Or climb a ladder to reach stock on a high shelf. A factory worker may use hand tools and heavy machines. An office worker may use a typewriter and a copy machine.

Always follow safety practices with all equipment. When you work with tools, have plenty of space round you. You do not want other workers bumping into you. You do not want others to be hit by flying sparks or chips.

Keep tools and equipment put away when not in use. Then things will not fall off your work table and injure someone.

There is a right and wrong way to use even the simplest tools. Find out how to use hand tools, electric appliances and electric tools, and machines. Follow the instructions.

When using electrical tools, turn them on yourself. Do not let anyone else turn them on. You may not be ready to operate them. Select the correct speed for the job. Keep your fingers safe. Know how to hold your work correctly with your hands. Or use another proper method such as a vise or pliers.

Turn off the power when you finish your job. Always unplug a tool or machine before trying to unclog it or repair it. Never operate an electric tool in a damp place or with wet hands. You can get a terrible shock.

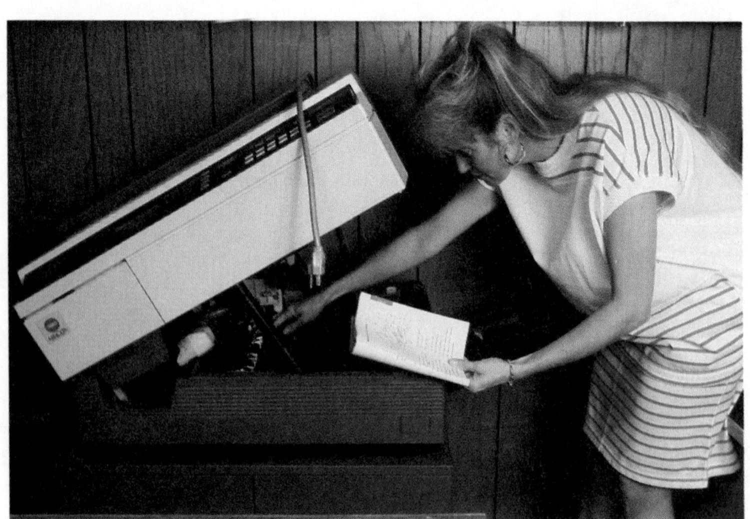

Always unplug a machine before trying to repair it.

Three-prong plugs **ground** tools so they cannot shock you. This means that electricity would flow to the ground rather than into your body. Use three-prong plugs whenever you can. Also make sure that plugs and cords are in good repair. Unplug tools the right way. Put your thumb and fingers on the plug. Then pull it from the outlet. Do not pull the cord.

If a cord is worn or cut, ask for a new one. Use long cords and extension cords safely. Do not stretch a cord where someone might trip over it. Do not attach more than one tool to a cord. The cord may get too hot and cause a fire.

Cutting machines can be very dangerous. As with any other machine, make sure that guards and shields are in place. Never put your fingers close to the cutting edge. Wear protective equipment. Keep alert. A saw, for example, may throw small pieces of wood with deadly force.

Follow correct procedures and take safety precautions with machines. Protective clothing and equipment can help prevent injury, too.

Ladder Safety

Many workers use ladders. Extension ladders may be made longer or shorter. They are used on construction jobs. Stepladders are used in most homes. Fixed ladders are used in factories.

There are safety rules even for something as simple as a ladder. You should follow these rules. Do you know how to use a ladder safely?

- A ladder must stand on a level place.
- Have someone help you set up a long ladder.
- Be sure all locks on an extension ladder are tight
- Be sure a stepladder is open all the way and locked.
- A ladder should reach three feet above the roof.
- On windy days, tie the ladder with rope to something strong, such as the house or a tree.
- Face the ladder when you go up or down.
- Never climb higher than three rungs from the top.
- Be sure your shoes grip the ladder rungs.
- Keep ladder rungs free of mud and grease.

Check the ladder before using it. See that it is in good condition. If a rung or side is broken, do not use that ladder. Store ladders indoors.

There is a special danger in using ladders near wires. Some wires are marked *DANGER* or *HIGH VOLTAGE*. Then you must be very careful! **High voltage** wires carry great amounts of electricity.

Never use a metal ladder near electrical wires. If the metal ladder comes near or touches a wire, you could be injured or killed. Always use a wooden ladder near wires.

Fire Protection

Fire can be a great danger. One fire can injure and kill many people. It can cause thousands of dollars worth of property damage.

Fires can occur almost anywhere. But they occur more often in some kinds of work than in others. Some of the most common causes of fire are

- machines and electrical wires.
- machine parts rubbing together.
- open flames.
- sparks from welding or from burning trash.
- hot surfaces and metals.
- workers who smoke.

You can help prevent fires by practicing fire safety rules. Follow the rules you learned about electrical tools. Keep your work area clean and tidy. Clean up oil spills. Keep your tools and machines working properly. Watch open flames carefully. Do not smoke on the job.

In this auto shop, what has been done for the workers' safety?

Watch for causes of fires, too. You might smell or hear something. Report a smell of smoke or gas at once. Report any fire hazards. If you hear an odd sound in your machine, stop it and check for problems. Know what to do in case of a fire. Then you can help save lives and prevent damage. Be prepared. Know how to do the following:

1. Find the exits. They are marked and lighted. Exits must never be blocked.
2. Find the fire extinguisher. A **fire extinguisher** is a container of chemicals that will put out a small fire. Learn to use it.
3. Find the fire alarm. Learn how to turn in an alarm.

Check Up:✓✓ True or False?

1. It is safe to use electric tools with wet hands.
2. Guards and shields can prevent injuries to hands and eyes.
3. You can help prevent fires by following safety rules and keeping your work area clean.

Working with Materials

Workers use many types of materials. Some workers unload and store materials. Others cut them to size. Handling materials can be dangerous. Bulky materials are dangerous because they may fall and hit someone. Flammable materials are dangerous because they can explode and cause fires. Chemicals give off harmful vapors.

Bulky Materials

Big items often have to be stored before they are used. One place that big materials are stored is a lumberyard. A lumberyard must be kept clean. Lumber, bricks, and bags of sand must be stacked carefully. Stacks cannot be top heavy or wobbly. Otherwise some of the items may fall and hurt someone.

Items must be removed carefully, too, so the stack does not fall. If a lift truck is taking heavy materials off a stack, stay clear. Stay a safe distance from the truck as it moves the materials.

Flammable Materials

Gasoline, paint thinner, and many other work materials are flammable. **Flammable** means able to catch fire very easily. Fire does not even have to touch flammable materials for them to catch fire. Their **vapors** (the gasses they put into the air) can explode into flames.

When not in use, flammable liquid in small cans must be stored safely in special cabinets. Mark each cabinet *FLAMMABLE*. Keep fire away from the cabinet. Have a fire extinguisher nearby.

Heavy items must be stacked and handled carefully so they don't fall on anyone.

Flammable materials are most dangerous when moved. For instance, gasoline being unloaded from a truck into a tank can easily explode.

You may have to pour flammable liquids from a large tank into a small can. If so, you can do two things to prevent fires. One, fasten a wire between the tank and a metal post. Two, attach a wire between the large tank and the small can. This will prevent electrical sparks from jumping between the two containers.

Chemicals

Working with chemicals can be dangerous, too. See that your work area is ventilated. **Ventilated** means that the air is moving around well. Some rooms have a fan that pulls out fumes and vapors. If so, open a door or window.

With some chemicals you should wear protective clothing and rubber gloves. Protective hand cream may keep chemicals off your hands. It also puts oils back into your skin.

Always know how you are supposed to handle each chemical. Do what the manufacturer says.

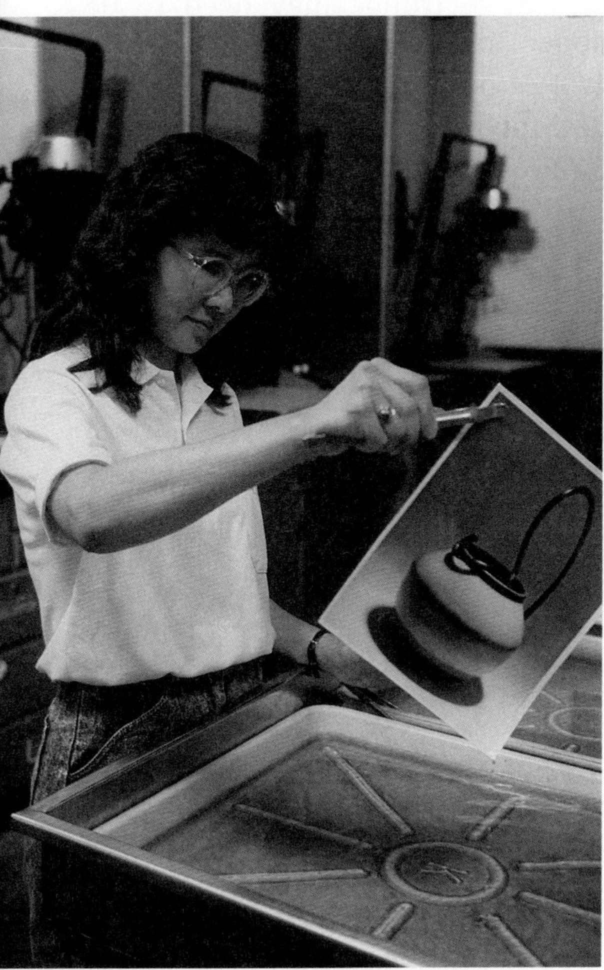

A photographer must be careful not to get chemicals on his or her hands and clothing.

When an Illness or an Accident Occurs

Even when everyone is careful, someone may get sick or hurt on the job. Do you know what to do? Learn what to do ahead of time. Then you will handle the situation well. Know what to do if you are hurt or get sick. Know what to do if a co-worker is hurt or sick. Practice first aid. Then you will do the right thing in an emergency. And always try to stay calm.

First Aid for Yourself

Sometime you may feel ill on the job. If so, stop work. If you are sick, you will not do very good work. And you might be careless and hurt yourself or someone else. Tell your boss you are sick. He or she can decide what to do. Many large workplaces have special rooms for first aid and medical care. Always go there if you are sick or hurt. A nurse or doctor will help you.

Many small businesses have a first aid kit for minor injuries. If you have a major injury, ask someone to take you to the hospital or call an ambulance.

First Aid for Others

"Report it to the boss." That should be your first thought when someone is hurt. Your boss can decide what first aid is needed.

Suppose a co-worker is injured and the boss is not there. If the injury is minor, you could wait for the boss to return. You could go find him or her.

Suppose, though, the injury is bad. If someone else is near, one of you should call an ambulance or the police. The other one should give first aid.

Three things may need to be done. Do them in this order.

1. Restore breathing
2. Stop bleeding
3. Prevent shock

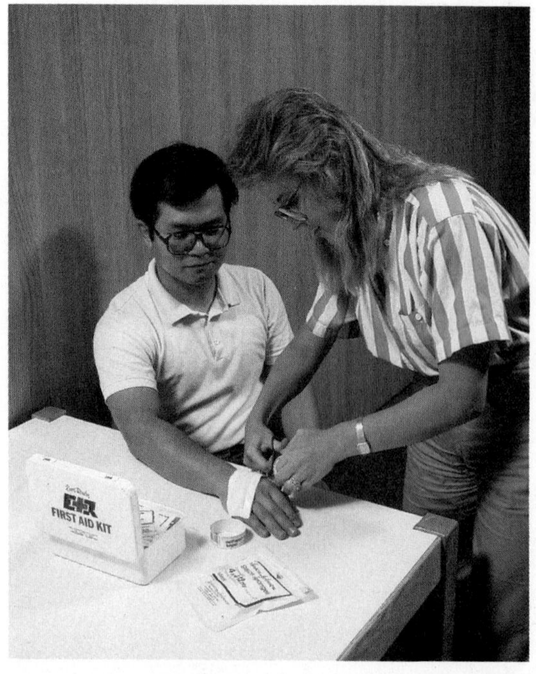

Go to the first aid room if you are hurt.

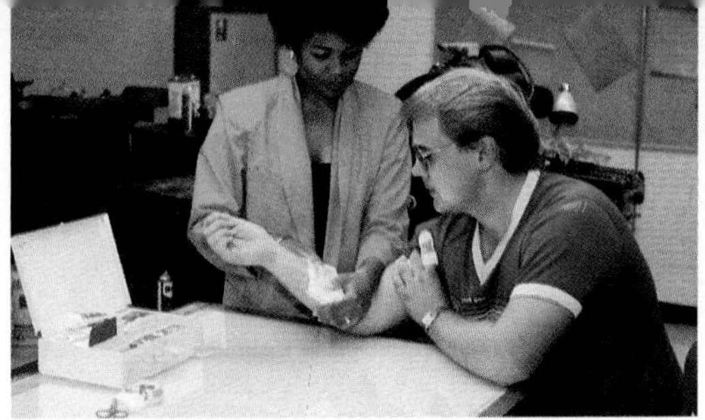

If an accident victim is bleeding, press hard on the wound with a clean cloth until help arrives.

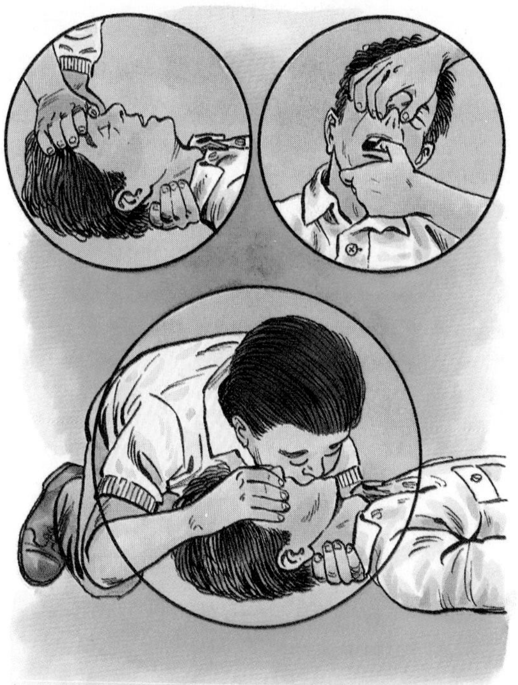

The first thing to do for an injured person is to see if he or she is breathing. If not, follow the steps to restore his breathing.

You may restore breathing by following these steps:

1. Tip back the head.
2. Put your thumb into the mouth. Hold the lower jaw. Open the mouth wide.
3. Tightly cover the person's mouth with your mouth.
4. Close the person's nose. Pinch it between your thumb and finger.
5. Blow air into the person's mouth. Do this until you see the chest rise.
6. Take away your mouth.
7. Do these six steps over and over until help comes.

To stop bleeding, cover the cut with clean cloth. Press your hand *hard* over the cut. Keep pressing hard until help comes.

When anyone is hurt badly, shock may follow. The person may perspire but feel cold. The face and lips will be pale. Keep the person warm, dry, and on his or her back. Keep the person's head low. Stay with the victim until a doctor comes.

After you have done these three things, do not try to give any more medical help. You may cause further injury if you try to move the hurt person. Stay calm and wait for help to come.

Check Up:✓✓ True or False?

1. Flammable materials must be handled with care to avoid explosions and fires.
2. If you are sick or injured, tell your boss right away.
3. The first thing to do for an injured person is to bring the person a drink of water.

The words

Listed below are the important new words that were used in this chapter. next to each word is the page on which you will find the word in bold, black print. Turn back and read again the paragraph in which you find the word. Then write each word and its meaning on a sheet of paper. Also write a sentence of your own using each word.

1. fire extinguisher (189)
2. flammable (190)
3. ground (187)
4. high voltage (188)
5. OSHA (181)
6. vapors (190)
7. ventilated (191)

The facts

1. Explain how a personal injury at work can cost you money. Explain how someone else's injury can cost you money.
2. What does *OSHA* stand for?
3. What three safety rules can you follow to avoid accidents?
4. Name four items of protective clothing.
5. Why is cleanliness important on the job?
6. What are five safety rules to follow when using an electrical tool or appliance?
7. Why must a metal ladder never be used near electrical wires?
8. Name six ways you can help prevent fires at work.
9. Why are bulky materials, flammables and chemicals each dangerous?
10. Name three things you should do for an injured worker.

What's right here?

Talk about your ideas

1. Have you ever had an accident? Why did it happen? Could you have prevented it?

2. Name three buildings that you are in regularly. What would you do in case of fire in each one?

3. Have you ever seen anything marked flammable? What was it? What special care was given to it?

Do some activities

1. Find the fire alarm in your school building. Tell how you would use it to report a fire.

2. Bring a hand tool or a small appliance to class. Demonstrate the proper, safe way to use it.

3. Have someone in the class show how to restore breathing.

4. Find a poster in a restaurant that shows what to do if someone is choking. Study it carefully. Practice the procedure in class.

Improve your basic skills

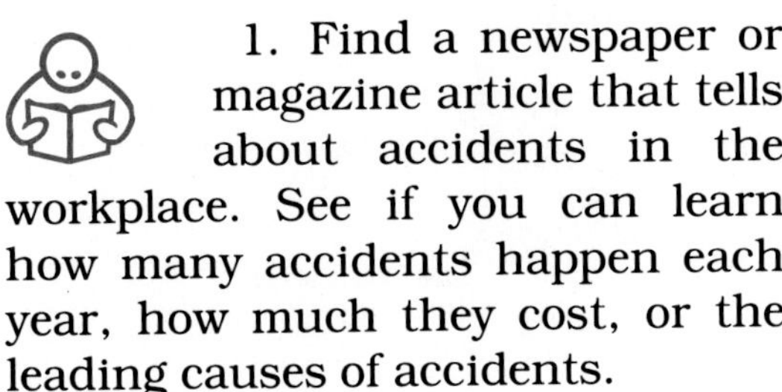

1. Find a newspaper or magazine article that tells about accidents in the workplace. See if you can learn how many accidents happen each year, how much they cost, or the leading causes of accidents.

2. Find a book about first aid in your school or local library. Read the procedure for removing a splinter, for getting something out of your eye, and for treating a sprained ankle.

1. Suppose your friend has had an accident and has missed a week of school. Write a letter to him/her telling what has happened at school while he or she was absent.

2. Think of an occupation you might like to have someday. Find out the special safety rules for that job by reading about the job or by talking to someone who has that job. Write a paragraph explaining safety precautions for the job.

1. Jo earns $4.50 an hour at the Country Store. She works six hours a day, 16 days a month. She is paid at the end of each month. How much does she get paid each month?

2. Last month Jo missed five days due to illness. But she will be paid for only 2 sick days. For how many days will Jo be paid? How much will she earn?

Chapter 10

Getting Along With Your Employer

What's wrong here?

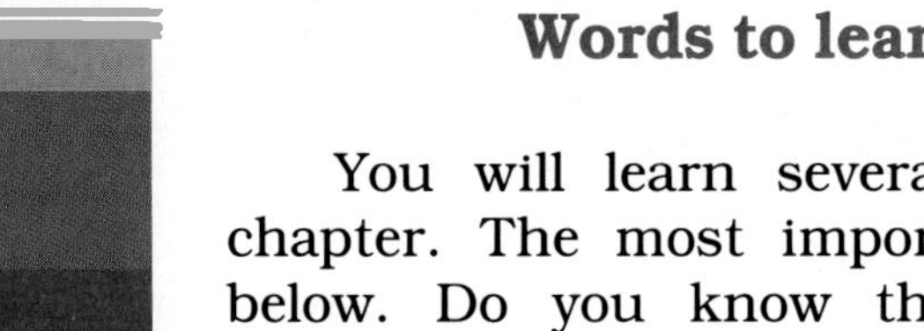

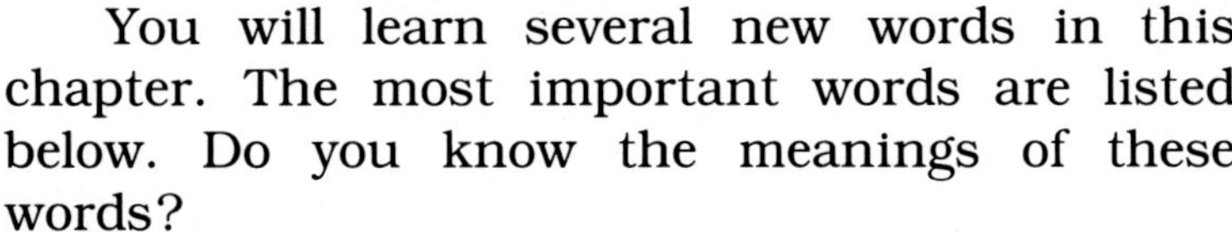

Words to learn and use

You will learn several new words in this chapter. The most important words are listed below. Do you know the meanings of these words?

cooperation
initiative
enthusiasm
criticism
raise
evaluation
promotion
adaptable
minimum-wage laws

Build on what you know

You already know. . .

- that understanding your personality can help you pick the right job.
- that your boss will want you to have a pleasing personality.
- that you can improve yourself by learning positive personality traits.
- that doing a job well may earn a pay raise.

In this chapter you will learn. . .

- what personality traits employers like.
- how to earn a raise or promotion.
- what you can expect from your employer in return for your work.

In Chapter 8, you learned about your first few days on the job. You know you want to make a good impression after you are hired. To do this you will be pleasant to your co-workers and work hard to learn your new job.

When you take a job, you are really making a deal with your employer. In this chapter you will learn what you can expect from your employer. You will also learn what your employer will expect from you.

What You Should Give Your Employer

In Chapter 2 you learned that your personality is different from everyone else's. By understanding your personality, you can choose a job you will like.

You also learned that an employer likes a worker with a good personality. Certain positive personality traits will make you a better employee. They will make you a more successful worker. Working hard to develop these positive traits will be well worth your effort.

Most employers want to see the traits listed below in their workers.

- Ability to understand and follow directions.
- Cooperation.
- Dependability.
- Initiative.
- Eagerness to learn.
- Enthusiasm.
- Loyalty.
- Honesty.
- Ability to accept criticism.
- Ability to please customers.

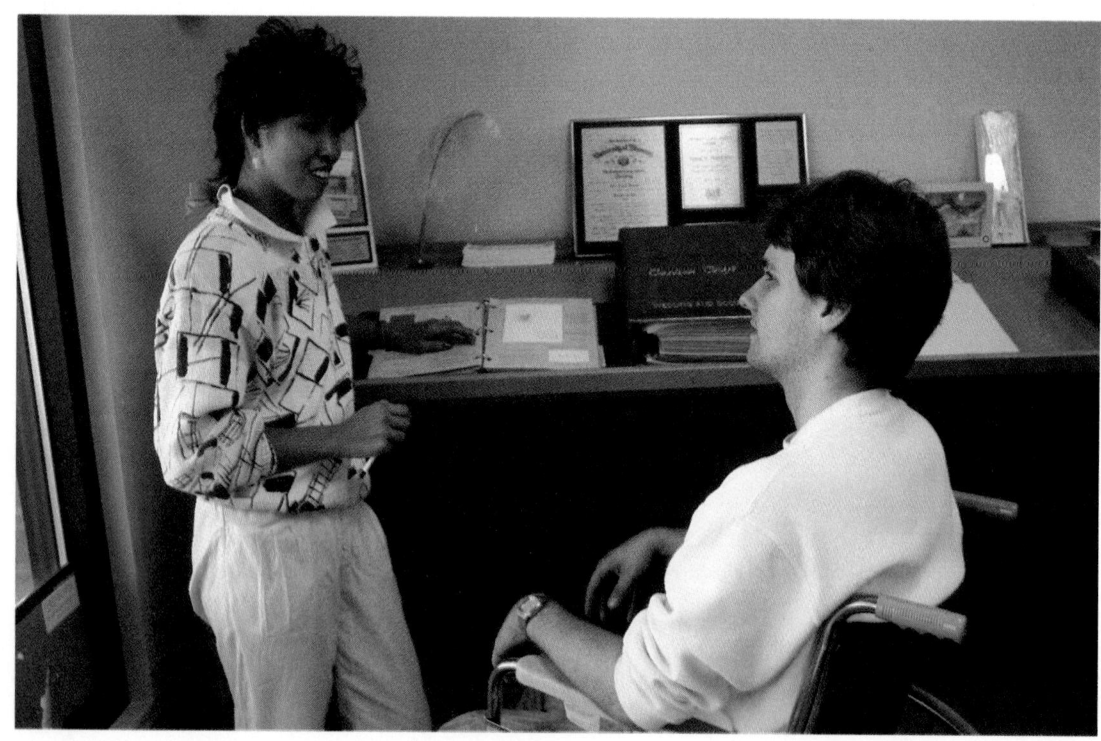

You can increase your positive personality traits if you try.

Ability to Understand and Follow Directions

Every job needs workers who understand and follow directions well.

The first step is to listen carefully. Do you daydream? Does your mind ever wander when someone is talking to you? If so, you may not hear your boss give you directions. To overcome this bad habit, concentrate on what your boss is saying. Give your total attention. Practice good listening skills. Soon you will become a good listener.

Next, make sure that you understand the directions. Ask questions. Ask your boss to explain things in a different way. Once you understand, remember what you are told. Make notes if necessary.

Last, follow the directions carefully. You may think you can do the job some easier way. Do not try it. Do exactly what your boss tells you.

Cooperation

Cooperation means working together well with other people. Employers like workers who cooperate.

Cooperation includes doing your part to get the total job done. For instance, you can help other workers if you finish your own tasks early. You can show cooperation by doing chores that nobody wants to do. These chores could be just cleaning up or watering plants. Your boss and co-workers will appreciate your extra effort.

Dependability

Dependability means that others can count on you. Part of being *dependable* is always being at work when you are supposed to be there. If you miss work, your employer must change the work plans. Other workers may have to do your job. So your absence is hard on everyone.

As a rule, being *dependable* includes getting the job done. Your employer should be able to assign you a task. And know that you will do that task. Your boss should not have to worry about the job getting done. If you have a problem doing a certain task, talk to your boss about it. Do not just ignore the problem.

Sometimes there is more work than usual. Your boss may ask you to do extra tasks. You may be asked to work extra hours. A dependable worker will pitch in when needed.

A Desire to Succeed

Working for a Normal Lifestyle:
Roger Meyers and Virginia Hensler

The church was decorated with flowers. The bride wore a long white gown. Organ music played.

For Roger Meyers and Virginia Hensler, this event was more than just their wedding. It was also a sign of their independence.

Both Roger and Virginia have been mentally retarded since they were born. Roger can learn, but he learns very slowly.

Virginia was injured at birth. Her left side is not as strong as her right side. She is partially blind in one eye. She has problems with her speech. Her spine is curved.

When he was twenty, Roger moved into a home for mentally handicapped people. There he learned many things. He learned personal grooming. He found out how to take a bus where he wanted to go. He learned to do many everyday chores. He learned to make decisions. Roger became a teacher's aide.

There he also met Virginia. They helped each other with their learning. Later they became engaged.

Roger applied for a job as a busboy and got it. His boss took time to explain exactly what Roger was to do on his job. Roger listened carefully. He remembered what his boss said. He did what he was told.

Roger and Virginia each moved into an apartment in a building called a transitional living project. A counselor lived in the building. They could go to him for help. But they were quite on their own.

After Roger and Virginia married, they moved into an apartment in their community. Now they were completely on their own. Not only did Roger and Virginia feel independent, they *were* independent. They made mistakes, but they learned from them.

Roger and Virginia had to work harder than many other people for the lifestyle they wanted. They had to convince their parents and teachers that they could accept responsibility. Although Virginia says they are slower than many people, they know what they want. They fight for the life they have chosen.

Initiative

Having **initiative** means doing work without being told. Workers with initiative are called *self-starters.* Keep your eyes and ears open. You may see chores that need to be done. If you know how, go ahead and do them. Do not wait to be told every little thing to do.

Employers like workers with initiative. Workers with initiative do not need as many directions. They do not need to be watched as carefully.

This worker is showing initiative. She is picking up a garment without being told to do so.

Eagerness to Learn

Employers like workers who are eager to learn. Being *eager* means showing you want to learn. Show a lot of interest in your work. Ask questions. Learn more than just your own job. Learn about the company, too. Those who are eager to learn often get better jobs with the company.

Enthusiasm

If you are eager to learn, you will likely show **enthusiasm.** *Enthusiasm* means being excited about what you do.

Of course, no job is all fun. There will be some work that you may not like. But accept your work. Do not complain. Do even the hard jobs with enthusiasm. You will probably find that the hard jobs are not so bad after all.

If you show enthusiasm in your work, you will look happy. You will work quickly and do your work well. Other workers will be glad to work with you. When you like your work, all of life seems more interesting. You will be a happier person at home, too.

Check Up:✓✓ True or False?

1. Once you get a job, you do not have to worry how you act.
2. You can develop some positive personality traits with practice.
3. Doing your own work well and helping others with their work will impress your boss.

Loyalty

There may be some things you do not like about the company you work for. After all, no company is perfect. But as long as you work there, be loyal to the company. Do not speak badly about the company. If you do, your employer may hear about it. You may lose your job. If you cannot be loyal to the company, get another job.

On some jobs, you may be told things in confidence. This means that you are not to tell other people. Do not even tell your friends. Part of being loyal to the company is to keep company secrets.

Honesty

Employers want their workers to be honest in all their work. Be honest with your boss. Do not steal time by not working a full day. Do not cover up your mistakes. Speak up when something goes wrong so it can be corrected.

Do not take even small items from your company. That is stealing.

Deal honestly with your co-workers so they will trust you. Tell customers the truth. This will help create a good name for your company.

Your reputation for honesty will follow you. Someday you will apply for other jobs. Future bosses may call your present employer to find out about your honesty.

You may know some confidential information about your company. Do not tell others.

Ability to Accept Criticism

Criticism is an explanation of what you are doing wrong. Most people do not like to be criticized. But on the job, criticism can be helpful. It helps you know what your employer expects of you.

When your boss criticizes your work, listen politely. Try to learn from your mistakes. Ask how to improve. Thank your boss for telling you how to do better. Then use the criticism to do a better job. Good workers learn to do this. It helps them do better work.

Ability to Please Customers

On many jobs you will meet customers. Whenever you meet customers, you must keep them happy. Be polite. Be courteous. Smile and be pleasant. Try to be helpful. It is your job to please the customers.

If customers get angry at you, they may quit doing business with your company. Employers do not often keep workers who do not please their customers. Never argue with a customer. Find out how to handle complaints without making people angry.

Carl Smith works at Phillips Furniture Store. He cleans and moves furniture. When Carl was hired, Mr. Phillips told him he wanted a fast worker. He had fired the last worker because she had moved too slowly.

Carl worked as fast as he could. He finished one job, then almost ran to the next one. One day he was moving a large desk. It was on rollers, so he pushed it quickly between rows of furniture. Carl did not see an expensive lamp. The desk hit the lamp and sent it crashing to the floor in pieces.

Carl knew he would be criticized. Mr. Phillips was upset, but he did not fire Carl. He just said that Carl was moving too fast in trying to do a good job. He said Carl should slow down a little bit. Then he could be more careful. Carl said he was sorry for breaking the lamp. He thanked Mr. Phillips for his advice.

How to Get a Raise or a Promotion

A **raise** is an increase in pay. Many companies give raises to good workers after six months. Some companies wait a year. At that time, each worker is evaluated. An **evaluation** is a written report saying how well you do your job. Your boss will show you your evaluation and talk with you about it. This should help you become a better worker.

If your report is good, you will probably get a raise. What if you get a bad evaluation? Then you may have to wait six months or a year for your next raise. Work hard to improve before your next evaluation.

Other companies give raises when they think raises are earned. Employers regularly check their workers. The best ones may get a raise every three to six months. Some may get raises every year.

At some companies your boss will sit down with you every so often and tell you how you are doing on the job. Use this information to learn how you can improve.

A **promotion** is a change of jobs within the company. It is a move to a job with more responsiblity and higher pay. The new job may be harder. The best workers may get promotions in the following cases:

1. The employer makes a new job. This is not often done. However, sometimes new jobs are made for very good workers. Other new jobs are made because of company needs.
2. Someone quits. A good worker is then promoted to the job.
3. Someone does not do a good job. Another worker is promoted to take his or her place.
4. Another worker is promoted, leaving a job opening.

Keep the following things in mind. They can help you get a raise or a promotion.

- Have a good work record.
- Get along well with everyone.
- Become a valuable worker.
- Improve your skills and knowledge.
- Prepare yourself for greater responsibility.
- Be adaptable.

Have a Good Work Record

Employers look at how well you do your present job. Do you do it well? If so, your employer will think you can learn a more responsible job. Employers also check to see that you are not absent very often. They look for workers who are always on time. They look for employees who are honest, loyal, and hardworking.

Doing your own job well is the first step toward getting a raise or a promotion.

Get Along Well with Everyone

Getting along well is always important. It is important in those first days on the job. It is important in keeping your job. It is also important when you want a promotion. On a responsible job, you must get along well with many people—your boss, your co-workers, and customers.

If you are the boss, you are responsible for the work of others under you. You must get along with your employees. You must see that they work well together.

Become a Valuable Worker

How can you become a valuable worker? Try to do your job better than any other worker. Learn all you can about other jobs in the company. Help do them. These actions help you become a valuable worker. You may be so valuable that the company will need you in a more responsible job.

Check Up: ✓✓ True or False?

1. You should tell everyone the bad things about your company.
2. Do not pay any attention when your boss criticizes. He or she will forget about your mistakes anyway.
3. A promotion may include a pay raise.

Improve Your Knowledge and Skills

Suppose you are only able to do one job. Then your boss may not think about you for a promotion. You may be stuck in that job. Work to improve both your knowledge and your skills. *Knowledge* is understanding facts. *Skill* is being able to do specific tasks.

You can improve your knowledge and skills in several ways.

- Take classes. You may have to work only part-time so you can go to the classes you need. Maybe you could take some night classes. Some employers even let their workers take courses on company time.
- Train on the job. Learn to do new tasks by practicing in your spare time at work. Ask your boss if you can learn to operate a new machine.
- Read. Read material put out by your company that would increase your knowledge. Your library probably has books that could help you better understand your work, too.
- Join groups. You can meet other people who do the same type of work. They may help you improve your knowledge or skills. Some groups have speakers. Others hold classes to improve members' skills.

Graduating from high school or college does not mean that you are finished with your education. Many adults take classes to improve on the job.

Prepare for More Responsibility

Promotions are made to jobs with greater responsiblity. Show your boss that you can take on more responsibility. Start by accepting more and more responsibility in your present job. Do not be afraid to take on extra duties. They will be good practice for a better job.

Look at jobs to which you might be promoted. Watch what those workers do. Watch your boss. See how he or she handles the job. Then think about how you would do it.

Try to learn when a good job will be open. Then learn all you can about it. Offer to help the person who does that job. Take a class that will help you learn how to do it.

There are two kinds of promotions:

1. To a job in which you are the boss of other workers
2. To a job in which you do important work but are not the boss

Can you get others to work hard? Can you be the boss and not be bossy? If so, you may like being a boss.

Many people do not like to be the boss. They are willing to take on harder or more important work. But they do not want to be responsible for the work of others.

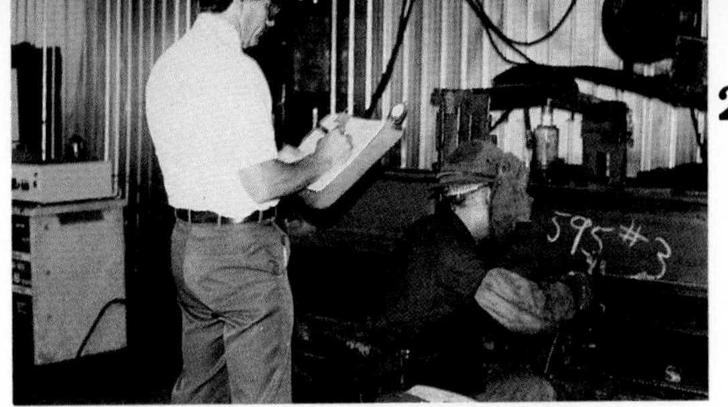

Being the boss means seeing that others do their jobs right.

Should you always take a promotion when offered? No. Sometimes you should turn down a promotion. You might not want to take a job that you would not enjoy. You may want to turn down one you are not suited for.

Be Adaptable

Being **adaptable** means being able and willing to change. Often it means changing when you do not really want to change. It may be a change in how you do your job. It may be a change in when you work. It may be a change in where you work. Are you able and willing to make changes? If so, your boss will see that you can change to a more responsible job.

Check Up: ✓✓ True or False?

1. Knowledge and skills are the same thing.
2. Before you get a promotion, you will need to show that you can handle more responsibility.
3. You should accept a promotion whenever it is offered.

What Would YOU Do?

The Boss or the Customer?

Suppose that you work in a car wash. Your job is to dry off the cars with a clean cloth. Your boss has told you to do a good job. But she has also said to spend only six minutes on each car. You can dry off a small car in less than five minutes. But you have to hurry to finish a big car in six minutes. So you always check your watch when you start on a car. Today you are drying off a very big car. You are doing your best. The boss is watching. So you give it a quick finish and go on to the next car. The owner of the big car complains that her car is still dripping. She asks you to spend more time on it. Will you go back to her car? If not, what will you tell her? If so, what will you tell your boss?

Your Boss or Your Co-Worker?

Yesterday, you began a new job. You are an assembler. You put parts together. Later, they are made into computers. Your supervisor showed you how to put the parts together. She said it will go slowly for a few days. Then you will pick up speed. But this morning another worker showed you a shortcut. He said he has done it this way for years. It is a lot faster. But sometimes the parts do not fit together as well. Some other workers check how well the parts fit. They are inspectors. When the parts do not fit well, they give them back to you. Then you take them apart and start over. Will you use the fast way and assemble more pieces? Or the slower way so fewer pieces will be returned? Or should you ask someone? And if so, whom?

Your Job and Friends

You began a new job last week. You drive the delivery truck for a flower shop. You have some friends who do not have cars. They ask you to give them rides. One wants to go downtown to play video games. One wants a ride to the skating rink. They say it will not be much out of your way. Another friend gets off work in the middle of the afternoon. He wants you to pick him up and take him home. You must deliver a lot of flowers. It will take extra time to haul your friends around. And it will take extra gasoline. But you want to please your friends. What will you do?

What Your Employer Should Provide

You may think employers expect a lot from their workers. Many of them do. But they give a lot, too. Some employers provide more for their workers than others do. You can expect these things from your boss.

- Your paycheck.
- A safe place to work.
- Help getting started on the job.
- Fair treatment.
- A regular check and criticism of your work.

Some jobs are not safe for young workers.

Your Paycheck

Your employer will pay you for the work you do. You will be paid regularly. It may be every week, every other week, or every month. How much you are paid will depend on such things as these:

- Minimum-wage laws.
- The kind of work you do.
- How well you do your work.
- How long you have worked.

Minimum-wage laws state that all workers must be paid at least so much money per hour. These laws apply to most jobs. Employers often pay more for some kinds of work than others. Beginning workers start at a lower wage. Workers who do the best work and who have worked longest usually get more than others.

A Safe Place to Work

Your employer should provide a safe place to work. Any tools you use should be safe, too. If you are under eighteen, you will not be allowed to do some dangerous jobs. A dangerous job is one on which you might get hurt. Some of the jobs that are not thought safe for those under eighteen are

- coal mining.
- logging.
- using big power machines.

Help Getting Started on the Job

Your boss should help you get started on your new job. For example, your boss will probably introduce you to other workers. This is a nice thing to do. Knowing people's names makes it easier to work with them. If your employer does not introduce you, introduce yourself. The way to do this was explained in Chapter 8.

Most companies have rules. Some have a lot of rules. Others have just a few. Rules help both the employer and the workers. Rules are like laws. They tell you what you can do and what you cannot do. They make it easier to treat everyone fairly.

Your employer should explain company rules to you. Sometimes rules are hard to understand. It is important that you understand the rules. Never feel badly about asking questions. If there is anything you do not understand, ask about it.

Most important, your boss should see that you learn to do your job the right way. He or she may work with you or have you watch another worker for a while.

On some jobs you may need some training. *Training* includes directions and practice doing the job. Your employer may train you. Sometimes another worker will teach you how to do the job. Training may take only a day or two. On some jobs it takes much longer. It may take several weeks or even months.

Fair Treatment

Your employer should treat you fairly. Company rules are for everyone who works for the company. So every worker must follow them.

This man is not following the rule. Why should he change his behavior?

A good boss will tell you when you are doing a task wrong so you can learn from your mistakes.

Some rules are written. Others are spoken. Either way, they must not be broken for some workers when others must follow them. That would not be fair. So you can expect company rules to be followed by every worker.

Every worker should have a chance to do a good job. The employer should provide the tools needed for every worker. Every worker should have his or her work checked and criticized. Doing these things for all workers is fair.

Each worker should be allowed to ask questions about his or her work and to make reasonable complaints. All workers should be given the chance to get pay raises and promotions. Doing these things for all workers is fair treatment.

A Regular Check and Criticism of Your Work

Your employer will check your work. This is to see that you are doing your tasks right. When you first start, your employer will check your work often. Many employers tell you when you are doing a good job.

Your employer should give you criticism, too. Criticism should be given in a helpful, friendly manner. That way, you will learn to do your tasks correctly. You will improve. You will become a better worker.

After a while, your boss will check your work less often. Still, your work should be checked from time to time. This helps your boss know which workers should get pay raises.

Check Up:✓✓ True or False

1. Everyone who works for a company gets the same pay.
2. Your boss should help you learn to do your job right.
3. You have a right to expect fair treatment from your boss.

The words

Listed below are the important new words that you learned in this chapter. Next to each word is the page on which you will find the word in bold, black print. Turn back and read again the paragraph in which you find each word. Then write the word and its meaning on a sheet of paper. Also write a sentence of your own using each word.

1. adaptable (207)
2. cooperation (199)
3. criticism (203)
4. enthusiasm (201)
5. evaluation (204)
6. initiative (201)
7. minimum-wage laws (209)
8. promotion (204)
9. raise (204)

The facts

1. Name five personality traits most employers want to see in their workers.
2. Give the three main steps to understanding and following directions.
3. How can criticism help you on the job?
4. Name four things you can do that may help you get a raise or promotion.
5. How can you improve your knowledge and skills after you start work?
6. Name at least five things your employer should provide for you.
7. What are three types of work thought not safe for workers under eighteen?
8. Give three examples of fair treatment on the job.
9. What is the difference between knowledge and skill? Between a raise and a promotion?

What's right here?

ADD TO YOUR KNOWLEDGE AND SKILLS

Talk about your ideas

1. Do you follow directions well? How can you improve?

2. What would you do if your boss told you to do a certain task and you did not know how?

3. What would you do if an angry customer began shouting at you?

4. What are some good reasons for taking a promotion? When should you turn down a promotion?

Do some activities

1. Interview an employer. Ask these questions:

   a. What do you look for in a worker?

   b. What should a worker do to get a promotion?

   c. What should an employer provide for workers?

2. Interview three people who work full time. Ask them the questions listed in number 1 above.

3. Write down the answers that the employer and the three workers gave. Do not use the people's names. Decide if the workers agree with the employer. Compare your answers with those your classmates collect. Discuss them in class.

Improve your basic skills

1. Look around your home for written directions telling how to do something. They may be instructions for putting together a toy or making a new recipe. Read the directions carefully. Notice where the directions are most clear.

2. Think of the first job choice you made in Chapter 4. Make a list of skills that would help you do that job well. Find a book in the library that tells how to do one of the skills. Read it.

1. Using the directions you found in Reading Exercise 1, rewite any parts that are not clear.

2. Think of a time when you were criticized by a parent, teacher, or friend. Write a paragraph about your experience.

5×7=?

1. You have been earning $4 an hour. Your employer gives you a 10% raise. How much will you earn after your raise? How much more will you make each 40-hour week?

2. You have been promoted to a supervisor. You have nine workers under you. Last week they worked a total of 333 hours. How long did the average worker work?

Chapter 11

Getting Along With Your Co-Workers

What's wrong here?

Words to learn and use

You will learn several new words in this chapter. The most important words are listed below. Do you know the meanings of these words?

self-respect	rumors
respect	emotions
stability	opinions
sense of humor	compromise
gossip	tactful

Build on what you know

You already know. . .

- how to get started properly on a new job.
- how to stay safe and healthy on the job.
- how to get along with your employer.
- that working well with others is an important part of your job.

In this chapter you will learn. . .

- what traits most people like in others.
- how to show positive personality traits.
- how to avoid problems with your co-workers.
- how to compromise and avoid arguments.

Pleasing your boss will help you keep your job. In Chapter 10 you learned some ways to get along with your employer.

Getting along with co-workers is important, too. Your positive personality traits will help you get along with others. In this chapter you will learn about some of these traits. No matter how hard you try, though, you will face problems at work. In this chapter you will learn some ways to avoid these problems.

Personality Traits Your Co-Workers Like

Do you like some people more than others? Why do you choose some people for your friends? Why do you choose *not* to become friends with others? Perhaps your closest friends have personality traits that you like.

But you do not pick your co-workers. Your boss does. So you may not like some of the people you work with. Some of them may even be hard to get along with. Yet it is important that you get along with everyone on the job. You and your co-workers must work well together.

There are a number of ways that you can make things easier at work. You can show positive personality traits with your co-workers. Your co-workers like to see many of the same personality traits that your boss does. Try hard to cooperate with your co-workers. It is easier to work with someone who is cooperative. Cooperation makes getting the job done easier and faster.

Be dependable. Workers feel better if they know they can depend on you to be at work. They like you to do your fair share of the work.

Show some enthusiasm. Other people like to see your enthusiasm. You are most pleasant and fun to work with if you are enthusiastic.

Be loyal. You are loyal to your company and your boss. You can be loyal to your co-workers, too. Do not say bad things about your co-workers. If they tell you something in confidence, keep the secret.

Treat everyone fairly. Do not play favorites. You will expect your co-workers to treat you fairly. Treat them fairly as well. Help everyone you work with.

There are other personality traits that you can show. These traits will help your co-workers like you, too. They will help you get along well with everyone at work.

- Friendliness.
- Self-respect.
- Respect for others.
- Stability.
- Understanding and empathy.
- Sense of humor.

Friendliness

You do not have to be close friends with co-workers. Yet everyone likes people who are friendly. It is easier to get along with your co-workers if you are friendly.

Speak to them when you first see them each day. Smile. Say, "Good morning," and call them by name. People like to hear you say their name. Show that you care about them as people. At the end of the week say something like, "Have a good weekend, Joe."

Self-Respect

Self-respect is feeling good about yourself. It is liking yourself. It is feeling worthy. *Self-respect* is seeing yourself as good.

You see yourself when you look in the mirror. You see yourself another way when you think about what you do. When you do a job well, you see yourself as worthy. This makes you feel good about being you.

Others see you whenever they look at you. They see the type of clothes you wear. They see the way you behave. They also see if you do good work. Others react to what they see. They may be friendly or unfriendly to you. Their friendliness helps you feel worthy. It boosts your self-respect.

You are happier when you respect yourself. You like yourself. This is important because having self-respect helps you do better work. It helps you like other people. It helps you get along with others.

In turn, when you do good work and like yourself, others like you better, too. Having others like you makes you feel even better about yourself.

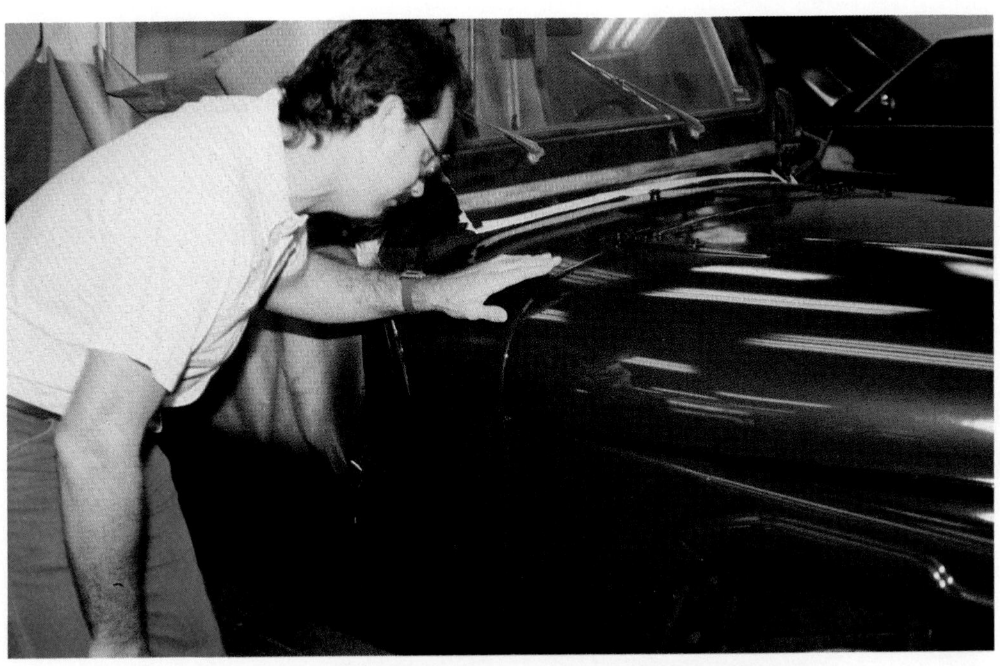

Doing a good job makes you like yourself better.

Respect for Others

Respect for others is showing them you think they are worthy. It is letting them know they are worth something. You do this when you are friendly and fair. You show respect when you speak well of others. You do not show respect when you speak badly of others.

Your co-workers will like you better when you treat them with respect. Make them feel worthy. It will help them have self-respect. Then they can do good work. They will like you. You will all get along well on the job.

Stability

Stability means being the same, even when things change. A *stable* person acts much the same way day after day. You show your stability by cooperating every day. You show stability by being friendly every day.

Are you friendly one day and grouchy the next? If so, people will not know what to expect from you. They will not want to work with you. They will not trust you.

Always be the same person. That way others will know how to get along with you.

When you respect your co-workers and understand their problems, you can work better together.

Understanding and Empathy

A person who cares about other people understands them and has empathy. If you know why other people feel as they do, you understand them. You may not feel the same way. But if you have empathy, you can accept their feelings.

When someone shares a problem, just listen. Listen quietly. Show your interest and concern. Listening tells the other person that you care.

You may want to talk about a similar problem of your own. But this may not help your co-worker. He or she may think you only care about yourself.

Perhaps you disagree with what is said. The person still has the right to say it. Continue to show him or her friendship anyway.

Sense of Humor

Do you know someone who never thinks anything is funny? Compare that person with someone who laughs a lot. Which of these people has more fun? Which one would you rather work with?

It is easy to be around a person who has a good **sense of humor.** That is, the ability to see the funny side of things. Of course, most people can laugh when the joke is on someone else. But those with a truly good sense of humor are different. They can laugh when the joke is on them!

Do you have a sense of humor? A good sense of humor brings you many benefits. Enjoying the funny side of life is relaxing. If you have a good sense of humor, you will have less illness. You will be happier and healthier. People will like you better. A good sense of humor makes getting along on the job easier, too.

Sarah and Jenny both have a sense of humor. They look for the funny things in life. They laugh a lot. They like going to funny movies. They both enjoy friendly jokes on others. But Jenny never thinks jokes on her are very funny. If others laugh, she often gets angry. Sarah sees the humor even when the joke is on her. Everyone enjoys Sarah.

Check Up:✓✓ True or False?

1. You can get along well with your co-workers much the same way you get along with your boss.
2. Do not call people by name. They usually do not like that.
3. Stability means that something is always changing.

How to Avoid Problems with Other People

You have read why it is important to get along with others. You may know some people who are hard to get along with. Some people even like to make trouble. You can have problems with anyone if you are not careful. Here are some ways to help you avoid problems:

- Admit your mistakes.
- Learn to work alone.
- Learn to give clear directions.
- Avoid practical jokes.
- Avoid gossip.
- Avoid being nosy.
- Respect company property.
- Control your emotions.
- Avoid arguments.
- Learn how to compromise.

Admit Your Mistakes

Do you know someone who will not admit a mistake? Many people are like that. Trying to cover up mistakes can lead to arguments. It will certainly prevent others from trusting you.

So admit it when you make a mistake. Others will respect you more. They will not feel a need to prove you wrong. Admitting that you made a mistake may even gain understanding and sympathy from your co-workers. After all, no one is perfect.

After you admit a mistake, say you are sorry. People forgive mistakes. Then work to correct your error. Try never to make the same mistake again.

Jane and Karen were hired as waitresses. They were both very courteous. But once in a while they had trouble getting customers' orders straight. So they made some mistakes.

Jane never admitted her mistakes. She would always say, "That's what the customer ordered." Karen was quick to admit her mistakes and say that she was sorry.

One day both girls made some mistakes on orders. One customer became angry with Jane because she said that he had ordered something different. The boss fired Jane on the spot. But Karen said she was sorry she had made a mistake. She took the order back to the kitchen. The customer told her that it was all right. He understood. Karen kept her job.

Some jobs require only one worker.

Learn to Work Alone

Many times you will work with others to get the job done. Sometimes, though, you will be expected to work alone. If you have a task to do by yourself, do it quietly. Do not bother other workers about it. Do not ask unnecessary questions. Let them do their own jobs.

Learn to Give Clear Directions

Being able to give directions can be as important as being able to follow directions. Do you give clear directions? Can you tell someone how to get to your house?

After you work awhile, you may give directions to new workers. You will want them to understand you.

Listen to how others give directions. That can help you learn how to give directions others will understand. It can help you avoid problems.

Working together may be part of your job. If so, you will need to communicate clearly with your co-workers at all times.

Check Up:✓✓ True or False?

1. It is important to learn to work with people and to work well alone.
2. You should admit your mistakes so you can correct them as soon as possible.
3. Only the boss needs to know how to give directions.

Avoid Practical Jokes

Do you know someone who likes to play practical jokes? Practical jokes are seldom funny. Sometimes they embarrass a person. Sometimes they hurt another person. They nearly always cause bad feelings.

Do not risk causing bad feelings among your co-workers by playing practical jokes. You want to work well together with the other employees on the job. Remember, friendliness and a sense of humor are positive traits. Playing jokes is a negative action.

Avoid Gossip

Gossip is talk about others. It is most often about personal things. Sometimes gossip is true. Often it is not. Gossip spreads **rumors,** stories that may not be true. If you hear a rumor at work, just forget about it. Do not pass it on.

Gossips seem to enjoy talking about others. They think you like them when they tell you about someone else's personal life. But gossip only causes problems. The person talked about may find out. Then he or she may be angry with those who gossiped. The person who gossips may gossip about you, too!

Do not listen to gossip. Change the subject if a co-worker starts to gossip. Avoid those who always talk about others. If people notice you talking with a gossip, they may think you are one, too, and they will not trust you.

Gossip can hurt other people's feelings. It can ruin their reputations. People don't trust those who gossip.

Avoid Being Nosy

Another way to avoid problems is to stay out of other people's business. Do not be nosy! Do not ask personal questions.

When others want to tell you about their personal lives, they will. Asking may make them think you want to gossip. Most people do not like those who are nosy.

Respect Company Property

Some people do not care about things that belong to others. They may write on school desks. They may wear muddy shoes into someone's house.

On the job, some people are careless with company property. They may not take care of machines. They may waste company supplies. They may leave their work area in a mess.

There are many ways to be careless with company property. Most of them cause problems.

Make it a habit to respect the property of others. Your boss will notice your good attitude. He or she knows that taking care of things saves money. Your co-workers will appreciate your actions, too. Being careful and neat makes their work easier. They do not want to clean up after you. They do not want to use equipment you have broken.

Being careless with company property is a good way to lose your job. It may also make your co-workers angry.

Check Up:✓✓ True or False?

1. Practical jokes are fun and helpful at work.
2. If you gossip, people will not trust you.
3. Taking good care of company property saves money for the company.

Control Your Emotions

Emotions are strong feelings. Love and anger are emotions. So is the hurt feeling you get when someone lets you down. Everyone has these feelings. Some people show them more than others.

Do you know someone who gets angry easily? Most children do. Perhaps you did when you were a child. But as you grew older, you probably learned to control your anger.

But you may still *feel* anger. Controlling it means you do not let your anger decide how you will *act*. If you do not control your anger, you may say things you do not mean. You may take your anger out on your co-workers. Such actions will only cause bad feelings and make working together harder.

Things will happen that make you angry. You have no control over them. But you do have control over how you react to them.

Learn ways to control your anger. One way is to give yourself some time to calm down before you do anything. You may count to ten. You may work by yourself for a little while before you discuss the problem. Then you can get over your first angry feeling. You can control what you say and do. You can face the situation calmly.

Another important thing to remember is not to let anger grow. If a certain situation is making you angry, face the problem. Try to solve it so it will not happen again. Do what you can to work things out.

Do not keep thinking or worrying about the problem. After work, get active. Hard physical activity such as running, handball, and tennis can help work off anger. So can doing something to help others.

Most employers will not keep workers who show anger on the job. Save yourself this problem. Learn to control your emotions.

People get along much better on the job when they control their emotions.

A Desire to Succeed

Wheeling to Success: Brad Parks

In 1976 Brad Parks was a freshman at the University of Utah. He planned to become a professional skier. He had also just read the story of Jill Kinmont, *The Other Side of the Mountain* (see page 108).

Then Brad had a skiing accident, too. Brad missed a backflip, landed in the snow, and broke his back. He knew right away that his legs were paralzyed.

Brad did not know anything about disability. But he knew he wanted to learn to do things right. He went through rehabilitation. He was anxious to build his upper body. He worked his muscles hard. He learned to use a wheelchair.

Brad built himself a racing chair so he could go fast. He competed in wheelchair races. He set several world records.

Brad thinks sports chairs are important for disabled people. The old-fashioned chairs are bulky. They make you look disabled, he says. Sports chairs are lightweight. They can go fast and turn easily.

Brad had never played much tennis before his accident. But after the accident he started playing with his family for fun.

Soon he met several other disabled men who played tennis. They set up several little tournaments. Then they started a group called The National Foundation of Wheelchair Tennis.

The purpose of the foundation is to get disabled people to play tennis for fun. Brad thinks that tennis is good therapy. Disabled players can meet others with similar problems and interests.

Brad is president of the National Foundation for Wheelchair Tennis. He holds clinics and sports camps. He teaches others how to play tennis. He also edits a newsletter about wheelchair tennis.

He has other interests, too. Brad also likes to go sailing and scuba diving.

A handicap, Brad says, is a mental thing. It is a feeling. He believes that becoming active in a sport helps handicapped people feel good about themselves.

Avoid Arguments

Do you like to argue? Do you like to *win* arguments? Have you watched people who argue a lot? If you have, you may have noticed that *nobody* really wins. This is true at home, at school—and on the job. It is good to discuss things, of course. It is even all right to disagree. When workers give their **opinions,** they say what they think. They help each other come up with new ideas. Discussion can lead to better ways of doing things.

To argue, though, is bad. It may result in bad feelings. Arguing causes people not to like you. It makes it harder to work together on a job. Those who argue on the job are often fired. The only way to win an argument is to avoid it.

Fred and Kate were friends, but they were always fighting. They both had their own ideas. They wanted to go different places or do different things. Kate told Fred that she did not want to go out with him anymore. She said it was not any fun.

Then Fred had an idea. He said, "Let's try to compromise." Kate said she would give it a try. So each of them gave in just a little. They found out that they both were able to do what they wanted much of the time. It was even fun to do what the other wanted to do sometimes. It was sure a lot better than fighting!

Discussion, not argument, can help workers decide the best way to do a job.

Learn How to Compromise

People often disagree. That is all right. Many times they do not need to agree. But there are times when it is important to agree. For example, you may need to agree with your co-workers on how to do a job.

One way to agree is to compromise. **Compromise** means that both people give in a little. No one gets his or her own way. It is often the best thing to do. Learn to give in a bit to your family and friends. Then you will be able to do it on the job.

These hints will help you compromise.

- Listen and think about the other person's point of view.
- Give facts that show your opinions.
- Avoid opinions that are not based on facts.
- Be **tactful.** (Speak politely. Try not to hurt people's feelings.)
- Decide what changes you can accept.

Employers often call workers together to discuss problems and decide good ways to compromise.

You will not get your way just by talking. You must listen to why the other person sees things differently. Then think about the situation. Maybe the other person is right! Maybe not.

If you still feel you are right, say why. Stick to the facts. Explain your reasons so the other person will understand. But do not show anger. If you do, the other person may get hurt or angry, too.

Both people must have a chance to say how they feel. Then they must think about how the other person feels. Both must change some. That is what compromising is all about.

Check Up:✓✓ True or False?

1. It is important to control your anger at work so others do not get angry with you.
2. If you are angry about a problem at work, just do not talk about it. It will go away by itself.
3. Discussion and compromise are usually better than an argument.

The words

Listed below are the important new words that you learned in this chapter. Next to each word is the page on which you will find the word in bold, black print. Turn back and read again the paragraph in which you find each word. Then write the word and its meaning on a sheet of paper. Also write a sentence of your own using each. word.

1. compromise (227)
2. emotions (224)
3. gossip (222)
4. opinions (226)
5. respect (218)
6. rumors (222)
7. self-respect (217)
8. sense of humor (219)
9. stability (218)
10. tactful (217)

The facts

1. Name five traits most people like in others.
2. What are three things you can say to show that you are a friendly person?
3. How can self-respect help you at work? In the rest of your life?
4. Why is it hard to work with someone who does not act the same every day?
5. How can you help a co-worker who wants to tell you about his or her problem?
6. List five ways to avoid problems with other people.
7. What four things should you do when you make a mistake at work?
8. What is the main difference between having a sense of humor and playing practical jokes?
9. List at least five things you could do to compromise in a work situation.

What's right here?

ADD TO YOUR KNOWLEDGE AND SKILLS

Talk about your ideas

1. How can you treat your co-workers fairly? How could working with one of your best friends make it hard to treat everyone the same?
2. How does the way other people treat you affect your self-respect? Give an example.
3. Name some ways you can control your anger. Have you used any of them? Did they work?
4. Tell about a time when you compromised with someone to get a job done. Explain how compromising is better than arguing.

Do some activities

1. Give clear directions for someone to get to your school. To your home.
2. Draw a chart or diagram. Show how your self-respect can help you get along with others. Also show how being liked by others can build your self-respect. If you wish, add pictures from magazines to help show your ideas.

Improve your basic skills

1. Look at the list on page 216. Then find and read an article on one of the traits listed. Your teacher may suggest some magazines.
2. Read a newspaper article about someone who got into trouble. Then look at the list on page 220 of this book. Can you find what the person in the article did wrong?
3. Find a magazine article about controlling an emotion such as anger. Read it and tell the class what the article said.

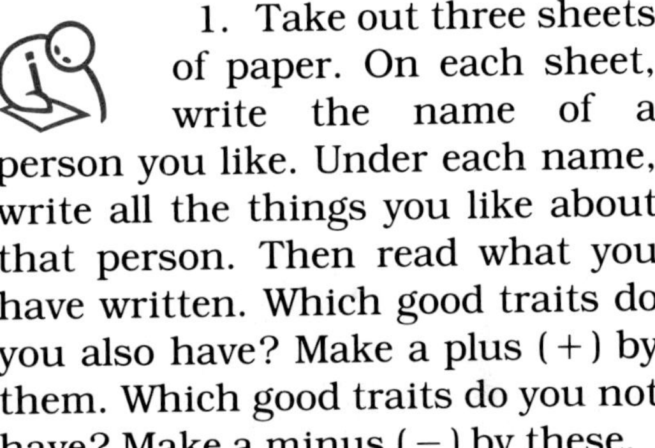

1. Take out three sheets of paper. On each sheet, write the name of a person you like. Under each name, write all the things you like about that person. Then read what you have written. Which good traits do you also have? Make a plus (+) by them. Which good traits do you not have? Make a minus (–) by these.
2. Write a paragraph. Tell about something you have done that made you feel good about yourself.

5×7=?

1. You and two of your friends want to buy and share a computer. The computer costs $990. The sales tax is 6% where you live. How much will the computer cost each of you?
2. You decide to buy a car to drive to work. You get a 24-month loan at $125 per month. What is your total cost?

Chapter 12

Situations That Affect Your Job

What's wrong here?

Words to learn and use

You will learn several new words in this chapter. The most important words are listed below. Do you know the meanings of these words?

absenteeism
sick leave
tardiness
suspended
traffic violation
stress
Alcoholics Anonymous
Al-Anon
addictive

Build on what you know

You already know . . .

- that attitude is an important factor in your job success.
- what employers expect of workers.
- how to get along with co-workers.

In this chapter you will learn . . .

- what types of behavior cause problems at work.
- what situations can affect your job behavior.
- how to manage stress.
- the right way to quit a job.

In the last few chapters you have learned how to make a good first impression. You have learned how to be a safe worker. You know how to get along with your boss and your co-workers.

Sometimes, though, people act in ways that keep them from being successful at work. These actions can keep them from advancing on the job. They can even cause them to be fired. In this chapter you will learn how to stop such behavior in yourself. Sometime you may want to take a different job. So you will learn the right way to leave a job.

Actions That Hurt Your Job Success

There are many ways to become a good employee. Have a good attitude toward your job, your boss, and your co-workers. Be dependable. Be enthusiastic. Accept criticism well. A good sense of humor and a pleasing personality help, too.

Do you know the main reason young workers are fired? It is *not getting along* with others on the job. In fact, *getting along* is more important to your success than anything.

There are other things that could cause you to not be successful on the job. They may keep you from getting a raise in pay. They may cause your boss to pick someone else for the next promotion. They can even cause you to be fired from a job.

Some of these negative actions are

- being absent a lot.
- being tardy often.
- being careless or unsafe on the job.
- not working hard enough while you are at work.
- breaking company rules.
- breaking the law.

Missing work causes problems for your boss and co-workers. Missing too much work could cost you your job.

Absenteeism

Absenteeism means missing days of work when you should be there. Absent workers make problems on the job. If you are absent, someone else must do your work. That person may not know just how to do your job. Less work may get done. The quality of work may be lower. Or your boss may have to hire an extra worker while you are gone. Absent workers cost a company money.

If you are too sick to work, call your boss. If you are injured off the job, call your boss to report the accident. Your absence may be excused for good reasons. Good reasons include sickness, the death of a family member, and sickness of a family member.

On most jobs, workers earn sick leave. **Sick leave** means time that you are sick for which you will be paid. For example, you may earn one day of sick leave for every month you work. After you have worked six months, you have earned six days of sick leave.

Find out your company's policy about excused absences and sick leave. Always be honest when you use excused absence days and sick leave. Do not lie about being sick.

Sometimes you may want to be absent from work for other reasons. You may want to go to a friend's wedding. You may have to take your car to a garage for repairs. For these things, use vacation time.

When possible, talk to your boss well ahead of the time when you will be gone. Your boss may be able to find someone to take your place while you are gone. Or you may be able to make up the time. Maybe you could work before or after normal working hours. You may even be able to switch hours with another worker.

Try not to be absent often. And never be absent without a good reason. Missing work can cause you to lose out on a raise—or even lose your job.

Jill thought sick leave was a free day each month. So she used it when she wanted time off. Other workers did her job when she was gone. And they did not like having to do it. Jill's boss noticed she was often absent but did not ask her about it.

Jill did not get a raise when her friend did. Jill wondered why.

A few months later, Jill lost her job. Her boss said the reason was that she was absent too often.

Check Up:✓✓ True or False?

1. Missing a lot of work can cost you your job.
2. If you need to run an errand, you should use your sick time.

Tardiness

Tardiness means being late for work. Tardiness, like absenteeism, costs a company money. Suppose you were just 15 minutes late to work every day. That would amount to 65 hours a year for a full-time worker. No employer wants to pay a worker for time that he or she is not on the job. Even a few minutes makes a difference. To be safe, be at work a few minutes early.

Suppose an emergency comes up so that you cannot be at work on time. You should phone your boss to say you will be late. Arrange to make up the time you missed. Perhaps you could take a shorter lunch break that day. Or maybe you could work late.

If you are late too often, you may lose pay for lost time. Even worse, you could lose your job.

Roy liked his work experience job at Nelson's Greenhouse. He was a good worker. But he seldom got to work on time.

At the end of the term, Roy's boss fired him. He said he wanted a student who could be on time.

Arriving late or leaving early is cheating your company out of valuable work time.

Carelessness, Unsafe Behavior

Sometimes employees are careless. Or they may not follow safety rules on the job. They may not be thinking about what they are doing. They may not be alert because they are tired. They may be showing off or clowning around.

None of these actions are acceptable in the workplace. Your boss can fire you for doing sloppy work. Your boss can also fire you for putting yourself and other workers in danger.

Not Working Hard Enough

An employer expects a day's work for a day's pay. This means you should work hard all the time you are on the job.

Some workers have poor work habits. They loaf on the job. They do not make the best use of their time. They either do not do enough work, or they do poor work. Develop good work habits by learning the best way to do each task. Then stick to your work.

Another bad habit is visiting on the job. Save your friendly talk for break time or after work.

Some workers come to work very tired. They move slowly doing their tasks. Some have even been known to fall asleep on the job. Try to stay alert on the job and work at a good rate.

Doing personal activities on the job is a bad thing, too. Do not write letters on company time. Do not visit on company telephones. These phones are for business use. Most companies permit emergency calls. Personal calls should be made during break time. All calls should be short.

Good use of company time is your responsibility. Wasting time is cheating. It can cause you to lose your job.

By finding the best way to do each task and working hard, you will make the most of your work time.

Breaking Company Rules

Many companies have rules that employees must follow. You may have to wear a uniform or dress. They may ban smoking or eating on the job or in certain areas. Almost all companies have rules against arguing or fighting.

Often company rules are made to protect the workers. Some are made to keep the work going smoothly. Whatever the reason, always follow company rules. If you do not follow the rules, you may be **suspended.** This means that you would be removed from your job for a certain length of time. It may cost you your job altogether.

Good workers obey company rules. This worker is doing so by wearing the face shield.

"Anyone fighting on the job will be fired." That was the rule at the Pitt Construction Company. But one day there was a fight.

Most of the workers did not like Ray, one of the helpers. He liked to tease and play jokes on other people. He bragged about himself and was lazy. Worst of all, he was an unsafe worker.

Nick was a carpenter. One Monday morning Ray was helping Nick. Nick was on a ladder. He asked Ray to hand him a tool. Instead, Ray threw the tool to Nick. Nick lost his balance and had to jump. Nick was not hurt, but he was angry. He jumped up and started punching Ray.

The boss saw Ray and Nick fighting. He fired them both at once.

Should both Nick and Ray have lost their jobs? Was the boss fair?

Both men broke the rule about fighting. Of course, the fight was Ray's fault. But Nick had other choices. He could have told the boss about Ray's behavior. He could have filed a complaint.

Do not act like Ray, breaking rules and behaving so that others do not like you. Do not act like Nick either, breaking rules because someone else does. Learn to control your own actions.

Breaking the Law

Sometimes a worker may break the law while on the job. This is a very serious problem. It usually leads to the worker losing his or her job.

Stealing is one example. Some workers think taking a little money from the company will not matter. They may think they will borrow the money without asking. They may plan to put it back later. But they get caught before they return it.

Other workers steal company products, a few at a time. Maybe they think that the company can afford it. No company can afford theft.

Workers who steal are usually fired. They may be arrested and sent to jail. They may be required to pay back what they stole. Stealing is not worth the risk. You may not only lose the job you have. You may have trouble finding another one.

Another way to break the law is to have a traffic violation. A **traffic violation** occurs when you disobey the law while driving a car.

Sometimes workers must drive on the job. If they drink and drive, they may be fired. They could also be in trouble if they speed or break other traffic laws. Be a safe driver both on and off the job.

Being in trouble with the law will often cause you to be in trouble at work.

Check Up: ✓✓ True or False?

1. Being just a few minutes late to work will not matter to your boss.
2. You may call your friends from work just to talk.
3. Breaking company rules or the law can cost you your job.

Causes of Bad Work Situations

Everyone wants to succeed on the job. No one likes to be fired. Then why do people do things that may cause them to lose their jobs?

Everyone has problems from time to time. And problems can lead to poor work situations. Some common problems are

- stress.
- alcohol or drug use.
- other negative behavior.

Stress

Stress is a feeling of physical, mental, or emotional strain. Your body feels stress if you work or exercise too hard. You feel mental stress if you worry too much or become upset.

Of course, some stress is good for you. Physical stress helps build muscles and keeps you strong. Mental stress helps you solve problems and learn new things.

Too much stress, though, can be harmful. It can make you angry. It can make you sad. It can even make you sick.

Feeling too much stress may cause you to behave badly at work. You might be rude to your boss or co-workers. You might not have your mind on the job. You might be worrying about your problems instead. You might start missing work or being late to work.

Job Stress. Sometimes a person's job can cause stress. You might feel stress

- if you are having trouble doing your job well.
- if someone at work is always telling you what to do.
- if another person gets the job you really wanted.

Family stress. Problems at home can cause stress, too. A fight with parents, a brother, or sister can be upsetting. You may worry about a family member who is ill. A death in the family causes stress. So does alcoholism, child abuse, or divorce.

How will you manage stress? Try not to worry about your problems while you are at work. Losing your job would only add to your problems.

Money stress. Yet another common cause of stress is lack of money. Some people have money problems all the time. They spend more money than they earn. Or they may charge too many items on their credit cards. This can cause a great deal of stress.

Again, try to think about your job when you are at work. Try to solve your money problems on your own time.

Managing Stress

You will not always be able to avoid stress. It is a part of life. But there are some things you can do to help manage stress.

- **Do what you can to solve your problem.** If you are having a problem at work, talk with your boss. Study or practice so you will become better at your job. Find out what you need to do to get a raise or promotion.

  If you are having family or money problems, talk with your family. Get help from an expert. Do not be afraid to ask for help. Asking for help shows that you are smart enough to want to solve your problem.

  Talk to your school counselor or ask your minister where to go for help. Check the yellow pages in the phone book. You can find a public service agency that could help you.
- **Work off stress.** Try to "blow off steam." You might run, play tennis, or swim. Even walking can help.
- **Talk out your problem.** It helps to share a problem with someone you trust. The person may be a friend, counselor, family member, or teacher.
- **Learn to accept what you cannot change.** The problem may be out of your control. Try your best to accept it until you can change it.
- **Take time to relax.** You may spend a lot of time working. But you also need recreation. It can lessen stress.
- **Do things for others.** While you are unhappy, you may do too much thinking about yourself. Get your mind off yourself. Do something for someone else. Besides, being with others often leads to new friendships.
- **Take one thing at a time.** You cannot do everything at once. Start with the job that must be done first. Then do the other jobs, one at a time.

Alcohol and Drugs

Using alcohol or drugs can be harmful in many ways. Drinking too much causes health problems. Some people spend too much money on alcohol. Drinking can cause family problems.

The greatest danger from alcohol is drunk driving. This is often called *driving under the influence.* Nearly half of all highway deaths are caused by drunk drivers. That is 25,000 deaths a year. Many others are hurt. Each year drunk driving causes nearly five billion dollars in property damage.

Drunk drivers pay fines and often go to jail. Some lose their driver's license. Most have trouble buying car insurance.

People who drink too much are called alcoholics. They cannot stop drinking on their own. They need to get medical help at once. **Alcholics Anonymous** is a group that helps alcoholics to learn to control their drinking.

Alcoholics also need help from their families. Family members can learn to help alcoholics through a group called **Al-Anon.**

Drinking too much is not just a problem at home. It can be a problem at work, too. Heavy drinkers often miss too much work. They often do poor work. Alcoholics often lose their jobs because of their drinking.

Like alcoholism, drug abuse is a behavior problem. Both affect a person on and off the job. Drugs are addictive. **Addictive** means habit forming, or very hard to quit.

Drugs are also illegal. Drug users may be arrested. They may be charged with driving under the influence. Drug addicts often turn to "pushing," or selling, drugs to make money to buy their own. They may also steal to get money for drugs. Like alcohol, drugs cause problems for workers that may cost them their jobs.

Drugs are dangerous. They cause personal tragedy and death. Say "No" to drugs so they will not affect your life and your job.

Check Up:✓✓ True or False?

1. Stress can be caused by many things. These include work problems, family problems, and money problems.
2. Suppose you have a family problem or a money problem you cannot handle. You should seek the help of an expert.
3. Using alcohol or drugs off the job cannot affect your work on the job.

A Desire to Succeed

Recovering from Alcoholism:
Betty Ford

In the 1970s Betty Ford was a very important woman. She worked hard for women's rights. She fought against child abuse. She talked to many women about the importance of getting check-ups at the doctor's office. She was married to President Gerald Ford.

Betty Ford was also an alcoholic and a drug addict.

Mrs. Ford says that she drank her first beer when she was in college. Drinking meant fun, celebrations, and a way to relax. She drank on dates to be part of the group.

Later in her life she got a pinched nerve in her neck. It was very painful. Her doctor gave her pills for the pain. Soon she was taking other pills for other things. She drank alcohol along with the pills.

Mrs. Ford's family had been watching her. They knew that she drank too much and that she took too many pills. But they thought she would get better.

One day they all sat down with her. They told her they thought she had a problem with alcohol and drugs. They all loved her and wanted to help her.

Mrs. Ford says she was shocked to hear them say such things. She did not feel like an alcoholic because she did not think she drank that much. She did not feel like a drug addict. Her doctor had given her the drugs she was taking.

But Mrs. Ford went to an alcohol rehab center. The doctors and other patients there helped her. And her family supported her all the time.

Later she and some friends started the Betty Ford Center in California. The center helps other people who have problems with alcohol or drugs.

Mrs. Ford now knows that she cannot have any alcoholic drinks. If she does, she will probably drink too much again. So she has learned to stay away from alcohol and drugs. "To the day I die, I'll be recovering," she says.

Behavior Off the Job

Do you remember reading about lifestyles in Chapter 1? You learned that your choice of lifestyle affects the type of job you choose. Even after you begin work, your lifestyle still affects your job. It affects how well you do on the job.

Your daily personal habits affect your work. Getting enough sleep makes you an alert worker. You do good work so your boss may notice you. You may get a raise or a promotion. If you go to work tired, you may not do well. You may even oversleep and miss work.

The same thing can be said for eating right. Eating the proper amounts of healthful foods keeps you from being sick. It makes you stronger. You do better work.

Your leisure activities affect your work performance, too. Getting plenty of exercise is a good thing to do. But too much recreational activity, which drains your energy for your job, is a bad thing to do.

Even your friends can affect your job performance. Choose friends that do not try to get you to do things you should not. You do not want friends who party too much or break the law.

Being arrested would certainly affect your job. You would miss work. You might lose your job because of your arrest. You would at least lose the respect and trust of your boss and co-workers. An arrest could cost you money. You might have to pay a fine, bail money, or a lawyer's fee.

Be a careful driver, too. The loss of your driver's license could hurt you on the job. You would not be able to keep a job that required driving. You may have trouble getting to and from work without a license.

What you do at home affects how well you do on the job.

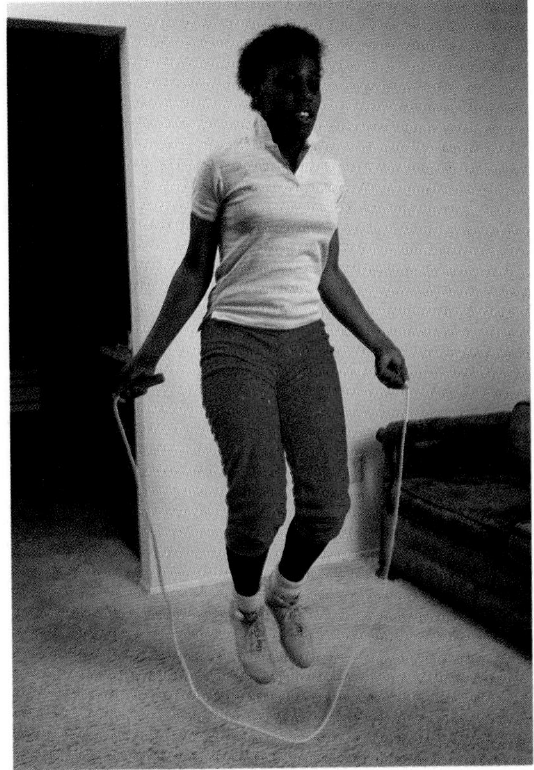

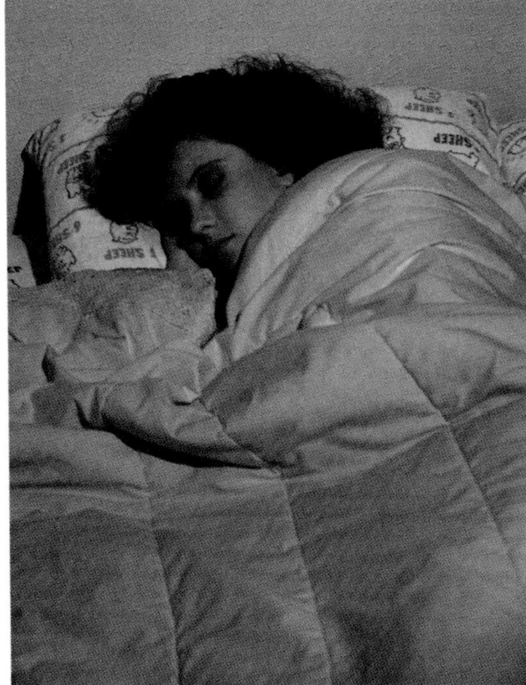

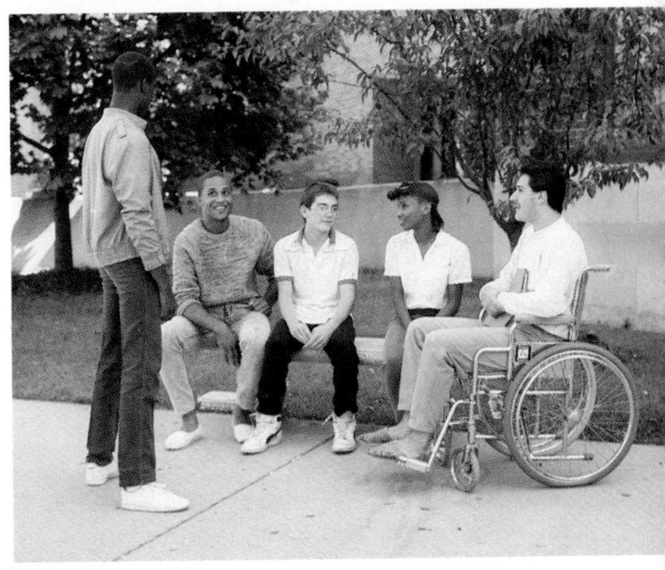

Good eating and sleeping habits, the proper amount of exercise, and having good friends can help you manage stress. This will make you a better worker.

Leaving a Job

You will not have the same job for your whole life. In fact, you may have many jobs during your working career.

Quitting a job should be a positive step, not a negative one. Do not quit a job in anger. Try not to leave with bad feelings. You may work together again someday.

There are good reasons for quitting a job. You may find a job that you will like better. Or one that pays more. It is better to have another job before you quit the one you have now.

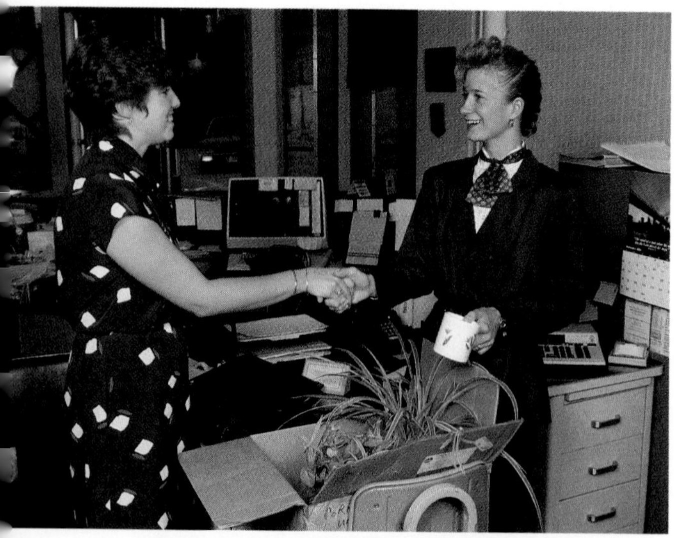

Each job should be a learning experience for the next one. Leave a job with a happy feeling and positive attitude.

Once you decide to leave your job, follow these steps.

- Tell your boss first. Tell your boss at least two weeks in advance.
- Keep a friendly attitude with your boss and co-workers.
- If required by company rules, write a letter explaining that you are quitting. See the sample letter below.
- Do not brag about your new job.
- Try to keep your co-workers as friends.
- Leave your work place neat and clean.
- On the last day of work thank your co-workers and boss for friendship and help.

Check Up: ✓✓ True or False?

1. Your eating, sleeping, and exercising habits make a difference in your work habits.
2. Changing jobs can be a good thing to do.
3. When you decide to quit your job, you should leave that day.

1020 Hill Street
New City, MO 63201
May 17, 1988

New City Auto Company
2366 Center Street
New City, MO 63201

Dear Mrs. Adams;

I would like to stop work at the New City Auto Company on May 31. I plan to begin working at the Jones Truck Lines on June 1, 1988.

I have enjoyed working with you and everyone else here. I have learned a great deal about cars during the last two years.

Thank you very much for all you have done for me.

Very truly yours,
John Doss

Sometimes you may need to write a letter saying you are quitting.

The words

Listed below are important new words that were used in this chapter. Next to each word is the page on which you will find the word in bold, black print. Turn back and read again the paragraph in which you find each word. Then write the word and its meaning on a sheet of paper. Also write a sentence of your own using each word.

1. absenteeism (233)
2. addictive (240)
3. Al-Anon (240)
4. Alcoholics Anonymous (240)
5. sick leave (233)
6. stress (238)
7. suspended (236)
8. tardiness (234)
9. traffic violation (237)

The facts

1. What are six negative actions that could cause you to lose your job?
2. What is sick leave? When should you use it?
3. What are three rules for using the phone at work?
4. How can stress affect your behavior at work?
5. Name four people you might be able to talk with about a stress problem.
6. Name six tips for managing stress.
7. Where can alcoholics and their families turn for help?
8. Name five things that you could do off the job that might affect your job.
9. What are two good reasons you might want to quit your job?
10. What are five things you should do once you have decided to quit your job?

What's right here?

ADD TO YOUR KNOWLEDGE AND SKILLS

Talk about your ideas

1. Do you have good study habits? How can good study habits lead to good work habits?
2. Should you always have to obey company rules? Why, or why not?
3. What would you do if you saw another worker stealing from the company?
4. Where could you turn for help if you owed too many bills? If your father hit you often? If your sister was using drugs? If you felt very depressed and sad?

Do some actitivies

1. Interview an employer. Ask the employer how an employee's actions off the job can affect job performance. Tell the class what the employer said.
2. Keep a chart of the foods you eat for a week. Also list all of the activities you do during a week. Note how long you do each activity. Read over your chart. Do you see any areas in need of improvement?

Improve your basic skills

1. Find and read a newspaper or magazine article about managing stress. Report the main points of the article to the class.
2. Read through the *Human Services* section of your phone book. Discuss the different agencies in class. Learn how each one can help you.

1. Imagine you have a job in a fast food restaurant in your town. Write a letter to your boss to quit your job. Have your teacher read your letter.

5×7=?

1. Read again the story about Roy's tardiness on page 234. Suppose last week Roy was 10 minutes late on Monday, 15 minutes late on Tuesday, 5 minutes late on Wednesday, 5 minutes late on Thursday, and 10 minutes late on Friday. Mr. Nelson pays Roy $4.25 an hour. How much did Roy's tardiness cost Mr. Nelson last week?
2. Jennifer just got a charge card. She charged items this month for $12, $16, $18.75, $70, and $42.50. What is her total bill this month? Suppose she only pays $20 on the bill when it comes. The charge card company charges 1.5% interest a month. What will her bill be next month if she doesn't buy anything else?

PART FOUR

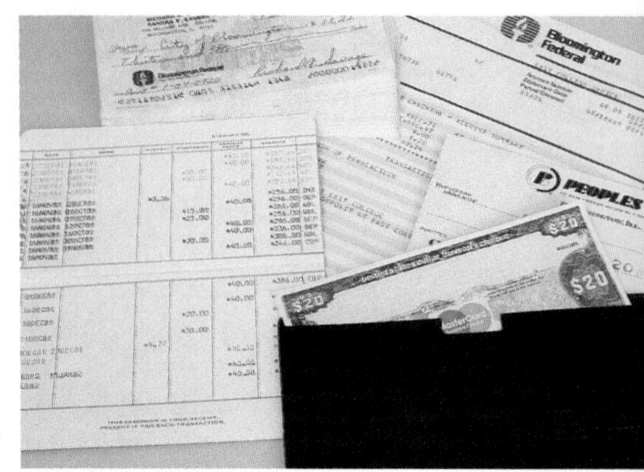

SKILLS FOR EVERYDAY LIVING

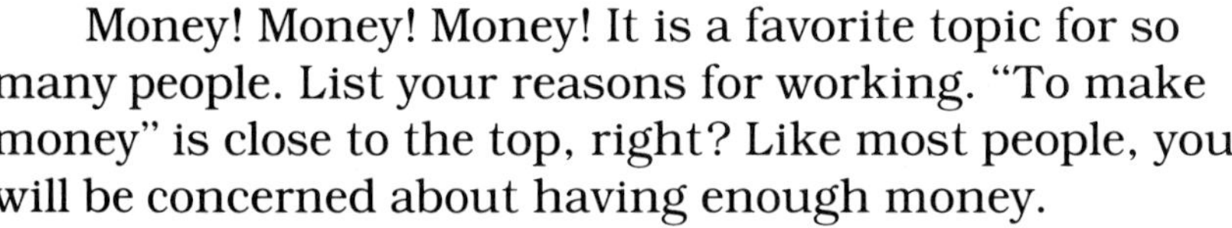

Money! Money! Money! It is a favorite topic for so many people. List your reasons for working. "To make money" is close to the top, right? Like most people, you will be concerned about having enough money.

Earning money is important. You need money to buy food and clothing. You will have to pay the rent. You will need to save for a rainy day. And there will be so many things you do not need—but want.

Earning money is only the first part of your money concerns. Managing the money you earn is the second part. Smart people get much more for their money than others. You want to be one of those smart people.

In Part Four you will learn about your paycheck. And about the many taxes you must pay. Then you will learn how to manage your money. You will learn how to be a good shopper. And what it means to live on your own. You will be on your way to a happy, successful life.

Penney
MasterCard
P.A. Bergner &
TEXACO
CREDIT
Sears
SEARS, ROEBUCK
FIRST CARD

Chapter 13

Your Paycheck and Your Taxes

What's wrong here?

Words to learn and use

You will learn several new words in this chapter. The most important words are listed below. Do you know the meanings of these words?

- payroll deductions
- pay stub
- gross pay
- net pay
- taxes
- FICA
- federal income tax
- Internal Revenue Service (IRS)
- state income tax
- Wage and Tax Statement

Build on what you know

You already know

- what decisions you must make during your first days on the job.
- how to get started on the right foot at work.
- how to get along with people at work.
- how to avoid situations that could hurt your career.
- how to fill out a W-4 form.

In this chapter you will learn

- why money is withheld from your paycheck.
- how to understand your pay stub.
- what FICA and the federal and state income taxes are.
- how to fill out a federal tax return.

Earlier you learned how to decide what kind of work you want to do. And how to apply for a job. Then you learned how to get along with others at work.

Now you will learn how to read your pay stub. And why your employer holds out some of your pay. You will learn how to fill out your first tax return.

A Look at Your Paycheck

Many beginning workers are disappointed when they get their first paycheck. They know how much money per hour to expect. And they know how many hours they worked. The two numbers multiplied together should be the amount on the paycheck, right? Wrong.

You will not usually receive this amount. Your employer must keep some of your earnings to pay for several things for you. Some of the things that must be paid for are

- FICA.
- Federal income tax.
- State and local income tax.

You may also ask your employer to keep some of your pay for other things. These things could include medical insurance, savings, or a retirement fund. The amounts the employer keeps are called **payroll deductions.**

When you get your paycheck, you will see that it has two parts. You can tear them apart along a dotted line. One part is the paycheck itself. You take your paycheck to a bank or somewhere else to exchange it for cash. You will learn what to do with your check in Chapter 14.

The **pay stub** is the section you keep. It gives a lot of information about your pay. Read it carefully so you understand it. Make sure the information on it is correct. Keep your pay stubs all together in a safe place. Then you will have a record of your earnings.

Look at Pat Smith's pay stub on page 253. It lists his name and social security number. The stub tells the last day of the pay period. In this case, Pat is paid every week. The last day of this pay period is December 6, 1987.

The pay stub lists the number of hours worked during the pay period. Pat worked 40 hours that week. Suppose Pat had worked more than 40 hours. Then the extra hours and pay would have been listed as overtime. The pay for overtime hours is figured at a higher rate of pay.

Gross pay is the full amount of pay for a pay period. Pat makes $4.50 per hour. His gross pay is $4.50 times 40 hours, or $180.

The next line shows the deductions. These are FICA, federal income tax, and state income tax for the pay period. It also lists other deductions. In this case Pat had $7.50 held out to pay for insurance.

Adding all the numbers on this line gives you the week's total deductions. Pat's total deductions are $41.72. The gross pay less the total deductions equals the **net pay,** or "take-home" pay. The net pay is the amount of the paycheck. It is the amount left over after your deductions are subtracted. Pat's net pay is $138.28.

The last line on the pay stub lists the year-to-date totals. These are the amounts earned and withheld so far during the whole year. So far Pat's gross pay is $6,428. His employer has held out $482.74 for FICA. He held out $578.52 for federal income tax. And he held out $160.70 for state income tax. Always save the last pay stub of the year. It shows the total earnings and deductions for the entire year.

Pat's Paycheck Stub

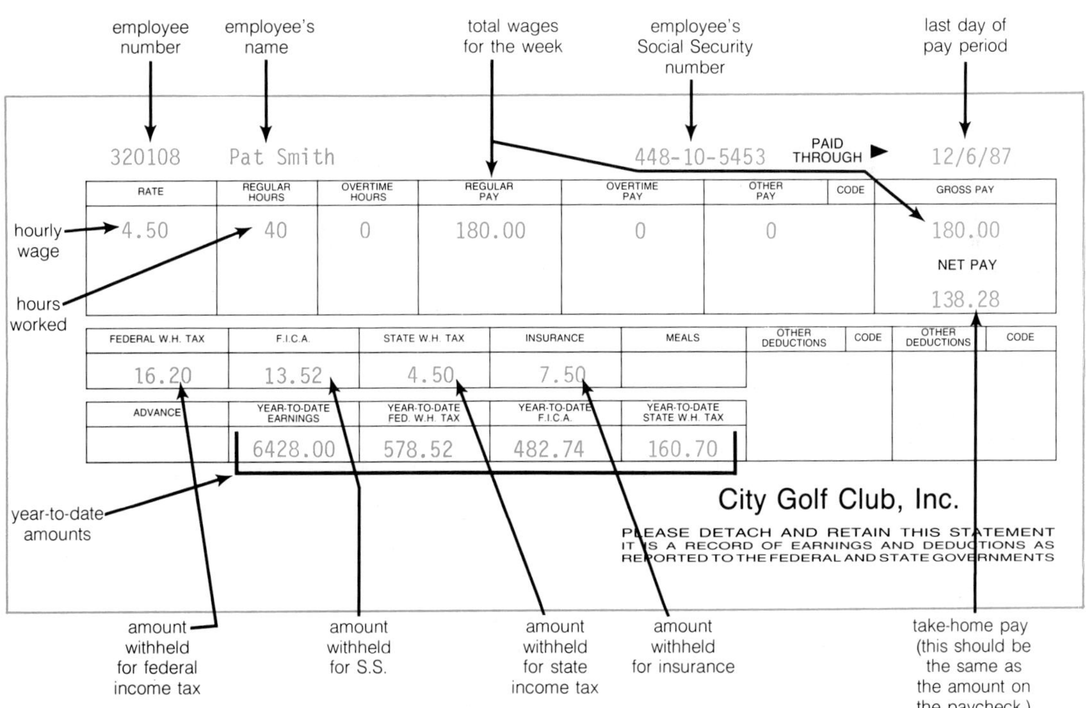

The paycheck stub tells the total wages for the pay period and what has been deducted from the wages. How much was deducted from Pat's paycheck this week?

Paycheck Deductions

Most of the deductions from your paycheck are for taxes. **Taxes** are money that you pay to the government. The government needs the money to do its work. The law requires that you pay taxes. You will also learn about other kinds of deductions in this section.

FICA

Almost everyone who works pays FICA tax. **FICA** stands for Federal Insurance Contribution Act. It is often called *social security* tax.

Social security collects a tax from almost all workers. During your working years, you and your employer make payments to the program. Most of the money is used to pay people who have retired.

The social security program gives four kinds of benefits.

1. Disability benefits help injured workers.
2. Survivor benefits help the families of workers who have died.
3. Retirement benefits help older people who no longer work.
4. Medical benefits help older people with medical bills. These benefits are called Medicare.

Someday you may retire. Or you may qualify for other benefits. Then you will get monthly payments, too. Your checks will come from FICA taxes paid by people who are still working.

Every time you get paid, your employer takes FICA taxes from your pay. The FICA rate is 7.51 percent of your gross pay. Pat's FICA payment is \$13.52 (\$180 × .0751 = \$13.52).

Your boss puts in the same amount for you. Then he or she sends this money to the government. These FICA payments are credited to your account. They are listed under your social security number. The government keeps a record of the months you work and pay FICA taxes. You get credit for the months you work. You must work a certain number of months before you can get any benefits.

Someday you may want to know how much has been credited to your account. If so, go to your nearest Social Security Office. Fill out a card to ask about your account. In a few weeks you will get an answer in the mail.

Tax money is used for the operation of all government services. Part of your federal tax money pays for the upkeep of the White House in Washington, DC.

Federal Income Tax

Another deduction from your check is for federal income tax. It is shown on your stub as "Federal W.H. Tax." It is also shown as "Federal Withholding."

Your **federal income tax** is money you pay to the United States government. This money pays for all the things the government does. For example, it helps pay for the armed services, federal highways, and Congress. It even pays for national parks and museums.

Your federal tax is collected by a federal agency called the **Internal Revenue Service (IRS).** Your boss withholds money from your check. He or she then sends that money to the IRS.

The first day on the job your employer will ask you to fill out a tax form. This form is called a *W-4.* Be sure to fill out your W-4 correctly. Then your employer should hold out the right amount for your federal income tax. Your employer will do this each pay period.

How much tax you must pay depends on many things. Some of these things are

- how much money you earn.
- if you are single or married.
- if you have children.
- if you support any other relatives.
- if you are blind.
- how many business and certain personal expenses you have.

Generally speaking, the more money you make, the more you will pay in income tax.

Check Up:✓✓ True or False?

1. *Gross pay, net pay,* and *take-home pay* all mean the same thing.
2. Your FICA tax is credited to your social security account.
3. *IRS* is a government agency that collects federal income tax money.

State and Local Income Tax

Most states also have an income tax. Only nine states do not. Alaska, Washington, Nevada, and Wyoming do not have income tax. Neither do South Dakota, Texas, Tennessee, New Hampshire, and Florida.

State income tax is money collected by the Department of Revenue of your state. This money is used to pay for the work the state government does. It pays for state highways, prisons, police, and courts. It also pays for welfare programs, job services, and many other things.

Your state income tax is withheld from your paycheck. It is withheld the same way your federal tax is. The state rate is usually lower than the federal rate. Every state makes its own income tax laws so each state is different.

Sometimes large cities have an income tax, too. Is there a city tax where you work? If so, money will be withheld for this fund, too.

Other Deductions

You may have some other deductions taken from your paycheck. This means that your boss will withhold money. He or she will then pay certain bills for you.

One example is insurance. You may decide to buy life insurance or medical insurance through your job. Insurance is often cheaper at work. You make your insurance payments through separate payroll deductions. This is the same way you pay your income tax and FICA. Your boss withholds the money. He or she pays the insurance company for you.

Look at Pat Smith's pay stub again. Notice that $7.50 was withheld to pay for his medical insurance.

You might join the trade union where you work. Then you need to pay union dues. These can be deducted from your paycheck.

Some employers have pension plans. A pension plan is a savings plan for your retirement. Through a pension plan you set aside money. That money earns more money. When you retire, you get your pension to live on. Pension plan payments might be another deduction you make.

Your company may have a credit union. If so, you can have part of your pay put into a savings account. This can help you save.

These deductions are most often not required. You choose them. You decide how much you want deducted from your paycheck. Then your employer pays these things for you. This helps you. When you cash your check, part of your expenses are already paid.

Your Wage and Tax Statement

Each year your employer will fill out a **Wage and Tax Statement** for you. This form is often called a *W-2.* Your W-2 tells how much you earned the past year. It also tells how much was withheld from your pay.

You will receive your W-2 at the first of the year. Suppose you worked for more than one employer during the year. If so, you will get a W-2 from each employer.

Check your W-2 carefully. Is the social security deduction correct? Are your earnings and income tax withholdings correct? If not, tell your boss right away. Keep your W-2 to help fill out your income tax returns.

Your employer has to give you a W-2. It must be ready by January 31. It may be mailed to you, or you may have to pick it up. You are responsible for getting your W-2s. Not getting one is no excuse. It is up to you to report your income on your tax return.

1 Control Number		OMB No. 1545-0008	
2 Employer's Name, Address, and ZIP Code The City Golf Club 8700 River Drive Pittsburg, IL 66762		3 Employer's Identification Number 26-492-8745	4 Employer's State Number
		5 Stat. Employee ☐ Deceased ☐ Legal Rep. ☐ 942 Emp. ☐ Subtotal ☐ Void ☐	
		6 Allocated Tips	7 Advance EIC Payment
8 Employee's Social Security Number 448-10-5453	9 Federal Income Tax Withheld $622.00	10 Wages, Tips, Other Compensation $6968.00	11 Social Security Tax Withheld $523.30
12 Employee's Name, Address, and ZIP Code Pat Smith 8500 River Drive Pittsburg, IL 66762		13 Social Security Wages $6968.00	14 Social Security Tips
		16	
		17 State Income Tax $174.20	18 State Wages, Tips, Etc. $6968.00 · 19 Name of State IL
		20 Local Income Tax	21 Local Wages, Tips, Etc. · 22 Name of Locality

Form **W-2 Wage and Tax Statement 1987**
36-2515832 APP. 4/84

Copy B To be filed with employee's FEDERAL tax return
This information is being furnished to the Internal Revenue Service

Department of the Treasury
Internal Revenue Service

The W-2 form is completed by your employer. It is used to report earnings, social security tax, and other information. Attach Copy B to your federal tax return.

Filing a Tax Return

Each year you must file (complete) a federal tax return. This return reports your income for the year before. It must be filed on or before April 15th.

On your tax return you add up your total income for the year. Then you figure your exact tax bill based on your income. The tax form and tax booklet will explain how to do this.

Next you compare what was withheld from your check to your total tax bill. You may have paid more than you actually owe. If so, you will get some money back. This money is called a *refund*. Getting a refund is like getting change when you buy something.

The amount withheld could be less than your tax bill. If so, you will have to pay more taxes. This extra amount is called the *balance due*.

The first few thousand dollars you make each year are not taxed. If you work part-time, you probably will not make this much money. In this case you would not have to pay any federal income tax. It is still important that you file your tax return. You must do this to get all of your withholding back.

There are two things to remember. One, your FICA withholding goes into your social security account. You cannot get that back each year. It stays in your account until you receive social security benefits.

Two, your state tax laws may be different from the federal tax rules. Find out if you need to file a state tax return. You may need to file a state return, but not a federal one.

You can get tax forms and instructions at your post office or bank.

Choosing the Right Tax Form

The IRS has several tax forms. Form 1040 can be used by all taxpayers.

Your tax situation may be quite simple. If so, you can use a 1040EZ or a 1040A form.

The 1040EZ is the simplest form. It has only one page. The instructions are printed on the back. You will want to use the 1040EZ if you fit *all* of the following:

- You are single.
- You do not support anyone.
- All your income is from wages, tips, salaries, and interest.
- Your interest income is less than $400.
- You got no unemployment during the year.

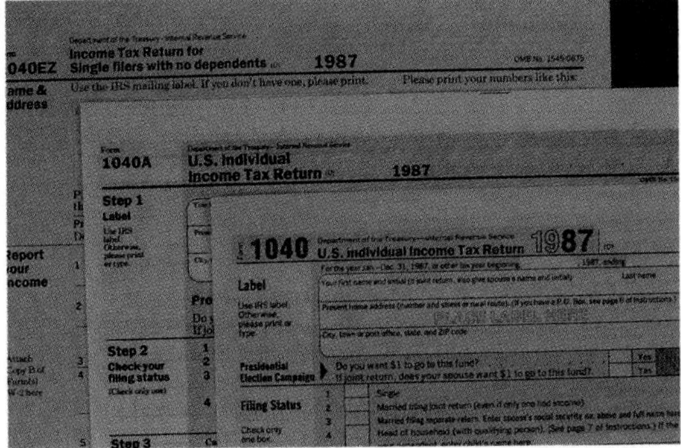

Taxpayers should choose the tax form that's best for them.

The 1040A is not quite as easy to fill out as the 1040EZ. You would use the 1040A in the following situations.

- You are married or support other relatives.
- You have income from dividends or unemployment.
- You have an Individual Retirement Account (IRA).
- You made contributions to political candidates.
- Your income is low, you support your child, and you qualify for Earned Income Credit.

The 1040 form is used by taxpayers in certain tax situations. They may have high incomes. They may have incomes other than wages, interest, dividends, and unemployment compensation.

Some expenses will help lower taxes. People with these expenses can list them on the 1040.

For the first few years you work you probably will be able to use the shorter form.

Check Up:✓✓ True or False?

1. Income taxes are the only deductions employers can make from paychecks.
2. Your W-2 tells how much you earned during the past year.
3. There is only one federal income tax form.

A Desire to Succeed

Excaping from Slavery: Harriet Ross Tubman

Many people learn to overcome an obstacle to achieve success. Harriet Ross Tubman lived from 1820 to 1913. She had a number of things against her. She was a woman. She was black. And she was a slave.

From the time she was little, Harriet's master mistreated her. He forced her to do hard work. A terrible thing happened when she was thirteen. Her master hit her with a heavy weight, cracking her skull. From then on she got dizzy easily. Sometimes she would fall asleep and no one could wake her.

When she was twenty-four, Harriet married a freed man. A few years later her master died. Harriet was afraid she would be sold and forced to move to another state. She decided to escape. Her husband refused to go with her. So she left with two brothers. The men became frightened and turned back. So Harriet escaped alone.

Harriet started a network of people to help other slaves escape. This network was called the *Underground Railroad.* Slaves traveled by back roads and through swamps and woods. And they hid in people's homes along the way.

Harriet worked eight years helping people to escape slavery. She guided over three hundred slaves to freedom. She carried a rifle with her for protection. She also used it when one of her "passengers" became afraid and wanted to turn back. "You'll be free, or you will die," she would say as she pointed the gun at the person.

There was a big reward for her capture. But Harriet Tubman was never caught.

During the Civil War, Harriet was a scout for the Union Army. She also worked as a spy and a nurse. In 1863, she led army troops on a raid that freed over 750 slaves.

She never lived a life of luxury. Or even earned much money. But Harriet Ross Tubman achieved her goal. She helped others to freedom, something she valued very much.

Getting Help with Your Tax Return

Will you need help completing your tax return? You may have questions about your return. Do you have to file one? Which one should you choose? Where do you enter your income? Can you list expenses?

There are several places you can turn for help. First, IRS prints a booklet with tax information in it. The booklet is free. You can usually get one at your bank. Study it carefully. You can also get the forms you need there.

An IRS agent can help answer your questions. Call the IRS office nearest you. Phone numbers are listed in your tax booklet. If there is an IRS office in your city, you can go there. An agent will help you fill out your return or answer specific questions.

Your employer may help you complete your tax return. Most adults fill out a tax return each year. You can ask your parents, a teacher, or an adult friend to help you.

You may decide to pay a professional tax preparer to fill out your return. Usually the fee is based on how hard your return is to do. Ask for an estimate of the fee before this person does your return.

Remember, if you do not understand something about your taxes, get help. In many cases you are required to file a return. Not doing so in these cases is against the law. Also be sure to file your return on time. You can be charged a penalty for filing late. You are responsible for reporting your income and paying your taxes.

If you have questions about your tax return, get help from someone who understands the laws.

How to Complete a Tax Return

Pat Smith used Form 1040EZ for his 1987 tax return. Look at his form on page 263 as you read the following information.

Name and Address

Pat printed his name, address, and social security number in the top section. You should use a pencil for the first copy. Then recopy your return in ink.

Pat did not want to give a dollar to go to the Presidential Election Campaign Fund. So he checked no.

Income

On line 1 Pat entered his wages for 1987. The $6,968 is the same amount as in box 10 of his W-2 form. You may have worked for more than one employer during the year. If so, add the gross wages from all your W-2s.

Pat's savings account earned $10 during 1987. He entered that amount on line 2.

He added the two incomes from lines 1 and 2. Then he entered the total on line 3. Pat's adjusted gross income is $6,978.

Pat is claimed as a dependent on his father's tax return so he checked yes on line 4. He completed the worksheet on the back of the form and entered $2,540 on line 4. He subtracted line 4 from line 3 and wrote $4,438 on line 5.

He wrote 0 on line 6. This amount is subtracted from line 5. Pat subtracted it and wrote $4,438 on line 7. This is Pat's taxable income.

Reporting your income and paying your taxes every year is your responsibility.

Form **1040EZ** Department of the Treasury - Internal Revenue Service
Income Tax Return for Single filers with no dependents (0) **1987** OMB No. 1545-0675

Name & address

Use the IRS mailing label. If you don't have one, please print.

Please print your numbers like this: 0 1 2 3 4 5 6 7 8 9

Print your name above (first, initial, last): PAT SMITH

Present home address (number and street). (If you have a P.O. box, see instructions.): 8500 RIVER DRIVE

City, town, or post office, state, and ZIP code: PITTSBURG, IL 66762

Your social security number: 448 10 5453

Please read the instructions for this form on the reverse side.

Presidential Election Campaign Fund Do you want $1 to go to this fund? *Note: Checking "Yes" will not change your tax or reduce your refund.* Yes ☐ No ☒

		Line	Dollars	Cents
Report your income	1 Total wages, salaries, and tips. This should be shown in Box 10 of your W-2 form(s). (Attach your W-2 form(s).)	1	6 968	00
	2 Taxable interest income of $400 or less. If the total is more than $400, you cannot use Form 1040EZ.	2	10	00
Attach Copy B of Form(s) W-2 here	3 Add line 1 and line 2. This is your **adjusted gross income.**	3	6 978	00
	4 Can you be claimed as a dependent on another person's return? ☒ Yes. Do worksheet on back; enter amount from line E here. ☐ No. Enter 2,540 as your standard deduction.	4	2 540	00
	5 Subtract line 4 from line 3.	5	4 438	00
	6 If you checked the "Yes" box on line 4, enter 0. If you checked the "No" box on line 4, enter 1,900. This is your **personal exemption.**	6	0	00
	7 Subtract line 6 from line 5. If line 6 is larger than line 5, enter 0 on line 7. This is your **taxable income.**	7	4 438	00
Figure your tax	8 Enter your Federal income tax withheld. This should be shown in Box 9 of your W-2 form(s).	8	622	00
	9 Use the **single** column in the tax table on pages 32–37 of the Form 1040A instruction booklet to find the **tax** on the amount shown on **line 7** above. Enter the amount of tax.	9	592	00
Refund or amount you owe	10 If line 8 is larger than line 9, subtract line 9 from line 8. Enter the **amount of your refund.**	10	30	00
Attach tax payment here	11 If line 9 is larger than line 8, subtract line 8 from line 9. Enter the **amount you owe.** Attach check or money order for the full amount, payable to "Internal Revenue Service."	11		

Sign your return

I have read this return. Under penalties of perjury, I declare that to the best of my knowledge and belief, the return is true, correct, and complete.

For IRS Use Only—Please do not write in boxes below.

Your signature: Pat Smith Date: April 1, 1988

For Privacy Act and Paperwork Reduction Act Notice, see page 31. Form **1040EZ** (1987)

Pat Smith used the 1040EZ form to report his income tax for 1986.

Tax

Pat looked in box 9 of his W-2. His employer had withheld $622 for federal income tax during the year. He wrote that amount on line 8. Did you work for more than one employer? If so, add the federal withholding from all your W-2s.

Then Pat turned to the tax table in his tax booklet. He read down the first column until he found his taxable income. $4,438 was between $4,400 and $4,450. Then he read across that line to the column for single taxpayers. His tax for the year was $592. He wrote $592 on line 9.

Pat had paid more money than needed for his 1987 taxes. He subtracted $592 from $622. He is entitled to a $30 refund. He wrote $30 on line 10. It could have turned out that he owed money for his tax bill. In this case he would have to pay. He would have written that amount on line 11, instead.

To figure your tax, find the right taxable income in the left column. Then read across that line to the column that applies to you. How much would Pat's tax be if he earned $5,155? If he earned $5,962?

COLUMN FOR SINGLE TAXPAYERS

PAT'S INCOME

		If 1040A, line 17, OR 1040EZ, line 7 is—		And you are—			
d	Head of a house-hold	At least	But less than	Single (and 1040EZ filers)	Married filing jointly	Married filing sepa-rately	Head of a house-hold
				Your tax is—			
3	230	3,800	3,850	502	454	514	47
7	232	3,850	3,900	509	461	521	481
1	235	3,900	3,950	517	469	529	489
4	238	3,950	4,000	524	476	536	496
8	241	**4,000**					
2	243	4,000	4,050	532	484	544	504
6	246	4,050	4,100	539	491	551	511
9	249	4,100	4,150	547	499	559	519
3	252	4,150	4,200	554	506	566	526
7	254	4,200	4,250	562	514	574	534
1	257	4,250	4,300	569	521	581	541
4	260	4,300	4,350	577	529	589	549
8	263	4,350	4,400	584	536	596	556
	265	4,400	4,450	592	544	604	564
	268	4,450	4,500	599	551	611	571
	271	4,500	4,550	607	559	619	579
	274	4,550	4,600	614	566	626	586
	277	4,600	4,650	622	574	634	594
	281	4,650	4,700	629	581	641	601
	284	4,700	4,750	637	589	649	609
	288	4,750	4,800	644	596	656	616
	292	4,800	4,850	652	604	664	624
	296	4,850	4,900	659	611	671	631
	299	4,900	4,950	667	619	679	639
	303	4,950	5,000	674	626	686	646

Continued on next page

This is Marie's first time to file an income tax return. She feels special. She is joining the adult world.

Marie is proud of having completed the form herself. She studied the instructions carefully. She kept all the records she needed. She was careful to attach the W-2 form to her return.

Marie asked her boss to check her work. It was correct.

Marie worked part-time and earned $1,500. That is not enough income to have to pay taxes. This means she will get a refund. She will get back all the taxes withheld from her paychecks. She mailed her return early in February so she would get her refund as soon as possible.

Finishing the Return

Pat signed his name in the space provided. He dated his tax return April 1, 1988. He also filled out his state tax return. He found that he was getting a refund on his state tax.

Next Pat made a copy of both returns for his own records. He stapled Copy B of the W-2 to the 1040EZ. He stapled Copy 2 to his state return. He stapled Copy C to his copies of the two tax returns. He put his copies away with his other important papers.

Then he mailed the returns. The address for the federal return was listed in the tax booklet. The next year Pat got a tax booklet from the IRS. It included tax forms, an envelope, and a mailing label.

Pat felt good about completing his tax form the following year. His experience with the 1987 return would come in handy. Because of it, he knew how to go about the task. He knew he had to keep good records. And he knew he had to follow directions very carefully.

Check Up:✓✓ True or False?

1. Knowing how to fill out a tax return is not important.
2. If your employer withholds too much income tax, you will get a refund.
3. Always keep a copy of your tax forms.

REVIEW

REMEMBER WHAT YOU LEARNED

The words

Listed below are the important new words that were used in this chapter. Next to each word is the page on which you will find the word in bold, black print. Turn back and read again the paragraph in which you find each word. Then write the word and its meaning on a sheet of paper. Also write a sentence of your own using each word.

1. federal income tax (255)
2. FICA (254)
3. gross pay (252)
4. Internal Revenue Service (255)
5. net pay (253)
6. pay stub (252)
7. payroll deductions (252)
8. state income tax (256)
9. taxes (254)
10. Wage and Tax Statement (257)

The facts

1. Explain what gross pay, net pay, and deductions are.
2. Name three taxes that may be withheld from your paycheck. Name four other deductions you could choose.
3. Where does your FICA tax withholding go?
4. Where do your federal and state income taxes go?
5. What does your W-2 tell you? How often do you get a W-2?
6. In what situation would you get back all of your federal withholding after filing your tax return?
7. What are the three federal income tax forms? Where can you get them?
8. How do you know what your tax bill for the year is?
9. What form must you attach to your tax return? What else might you have to attach?

What's right here?

ADD TO YOUR KNOWLEDGE AND SKILLS

Talk about your ideas

1. Do you think all workers should have to pay FICA tax? Why, or why not?
2. Should people who make more money pay more taxes? Why, or why not?
3. Should single taxpayers pay more taxes than married ones? Why, or why not?

Do some activities

1. Everyone has important papers. You should keep your papers where you will know where they are. Figure out a way to organize and keep your papers neat and safe. Explain your system to the class.
2. Get a card from your social security office to request information about your account. Fill it out and mail it in.
3. Talk with your parents or other adults about taxes. Ask them which 1040 form they use and why.

Improve your basic skills

1. Get an instruction booklet for filling out a 1040EZ tax return. Read through it. Can you fill out a 1040EZ?
2. Read the instructions for filling out a 1040A. When would you use a 1040A instead of a 1040EZ?

1. Write a paragraph telling how you feel about paying income tax.

1. Suppose you have a job at Carl's Cafeteria. You make $3.75 per hour. Last pay period you worked 26 hours. What is your gross pay?
2. Suppose you had the following deductions.
   - FICA—$6.96
   - Federal withholding—$5.50
   - State withholding—$1.75
   - Gift to United Way—$2.50

   What are your total deductions? What is your net pay? (Subtract your answer for 2 from your answer for 1.)
3. Suppose you worked two jobs last year. One employer withheld $316 for federal tax. The other withheld $351. You figured your tax to be $646. Do you have a refund coming? Do you owe more?
4. The rate of FICA tax is 7.15 percent of your earnings. If you earned $88 last pay period, what is your FICA withholding?

Chapter 14

Managing Your Money

BANK IV Pittsburg, N.A.
Pittsburg, Illinois
83-24/1011
No.

022
BANK IV

Date

$15.75

Dollars

Pay to the Order of City Cleaners

15 and 75/100

Account No. 200-4-6623

Name James B. Jones

Address 1900 Lake Drive

Phone 251-0200

Signature Jimmy Jones

⑆101100200⑆

What's wrong here?

Words to learn and use

You will learn several new words in this chapter. The most important words are listed below. Do you know the meanings of these words?

budget	endorse
service charge	check register
bank balance	bank statement
interest	overdraw
deposit	withdraw

Build on what you know

You already know . . .

- that you will receive a paycheck when you work.
- that you must pay taxes out of your paycheck.
- that you can use your money to pay bills and buy things.
- how to handle small amounts of money.

In this chapter you will learn . . .

- how to budget your money.
- how to open and handle a checking account.
- the importance of saving money.
- how to use a credit card.

Getting a job and earning money are important parts of your life. The money you earn at your job will help you live the lifestyle you choose.

Earning a paycheck is the first part of your money responsibility. Knowing what to do with your money is the second part. In this chapter you will learn how to make a budget. You will learn how to use bank services. You will learn some different ways to save money. You will also learn how to use a credit card wisely.

You and Your Money

Probably you have handled money, at least small amounts. Perhaps you have an allowance. You may receive money as a gift once in a while. You may earn money on a part-time job.

You may already pay for some expenses. Do you pay part of your own expenses? You may pay for your lunches out of your own money. You may also pay for your school books and for your entertainment. Perhaps you have been responsible for buying your own clothing.

As you grow older, you will become more responsible. As this happens, you will earn more money. You will pay for all of your expenses. At first your pay may seem like a lot of money. As an adult, your money must pay for many things.

Money is something that has trading value. The value becomes real only when it is spent.

Is this the best way to take care of your money?

Keeping your money in a savings or checking account is safer than keeping your money at home or on your person.

Your expenses can be divided into four groups.

- **Fixed expenses.** Fixed expenses are things you must pay for each month. Suppose you live in an apartment after you graduate. You would pay rent. You would pay for food. You might have a car payment. And you would probably pay for insurance.
- **Other spending.** You may want to buy some other things from time to time. Entertainment and hobby expenses are examples. Clothes and grooming products are also such expenses.
- **Short-term savings.** Let's say that you want to buy a certain item. It could be a TV, a cassette player, or a vacation trip. You probably will not be able to pay for it with one paycheck. You would need to save money. You would continue to save until you had enough to buy that item. Or you could save enough to make a down payment.
- **Long-term savings.** If you save only a small amount each paycheck and leave it alone, you will have a good sum in a few years. This savings could be kept for emergencies. It could be used to help pay expenses after you retire.

Make a Budget

A **budget** is a plan to manage your money. Large and small companies have budgets. So do governments. Individual people should have budgets, too.

There are five steps to making and keeping a budget.

1. Keep a record of your spending now.
2. Look carefully at your spending.
3. Decide how to change it.
4. Stick to your plan.
5. Review your budget regularly.

Here is how you can keep a record of your spending now. First you need a sheet of paper with lines on it. Draw lines up and down to make columns. The record on page 273 is one example.

In the first column, write the days of the week. At the top of each of the other columns, write an expense. Change the names of the headings to fit your own budget. For example, you may have car expenses instead of bus fare. You may have medical or dental expenses of your own. If so, add a column for these costs. Each day write what you spend for each expense.

Add across to find what you spent each day. Add down to find what you spent for each type of expense. Add across the bottom line to find your total expenses. Keep this record for four weeks. It will show how much you spent in a month.

Now take a good look at your spending. You may be surprised that you are spending so much in one area. You may wish you were saving more money.

If you have a personal budget, you will know how much money you have to spend on fun things.

Date: ____________________

Income this week: ____________________

SPENDING:	FOOD	CLOTHES	LIVING COSTS	BUS	SCHOOL	RECREATION, GIFTS, AND CHURCH	SAVINGS	TOTAL FOR DAY
SUNDAY								
MONDAY								
TUESDAY								
WEDNESDAY								
THURSDAY								
FRIDAY								
SATURDAY								
TOTAL FOR WEEK								

This record will show how you spent your money each day for a week.

Next, decide if you want to change your spending habits. Maybe you are happy with your current budget. If not, think how you want to change. For example, you may decide that you are spending too much money on entertainment. You may decide to go to the movies less often. Maybe you did not realize you were spending so much money on clothes. You could decide to spend less there.

Once you decide how to change your budget, stick to your plan. Try your new plan for several weeks or months.

Finally, look at your budget again. Is your new plan working right? Are you happy with your spending habits? Can you improve your budget even more?

You may want to keep a record of your spending all the time. Then you can review your budget every month or so. Or you may decide to write and review your spending only at certain times. Your income will change from time to time. These are good times to review your budget. At other times you will take on new expenses. These are also good times for budget review.

Check Up:✓✓ True or False?

1. Fixed expenses are the bills you pay each month.
2. Once you make a budget, you should never change it.
3. Saving is for older workers only.

Do You Need a Checking Account?

What do you do with your allowance when you get it? Where do you keep the money you earn from your part-time job? Maybe you carry it in your wallet. Maybe you keep some of it in your room.

These ways may work fine for small amounts of money. They may be all right when your parents pay most of your expenses. But soon you will want to open a checking account. You can open one at a bank or a savings and loan (S&L) company.

Here are some good reasons for having a checking account.

1. It is easier to cash your paycheck at a bank where you have an account.
2. In a bank account, your money is safe until you need it. It will not be lost or stolen. When you carry cash, you might spend it too fast or lose it.
3. You can pay your bills by mailing your checks. Mailing payments will save you time and money. You will not have to go to each business to pay your bill.
4. If a check is lost in the mail, you will not lose the money. You can tell the bank the check is lost and write a new one.
5. After the bank makes payment on your checks, it will return them to you. You can keep them for your records. They will help you keep track of your spending. They will be proof that you paid your bills.

Check the bank's service charges before opening an account.

Choosing a Bank

There are many banks. Choosing a bank is like shopping for other things. Choose one that offers what you want. It should match your needs. Shop for price, too. Not all banks charge the same for their services.

Some things to consider when choosing a bank are

- location.
- hours.
- fees.
- services.

When choosing a bank, visit several banks. Employees at the information desks can help you.

Ask what types of accounts they have. Compare the fees and interest rates. Ask about their hours and other services. Then decide which bank is for you.

Location. You will want to choose a bank that is easy to reach. It should be close to your work or home. You do not want to spend much time driving or walking to your bank.

Hours. Check the bank's hours. Is it open before or after your working hours? Will you be able to go to the bank when you want to? Is there a drive-up window that is open extra hours?

Fees. Many banks charge fees for their services. A fee to manage your checking account is called a **service charge.** Banks make service charges in different ways. Some charge a certain amount each month. Others charge for each check you write.

Service charges may depend on your **bank balance.** Your balance is the amount of money you have in your account. The bank could add your balance from each day of the month. They would then divide by the number of days in the month. That would show your average daily balance. Your fee that month would be based on that average balance. The higher your average balance, the lower your fee.

Another way is to use a minimum balance. Suppose you keep $500 in your account. In this case you would probably not pay a fee.

Other banks have special checking accounts for customers who write very few checks. For this type of account, you would pay a fee for each check.

Some banks will pay interest on your bank balance. Earning **interest** means the bank pays you to keep your money at their bank. The bank will tell you the interest rate. A 5.5% rate means for every $100 of savings you earn $5.50 ($100 × .055 = $5.50). Suppose you have $100 in your account. And suppose it earns 5.5% interest. At the end of the year you will have $105.50.

Services. Banks often offer other services in addition to checking accounts. Some of these services are

- loans.
- credit card services.
- electronic fund transfer.
- savings accounts.
- government bonds.
- certificates of deposit.
- lock boxes.
- traveler's checks.
- advice on money matters.

You may not need all of these banking services right away. You may want to use these services later on, though.

Opening an Account

A new accounts clerk will help you open an account. You may be unsure about the account that is best for you. If you are unsure, say so. Tell the clerk how much money you plan to keep in your account. Tell him or her how many checks you will write each month. Then the clerk can help you choose the best type of account.

The clerk will type a signature card. You will give your name, address, and phone number. You will also give the name, address, and phone number of your place of work. Your social security number and the date will also be needed. You will then sign the card.

Next, the clerk will assign you an account number. The bank will keep your money recorded under your account number. The clerk will also give you some checks and deposit slips. Each one will have your account number on it. You may use these checks and deposit slips right away.

You may give the clerk cash. Or you may give the clerk a paycheck. He or she will put this money into your account.

The clerk will then ask you to choose the checks you want. The bank will have your name, address, and account number printed on the checks and deposit slips. Then they will be mailed to you. When you have used most of them, you may order more. There is usually a fee for check printing. The clerk should explain how much that fee is. It can be taken out of your account.

DEPOSIT TICKET

FOR DEPOSIT TO THE ACCOUNT OF

ACCOUNT NUMBER 60 1107 11

NAME Pat Smith

DATE 2-15 19 85

ACKNOWLEDGE RECEIPT OF CASH RETURNED BY SIGNING ABOVE.

The National Bank OF PITTSBURG
MEMBER - FDIC
P.O. BOX 599 - PITTSBURG, KS. 66762

CASH	40	00
TOTAL	40	00
LESS CASH RECEIVED		
NET DEPOSIT	40	00

83-24
1011

In receiving items for deposit or collection, this bank acts only as depositor's collecting agent and assumes no responsibility beyond the exercise of due care. All items are credited subject to final payment in cash or solvent credits. This bank will not be liable for default or negligence of its duly selected correspondents nor for losses in transit, and each correspondent so selected shall not be liable except for its own negligence. This bank or its correspondents may send items directly or indirectly to any bank including the payor and accept its draft or credit as conditional payment in lieu of cash; it may charge back any item before final payment whether returned or not also any item drawn on this bank not good at close of business on day deposited.

⑆101100249⑆

Pat Smith deposited his paycheck on payday. He wanted $50 in cash. He put the rest into his account. His net deposit was $66.78.

Making a Deposit

The money you put into your checking account is called a **deposit.** You will probably want to make a deposit every time you get paid.

Fill out a deposit slip carefully. Write the date on the slip. At first, you will use the slips you received when opening your account. On these you must write your name and address, too. The printed slips you get later will have your name and address on them.

Fill in the name of the person or company who gave you your paycheck. Then write in the amount of the check. If you are depositing other checks, list them, too. You may deposit cash. List the coins and currency (paper money) separately.

Then add all these amounts. Enter the total. You may want to deposit only part of your paycheck. You may want part of your pay in cash. Enter the amount of cash you want by "Less Cash Received." Then subtract that from the total. The remainder is your net deposit.

Endorse your check. This means to sign it on the back.

Wait until you get to the bank to endorse your check. No one else can cash your check until you sign it. What might happen if you lost an endorsed check? Someone else might cash it.

Give your deposit slip and paycheck to a bank teller. The teller may give you a receipt. He or she will give you the cash you ask for. Make sure the amount is correct. Keep the receipt for your records.

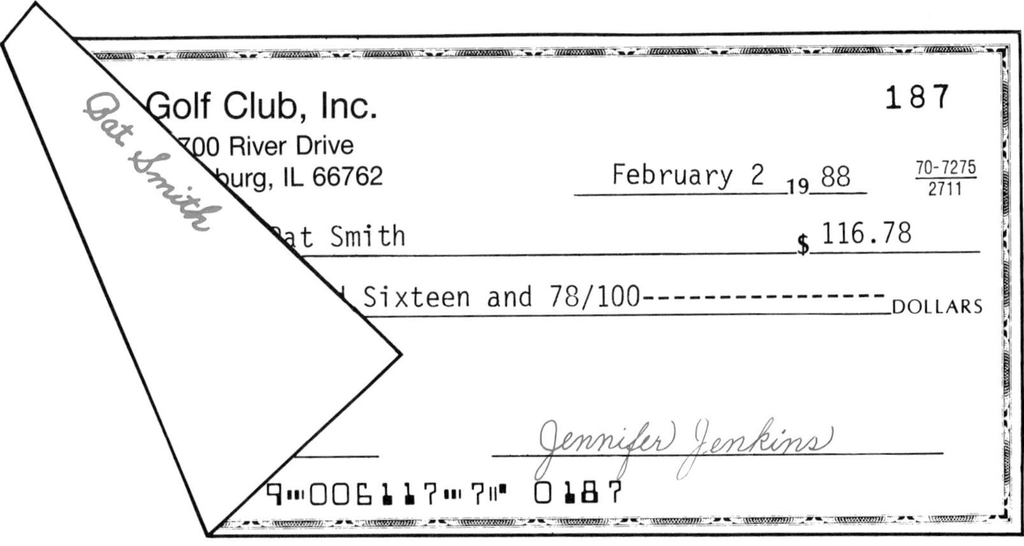

Endorse your check on the back. Sign your name the same way it appears on the front.

Writing a Check

You can write a check to pay a bill. You can write one to buy something. Write a check very carefully. Use a pen. That way no one can erase the numbers you wrote and write in bigger ones.

Look at the check below. Pat Smith wrote a check to pay for a pair of shoes. First, he wrote the date on the check. Then he wrote the name of the store where he was buying the shoes.

He wrote the amount of the check twice. First he wrote it in numbers, $25. On the next line, he wrote the amount in words, "Twenty-five and 00/100." This means that the check was for exactly $25. If Pat's check had been for $25.99, he would have written "Twenty-five and 99/100."

Note the line drawn after the amount. This is important. It makes sure no one can fill in a higher amount.

In the lower left corner is a space called "Memo." Pat wrote "tennis shoes." That will help him remember what that check was for. Last, Pat signed the check. Notice that he wrote his signature. He used his full name. A bank worker might wonder if this is really Pat's signature. If so, the clerk can look at Pat's signature card. Pat would have filled out this card when he opened his account. The bank clerk can use it to compare the signatures.

Pat then gave the check to the store clerk. In exchange, the clerk gave Pat the shoes he wanted. Pat's bank will give $25 to the shoe store. Then, $25 will be subtracted from his account.

PAT SMITH
8500 River Drive
Pittsburg, Illinois 66762

187

Mar. 6 19 88 70-7275/2711

PAY TO THE ORDER OF Bill's Shoe Store $ 25.00

Twenty-five and 00/100 DOLLARS

1 FIRST NATIONAL BANK
Pittsburg, Illinois 66762

MEMO Tennis shoes Pat Smith

⑆271172754⑆ 9⑈006240⑈7⑈ 0187

Writing a check for what you buy is an easy way to pay for a purchase. You may need to show your driver's license and another form of identification when you write a check.

Using a Check Register

A **check register** is a record of your account. Always fill out the check register when you deposit money or write a check.

Look at Pat's register below. He opened his account with a $66.78 deposit. The next week he bought a pair of shoes. He entered the check number, 101. He wrote the date. He issued the check to Bill's Shoe Store. He noted that the check was for tennis shoes. He entered $25 under "payment/debit."

Next, he wrote $25 in the right-hand column. He subtracted $25 from $66.78. His balance on February 10th was $41.78.

On February 20, Pat deposited $50 and added this to the $41.78 balance. Pat then had $91.78.

On February 25, Pat bought a watch. It cost $19.50. The check was issued to Ray-Co. Pat subtracted $19.50 from $91.78. Pat's new balance is $72.28.

Follow this plan. Never write a check for more money than is in your account.

Check Up:✓✓ True or False?

1. You should choose a bank that has the services you want.
2. Taking money out of your account is called *making a deposit.*
3. Your check register is a record of your checks and deposits.

RECORD ALL CHARGES OR CREDITS THAT AFFECT YOUR ACCOUNT										
NUMBER	DATE	DESCRIPTION OF TRANSACTION	PAYMENT/DEBIT (-)		√ T	FEE (IF ANY) (-)	DEPOSIT/CREDIT (+)		BALANCE	
									$ 66	78
101	2/10	Bill's Shoe Store	$ 25	00		$	$		25	00
	88	tennis shoes							41	78
	2/20	deposit					50	00	50	00
	88								91	78
102	2/25	Ray-Co	19	50					19	50
	88	watch							72	28

Keeping your check register up-to-date lets you know exactly how much money you have in your account.

Reading Your Bank Statement

Your bank will mail you a statement regularly. You may get a statement every month or you might get one every three months. A **bank statement** is a printed list. This list shows each amount that you have put into your account. It also shows each amount that you have taken out.

When you get the statement, look in your check register. Note the amount you had at the beginning of the statement time. Compare this with the first amount shown on the statement.

Next, put a mark in your check register beside every check listed on the statement. Do the same for the deposits. See that you wrote each amount correctly. Enter in your register any service charge. Subtract it. Enter any interest your account earned. Add it. Now compare the statement to the register. Do they match?

Some checks may not have reached the bank for payment yet. Use a scratch pad to add all missing checks. Add this total to the last balance shown in your register. Also look at the date of the statement. Did you deposit any money after that date? If so, add that amount to the balance.

Now does your register balance match the statement balance? If not, check your addition and subtraction.

Maybe you cannot find why the statement and register do not show the same amount. Take the statement and register to the bank. Someone there will help find the problem.

It is important that you know your register is correct. Then you know exactly how much money you have. Knowing this you will not accidently **overdraw** your account. This means that you will not write a check for more than your balance.

Keep each statement with its checks and deposit slips.

This woman's bank statement and register do not show the same amounts. What should she do?

Why Start a Savings Account

You know that it is a good idea to save some money each week. You may be able to think of many reasons for saving money.

- Saving money earns you more money. Putting your money in a savings plan earns you interest.
- Saving money lets you build up enough money to pay for something expensive.
- Saving for expensive items costs less than borrowing.
- Your savings can help you in an emergency.
- You may need your savings if you are unable to work. You could be in an accident, have an illness, or lose your job.
- You may need your savings to pay your bills after you retire.

How many other reasons can you think of? Whatever your reasons, saving money is a good habit.

Where to Save

There are a number of places where you can save your money. A bank is one. A savings and loan company is another. The company where you work may have a credit union you could join. You can save money through your credit union. You can have a certain amount deducted from each paycheck for savings.

Saving money to buy a computer might be a short-term savings goal.

Saving money to buy your own business might be a long-term savings goal.

Types of Savings Plans

There are several different ways you can save your money. All of them pay interest.

Savings Accounts. You can open a regular savings account. You can do this at a bank, savings and loan company, or a credit union. You open a savings account by depositing some money. You will sign a signature card. When you make deposits, the teller will give you a receipt. This receipt shows your account number, the date and the amount deposited. You can **withdraw,** or take out, money in the same way. But this time the receipt will show the amount withdrawn. Keep all these receipts in a safe place.

Usually banks mail savings account statements every three months. Match all your receipts to the statement items. Notice that interest has been added to your account. If you do not agree with the statement, ask about it at your savings department.

Interest on money in your account is added daily. It is put into your account once every month or every three months. Each year you will get a statement called *Form 1099.* It tells how much interest your account earned during the year. You must report this interest income on your tax return. You pay taxes on interest you receive.

Savings Clubs. Some banks, savings and loans, and credit unions offer savings clubs. One example of a savings club is a Christmas club. In a Christmas club, you make a certain deposit each week or month. Just before Christmas a check is mailed to you. The check total is for all your savings plus interest. Then you can do your Christmas shopping with the money.

Certificates of Deposit. You can buy certificates of deposit (CDs) at banks. You can also buy CDs at savings and loans and credit unions.

You need a large amount of money to buy a CD. It may be $500 or more. You must leave your money in the CD for a certain length of time. This time period could be anywhere from six months to five years. At the end of that time, you may take out your

A credit union is a good place to save money.

money. You choose the amount and the length of time when you buy a CD.

CDs are a good way to save. They pay a higher rate of interest than regular savings accounts. But there is a negative side to CDs. Suppose you have to withdraw your money before the time is up. In this case you would lose your interest. And this can be quite expensive.

Government Bonds. U.S. Government Bonds pay good interest. They are also a safe way to save. If the bonds are lost, stolen, or destroyed, they can be replaced. Also, you do not pay taxes on interest earned until you cash in the bonds.

You can buy bonds at banks or savings and loans. Some companies have payroll savings plans. If yours does, you can buy through paycheck deductions.

The EE Bonds come in different amounts, from $50 to $10,000. You pay $25 for a $50 bond. In ten years, the $25 bond will be worth at least $50. If you can save $12.50 each week for bonds, your savings may be $8,000 in ten years.

You must keep government bonds for six months. After six months, you can cash them. The longer you keep them, the more they earn. You could double your money in ten years.

Tim Martin is starting his first full-time job. Each month he plans to invest $100 in a U.S. Government Bond. He expects to have an average interest rate of 6%. In ten years his bonds may be worth almost $17,000. With that amount of money he can start a small business. Tim wants to be his own boss. It will take some time to earn enough money for a business. But Tim thinks it will be worth it.

Tim Martin's dad started buying government bonds when he was young. He bought them regularly for 35 years. When he retired, he had enough income to pay his living expenses. This income came from the interest on the bonds.

Check Up:✓✓ True or False?

1. You should use your bank statement each month to double check your register.
2. CDs often pay higher interest rates than do regular savings accounts.

Using Electronic Fund Transfer

Many banks now offer electronic fund transfer (EFT). You may sign up for this service. If you do, you can use the automatic teller machine at any time. It is open 24 hours a day.

At the machine, you can

- withdraw cash from your account.
- make deposits to your account.
- transfer funds from one account to another.
- check your bank balance.

With some EFTs you can pay for purchases automatically. You use a sales terminal in a store. The machine takes the money out of your account. It pays the store for your purchase.

With some EFTs your paycheck can be placed directly into your account. You can even pay bills automatically. You do not even need to write a check. You just call and tell the system what bills to pay. It will automatically pay the bills for you.

You may decide to sign up for EFT. If you do, the bank will give you a plastic card. They will also give you a personal identification number. You will need both to use the automatic teller machine. Memorize your number so you can use the machine.

To be safe, follow these tips:

- Do not keep your secret number and EFT card in the same place. If someone steals both, he or she can take all your money.
- Never tell anyone your secret number. Never write your number on your card.
- Do not let others see you punch your number into the terminal.
- Keep a record of your account. If theft or error happens, call the bank as soon as possible.

Automatic teller machines make your money available any time.

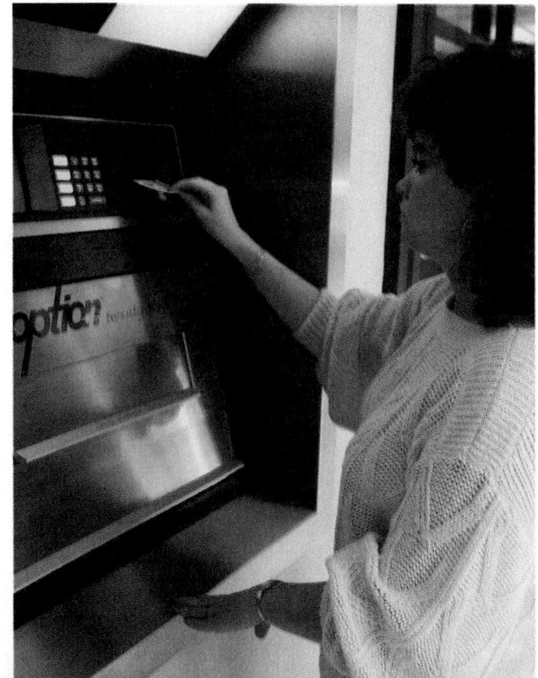

A Desire to Succeed

Winning Over Polio: Alan Alda

Alan Alda's father was a famous movie star. Alan lived on an estate. He went to a private school. You would think that Alan would have an easy, happy life.

But when Alan was seven, he suddenly became ill. He got a fever and a terrible headache. He lost his balance, and his body stiffened. He could not even move his head. The doctor said Alan had polio.

In those days, many people died from polio. Most of those who did not die had to wear braces or stay in a wheelchair for the rest of their lives.

Alan's mother was determined that he would get over this terrible disease. She learned about a treatment for polio. She cut up wool blankets. She put the pieces into boiling water. Then she placed them on Alan's back and legs. She did this every hour for months. The hot packs hurt.

Finally Alan was able to get up. He swam to strengthen his muscles. He took therapy, too. Instead of going to school, he had a private tutor.

Alan was very shy. By staying at home he did not have to compete with his classmates.

By junior high, Alan was able to go back to school. The other boys teased him.

As a teenager, Alan had a good sense of humor. He put on skits.

One day his English teacher made him write a play for the senior class. That was the beginning of his writing career.

He continued writing and began working on the stage, on TV, and in the movies.

His most famous role was probably that of Hawkeye Pierce on the TV series *M*A*S*H.* That show ran for over ten years. Both Alan and the series won many awards. Reruns from *M*A*S*H* are still being shown on TV. Today Alan makes over $5 million a year.

Alan is also famous for helping others. He works hard for the rights of minorities and women.

Credit Cards

Many people today use credit cards. Large stores and oil companies offer credit cards. Certain banks issue national credit cards.

To get one, you need to fill out an application. The credit card company will want to know some personal information about you. It will want to know your income. You will need to put down the name of your bank and where you work.

When you get your credit card, the company will tell you your credit limit. This is the amount you can have charged at any one time on your account.

You may make purchases with your credit card. When you buy something, hand your card to the clerk. The clerk will fill out a sales ticket. You will need to sign it. Get your card back before you leave that clerk. Never leave your card! The amount of the purchase will go onto your account.

Once a month you will get a bill from the credit card company. Your bill will list all the charges you have made. It will give the due date of the bill. Before the due date, write a check for all or part of your bill. Mail your check with the return section of your bill. Be sure the envelope shows the correct address.

Credit cards make shopping easy. But they can be a problem for some people.

Advantages of Credit Cards

Credit cards offer many advantages:

- You will not need to carry as much cash if you have a credit card. This can be helpful, especially if you travel.
- You can make several purchases and pay for them all at once. You do not have to write as many checks. You do not have to pay as many separate bills.
- You can make a purchase without having the money to pay for it. Suppose an item is on sale for two days. You do not get paid for five days. You can take advantage of the sale price by buying it now.

- You can use your credit card for an emergency. Suppose your car needs repair when you are in a strange city. A garage owner there may not take your check. He or she may, however, accept your payment with a credit card.
- Having a credit card is one way to build a good credit rating. To do this you must pay your credit card bill on time. Then you may find it easier to get a loan when you need it.

Disadvantages of Credit Cards

Credit cards have some disadvantages as well:

- Credit cards can cost money. Most national credit card companies charge a yearly fee.
- Usually you will be charged interest. This kind of interest is money you pay to the company for owing them money. Interest rates on credit cards are usually high. Charges can add up quickly.
- You may be tempted to buy more than you can afford. Buying on credit seems easy. People sometimes lose track of how much they charge. Soon their total bill is bigger than they can pay.

Using a Credit Card

Using a credit card requires some good money management. Remember that your credit card purchases are part of your budget. Figure them into your budget plan. Stick to your plan.

Keep your sales tickets. You might want to keep a total of the unpaid purchases. Then you will know exactly how much you have charged. That will help you not to overspend.

When your monthly bill arrives, compare the charges to your sales tickets. Be sure all the charges listed are yours. If there is a problem with your bill, call or write the company. Pay your bill on time.

Keep your card secure. Do not let other people have your number. Keep a list of your credit card numbers in a safe place. If your card is lost or stolen, call the company right away.

Check Up: ✓✓ True or False?

1. Do keep your identification number with your EFT card so the number will not get lost.
2. Credit card companies often charge a yearly fee to credit card holders.
3. The interest rates on credit card bills are usually high.

The words

Listed below are the important new words that were used in this chapter. Next to each word is the page on which you will find the word in bold, black print. Turn back and read again the paragraph in which you find each word. Then write the word and its meaning on a sheet of paper. Also write a sentence of your own using each word.

1. bank balance (275)
2. bank statement (280)
3. budget (272)
4. check register (279)
5. deposit (277)
6. endorse (277)
7. interest (275)
8. overdraw (280)
9. service charge (275)
10. withdraw (282)

The facts

1. Name the five steps in making and keeping a budget.
2. What four things would you think about when choosing a bank?
3. What is an average daily balance? A minimum balance? How do banks use these figures?
4. Explain how to make a bank deposit.
5. Explain how to write a check. Explain how to enter a check in your check register.
6. Why should you save your bank statements, checks, and deposit tickets?
7. Give five reasons for having a savings account.
8. What is an advantage of a CD over a regular savings account? What is a disadvantage?
9. What are three advantages of owning a credit card? What are three disadvantages?

022

BANK IV

BANK IV Pittsburg, N.A.
Pittsburg, Illinois

Date April 1, 1988 No. 19 83-24/1011

Pay to the Order of City Cleaners $ 15.75

Fifteen and 75/100 Dollars

Name James B. Jones Account No. 200-4-6623

Address 1900 Lake Drive

Phone 251-0200 Signature James B. Jones

⑆101100200⑆

What's right here?

ADD TO YOUR KNOWLEDGE AND SKILLS

Talk about your ideas

1. When do you think someone should start saving money? Why?
2. What are your short-term savings goals? Your long-term savings goals?
3. Should everyone be allowed to have a credit card? Why, or why not?
4. Explain interest earned and interest paid out. Which rate is usually higher?
5. What happens to your checks after you write them?

Do some activities

1. Make a spending chart like the one on page 273. Make it to fit your own needs. Keep track of your spending for two weeks. Are you happy with your spending habits? If not, change your budget.
2. Make a list of fixed expenses you would have if you lived alone.
3. Go to a bank. Ask if you may have a signature card. Tell the class what information you need for the card.

Improve your basic skills

1. Go to two banks. Ask for brochures about checking and savings accounts. Read them. Which checking account best fits your needs? Which savings account best fits your needs? Are the interest rates the same at both banks?
2. Find a magazine article about managing your money. Read it. Tell the class one thing you learned from the article.

1. Write a note to a friend. Tell him or her why it is wise to start a savings account. Give your paper to your teacher.
2. Write a paragraph telling how you would use a credit card. Tell how you would keep your card safe. Tell ways you would be careful not to spend too much.

5×7=?

1. Suppose you open a checking account with \$75. You make another deposit of \$36.75. You write a check for \$12.50. You write other checks for \$7.12, \$37, and \$10. You deposit \$25. Your bank statement comes. It shows your account earned \$3.10 interest. What is your balance?
2. Suppose you buy a stereo for \$350. You pay \$50 as a down payment. You take out a loan for the rest. The loan is for one year. The interest rate is 12 percent. What do you pay for the stereo?

Chapter 15

Being a Smart Shopper

What's wrong here?

Words to learn and use

You will learn several new words in this chapter. The most important words are listed below. Do you know the meanings of these words?

consumer
goods
services
guarantee
installment plan
down payment
contract
fraud
premium
liability

Build on what you know

You already know . . .

- the importance of budgeting your money.
- how to make small purchases.
- how to handle a checking account and a savings account.
- how to use a credit card wisely.

In this chapter you will learn . . .

- to make smart shopping decisions.
- how to get the most for your money.
- what a contract is.
- some sales tricks to avoid.

In the last two chapters you learned some things about your paycheck. You learned how to read your paycheck stub. You know what taxes you must pay. You know how to fill out a federal income tax form. You also learned how to keep money safe. And you learned about other banking services.

In this chapter you will learn how to be a good shopper. You will learn that there are several ways to pay for your purchases. You will learn some shopping tips.

What Is a Consumer?

A **consumer** is a person who buys goods and services. **Goods** are products that you buy. Goods can be big or little. A house, a diamond ring, and a piano are examples of big goods. They cost a lot of money. A bar of soap, a potted plant, and a belt are examples of little goods. They do not cost very much money.

Services are things that you pay other people to do for you. An example of a service is the repair of a motorcycle. Other examples are cleaning teeth and teaching people to swim.

You have been a consumer for a long time. You are a consumer when you pay for your lunch in the school cafeteria. You are a consumer when you purchase magazines or and go to the movies. As you grow older, you will buy even more goods and services for yourself. You will not rely on others to buy them for you.

You have been a consumer for a long time.

When you become an adult, you have more needs and wants. You buy more things.

When Should You Buy?

Being a smart consumer is not always easy. Your first decision as a consumer is whether or not to buy an item. Think about why you buy. You buy goods and services to satisfy your needs and wants.

Your first shopping decision is "Should I buy one?"

Needs and Wants

Everyone needs certain things. You need a place to live. You need food to eat. You need clothing to keep warm and to protect your body. You may need the services of a doctor or dentist. You may need medicine.

You also buy goods and services that you do *not need.* These are things that you *want* to buy. They are fun to have or to do.

People often say they *need* things when they mean they *want* things. Have you ever heard someone say, "I *need* a new record. I am really tired of listening to my old ones." Or, "I *need* a new outfit for the party Saturday night"? These people mean "I *want* . . . ," not "I *need* . . . ."

Listen to others when they say they need things. Do you ever say, "I need" instead of "I want"? Few people can buy everything they want. They must decide which items to buy and which not to buy.

Know Your Reasons

There are good reasons for buying things. There are bad reasons, too. When you are thinking about buying something, think carefully. Take your time deciding.

Suppose you want a bike. Ask yourself, "Do I really want a bike more than I want anything else?" Think about why you want the bike. List all the reasons why it would be good to have a bike. Do your reasons seem to fit in with your interests? Your values? Your personality?

Next, list all the reasons *not* to buy a new bike. Now compare your lists. Which list has the most, or the best, reasons? Think about both lists. Be honest with yourself. Take your time. Then decide if you still want that bike.

Influences on Your Decision

Many things affect your decision to buy. More than anything else, your income influences your buying. People with high incomes spend more. Those with low incomes spend less.

Always ask yourself, "Can I afford this?" Do not forget costs that may come later. If you buy a stereo, you will want records or tapes later. A car will need repairs—and insurance. A radio will need new batteries. You will want film for your camera.

Your work affects your buying. Different jobs require different clothes or tools. Your job even affects how much food you buy! An outdoor worker may need more food than a typist, for example.

Where you live affects your buying. In warm climates, you want clothes and housing to keep you cool. In cold climates, you want warm clothes and a warm house. You may have indoor recreation.

What you do for leisure activities also affects your buying. Most sports require special types of equipment. Hobbies require tools. You may want to buy items to add to a collection.

Buying Checklist

Before you buy something, ask yourself these questions. If you are happy with your answers, go ahead with your purchase. If not, think again.

- Can I afford it?
- Do I really want it?
- Will I use it after I get it?
- Do I need it?
- Will I enjoy it?
- Will it cost me more than just the price? Does it have upkeep costs? Will I need to buy other things after I buy it? Can I afford them?
- Would I rather save my money for something else?
- Is this a good buy? Is it well made? Is this a good price for it?
- Am I making my own decision? Am I being influenced by other people or by flashy advertising?

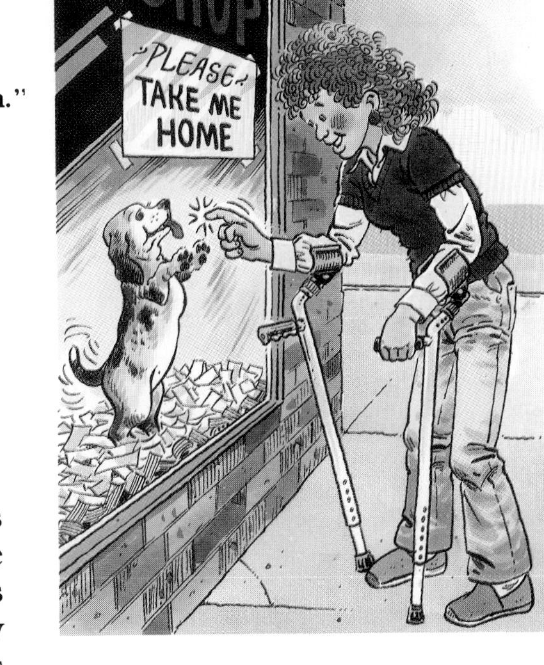

Be able to say "No" to a "sales pitch."

Your values and interests influence what you buy. Someone who loves to read may buy books and magazines. A movie fan may see a movie once a week. A tennis lover may save money to go to a tennis camp.

You may be tempted to buy the same things as your friends. Can you remember buying something because a friend had one? Do not let friends decide for you. Ask yourself, "Do I buy things because *I* want them? Or do I buy to be part of the group?" Do not buy just to be part of the group.

Do not ever be pushed into buying something. Do not let a salesperson talk you into buying something. You may not be able to afford it. And you may not really want it. Do not buy something because of an ad or a low price tag. Especially do not buy it if it is something you will not use later.

Check Up:✓✓ True or False?

1. People buy goods and services to satisfy their needs and wants.
2. You should make up your mind to buy quickly before the price goes up.
3. Your income greatly affects your buying decisions.

How to Find the Best Value

One important part of being a good shopper is finding the best value for your money. You can do a number of things to get the best value.

- Use advertising.
- Comparison shop.
- Shop sales.
- Read the guarantee.
- Look at used items.

Advertising

Companies advertise their products to try to get you to buy them. Do not be tempted by advertising to buy things you do not want. Nothing is a good buy if you do not use it.

However, ads also give a lot of information. They tell you what is on the market. They tell you about the features of their products. They explain ways to use certain products. You can also read ads to learn about prices. Then you will know a good price when you see one.

Comparison Shopping

Comparison shopping is looking at different products before you buy. Suppose you want to buy a typewriter. Look at the different brands. See what features each one has. Compare prices.

You can go into stores and look at typewriters. Try them out. Ask the clerk questions. Then decide which one you want. Sometimes different stores carry the same brands at different prices. Find out the prices at several stores. Then you will know which is the best buy.

Buying during a store sale may be the best way to get the most for your money.

Shop Sales

If you plan ahead, you can often buy things on sale. After Christmas is a good time to buy clothes and toys. Toward the end of winter might be a good time to buy a heavy coat. Bedding and furniture often go on sale in January and July.

Many stores regularly mark down their products. You can even ask a clerk if a sale is coming soon. Waiting a few weeks can save you a lot of money.

Guarantees

Always read the guarantee that comes with a product. The **guarantee** will tell you what the manufacturer will do if something goes wrong. This can be a clue to value. An item that you must replace or repair often may not be a good buy. See if the manufacturer or seller will stand behind the product.

Used Items

You may not need to buy everything new. There are many places where you can buy used items. Used items may fit your needs for some things. Perhaps there is a thrift store in your area. Some people will sell used items by advertising them in the newspaper. You can shop garage sales, too.

You can save money if you shop at garage sales.

How to Pay for a Purchase

One part of shopping is deciding which goods and services to buy. Another part is deciding how to pay for the goods and services you buy.

Cash

One way to pay for your purchases, of course, is with cash or a check. You will pay for many things this way. You usually pay cash for food, clothing, and other small items.

Credit

You may decide not to pay for some items when you buy them. Do you have a credit card? If so, you can charge some of your purchases on your credit card. Some stores and companies will let you buy on an **installment plan.** This is another type of credit. It allows you to use the product before you pay the entire amount. You make regular payments to the company. These payments usually include a credit charge.

Before you decide to buy, figure out how you will pay the price.

Be sure you can pay for what you buy on credit. If you do not pay when you should, you may lose what you bought. You may also lose the money you have already paid. People who do not keep up their payments have a poor credit rating. Then they cannot continue to buy on credit.

Loans

Suppose you want to buy a large item like a car or motorcycle. You could take out a loan to borrow the money you want. You could get a loan at a bank or a savings and loan. You might be able to get one at a credit union.

Usually you pay for part of the purchase when you buy it. The part you pay right away is called the **down payment.** You take out a loan for the rest.

The loan company charges you interest on your loan. Loan interest is just the opposite of savings account interest. Interest on a loan is money you pay the loan company for using its money. You agree to pay back the money plus the interest in monthly payments.

Figuring Credit Charges

Be sure you figure the total charges. Do this before you agree to buy the product. Add the down payment plus all the monthly payments. Compare this total with the cash price.

After figuring the credit costs, decide if you want to buy the item on credit. You may decide to save your money and pay cash for it later. And save the interest charges.

The computer John wants costs $1500. He figures he can afford between $80 and $90 a month. These are his choices.

- John can charge this computer on his credit card. The interest rate is 18%. He can pay $89.34 a month for two years. His total cost would be $2144.16.
- John can take out a loan for $1500 at 13 percent interest. He would pay $80.95 a month for two years. The total cost would be $1942.80.
- John could save $80.95 a month for 18½ months. Then he could pay cash. The total cost would be $1500.

Which option would you choose?

Check Up:✓✓ True or False?

1. Advertising can tell you a lot.
2. Buying new items on sale or buying used items can save you money.
3. Three ways to pay are cash, credit card, and taking out a loan.

A Desire to Succeed

Staying Independent: Denise Karuth

For Denise Karuth, staying independent is very important. It is also a lot of hard work. Denise is blind and she has multiple sclerosis (MS).

Denise has nerve damage in her left leg. She cannot walk. Her back and arms are too weak to use crutches. So Denise uses a wheelchair to get around. In fact, she has one for indoors and one for outdoors.

Denise has a guide dog named Irene. Irene is with her at all times. She makes it possible for Denise to go places. Denise considers Irene her best friend.

Denise also hires personal care attendants to help her. These workers help her with her physical needs. They shop, cook, clean, and run errands for her. Without them she would not be able to live in her own apartment.

One of the worst things about MS, says Denise, is that it makes her tired. She can only be active for about five hours each day.

Everything she does takes a lot of effort. Sometimes by the time she gets all her tools ready to start a task, she has no energy left.

MS affects Denise's memory, too. So Denise makes lists to help her remember.

Denise says that she did not like school because the other children took advantage of her. But several caring teachers helped her. She also found comfort in her church.

Denise became good at music. She won a scholarship. She earned a degree in music. Then she continued her schooling. She earned a master's degree in rehabilitation counseling.

Denise has worked with blind people. She is active in her church both on committees and in the choir. And she works to make buildings accessible to people in wheelchairs.

Denise knows that her illness may get worse. Yet she continues to solve her problems. For her, independence and a happy life are worth planning and fighting for.

What Is a Contract?

When you take out a loan, you must sign a contract. A **contract** is an agreement. It can be between two persons, two groups, or a person and a group. It is a promise. Both people promise to keep their parts of the contract. Contracts may be written or unwritten.

You use unwritten contracts every day. Buying a quart of milk is a sales contract. You pay the price and the milk is yours. The store promises fresh milk. If the milk is spoiled, the contract is broken. The store did not keep its part of the contract. You will get your money back, or you will get a quart of good milk.

When you take your shoes to be repaired, you also enter into an unwritten contract. The shoe repairer agrees to repair your shoes. You agree to pay for the work.

Unwritten contracts are used for many kinds of work and sales. They most often involve small amounts of money. Most service jobs use unwritten contracts. One example is taking a roll of film to be developed. Another is getting your hair cut.

There are many kinds of written contracts.

- A contract to use a charge account.
- A contract to buy on time payments (a loan or installment sale).
- A contract to buy or sell a house or land.
- A contract to sell something for $500 or more.
- A contract to work for a company.

A *written contract* is a legal promise. The persons making the contract sign it. It is important to know what you sign. Read a contract carefully. If you are not sure what it means, have someone else read it, too. Do not sign a contract until you understand all parts of it. If you do not understand, you may sign a contract that you should not sign. Then you may have to pay more than you expected.

Do not sign a contract you do not understand.

Special Shopping Needs

When you shop, you want to get good value. You want an appliance to work well. You want it to last for a long time. You want the food you buy to taste good. You want your clothes and furniture to look good and wear well. You want your car to start every morning and to run smoothly.

When you shop, you also want the best price. You do not want to pay any more that you have to. Usually the price will be higher if

- the item is well-made and of good material.
- there are few of the items for sale.
- many people want the same item.

Learn how to be a good shopper. In the future you will buy food, clothing, cars, and many other things. Learn shopping tips that will help you get the most for your money.

Shopping for Food

Grocery shopping is probably the biggest shopping chore. You can save money by shopping regularly. Stay organized. Know what you need.

Always make a shopping list before going to the grocery store.

Do not get in the habit of going to the store every day. You will waste time and transportation costs. And you will probably spend more.

Keep a grocery list. When you run out of an item, write it on your list. Before you go to the store, add the other things you need. Look in the cupboards and refrigerator. Do you need milk, bread, eggs, or cereal? Do you have vegetables, fruits, and juice? See if you have the other foods you eat often.

Study the newspaper grocery ads. Add to your list sale items that you know you will use. Plan meals around sale items. Read the ads and sale signs posted in the store.

When you get to the store, stick to your list. Buying extra foods and junk foods can really increase your bill.

The store's own brand of food is almost always the best buy. Compare store brands with national ones. If they are lower and you like the food as well, buy store brands. Remember, though, do not buy foods you will not use just because they are on sale. That would not be saving money. It would be wasting it.

Read package labels. There is a law about food packages. The contents must be listed on the label. They must be listed in order of amounts. This means that the ingredient making up the largest amount is listed first. Then the ingredient second in amount is next. The list goes on to the least amount.

The list of ingredients can be a clue to the value of the package. For example, look at a can of fruit. If the first ingredient is water, you know there is more water than fruit in the can. Compare it to other cans. The cheapest can may not be the best buy. It may not contain as much food.

Think about the size of packages you buy. Compare the price per ounce between package sizes. Larger packages may save you money. They usually are priced at less per ounce. If you will use the whole package, they may be good buys. Perhaps you can take part of the food out of the package and freeze what you wil not eat right away. Do not buy packages so big that you throw out part of the food. That would certainly be a waste of money.

Check Up:✓✓ True or False?

1. A contract may be either written or unwritten.

2. Usually a product that is well made costs more than one that is poorly made.

3. The best way to grocery shop is to buy everything that looks good.

Shopping for Clothes

There are three kinds of clothing. Some clothes are for work. Others are for parties, church, and special times. Still others are for sports and casual wear around home. So you need to plan for three kinds of clothing.

Plan what clothes you will buy for the year. First, check what you have of the three kinds of clothes. Then plan what you *need.* Plan what you *want* to buy. Last, decide what you *can* buy.

Few people can buy everything they want. They must decide what and how to buy. Follow these tips.

- Think about *how* clothes will be worn. Work clothes are worn often. They need to be well made of strong cloth. Clothes for special times need not be so well made or strong.
- Always check for quality. Is the material what you want? Are the seams carefully stitched? Good quality clothing fits and wears better.
- Read the care label. You may not want an article of clothing that needs ironing or dry cleaning.
- Learn what clothing *should* cost. The material and the way the clothing is made should decide the cost.
- Buy what fits into your wardrobe. For example, buy a shirt that matches slacks you already have. Buy a coat that you can wear many places.
- Buy clothing at the end of the season. Buy winter clothing late in the winter. Buy summer clothing late in the summer. Those are times when stores have big sales. You can wear your sale clothing the rest of the season. Then, when that season comes next year, you will still have good clothing.
- Learn *where* to buy clothes. Where a store is located affects its prices. Also, some stores give lots of service. This raises prices. And remember, the number of items available affects the price. A store that has only one of each style will charge more.

Cleaning costs can add to the total cost of clothing.

Watch Out for Sales Tricks

Some salespeople try to cheat buyers. Cheating someone is called **fraud.** Fraud is against the law, of course, but it is hard to stop.

Beware of fraud. Before you buy, ask questions to find out all you want to know. After you buy, be sure the item is what you thought you were buying. Did the salesperson tell the truth about it.

The *contest winner* plan is sometimes fraud. Suppose you are called on the telephone. You are asked a question anyone could answer. You are a winner if you say the right answer. You win a chance to buy something for $20. It is said to be worth $50. But it may not even be worth $20. If it is not, that is fraud.

Another plan is called *bait and switch.* Suppose a coat is advertised for $25. That is the *bait.* At the store you find only large size coats. The salesperson then tries to sell you a $50 coat. That is the *switch* to a higher priced coat. The advertising misled you. This is fraud, too.

A salesperson may come to your door selling something you want. The price might be less than the store price. A salesperson will take your order and your down payment. You are to receive your order in the mail. But it never comes. You never see the salesperson again. This is another kind of fraud.

There is fraud in the car repair business. Workers may make repairs that are not needed. They may charge for repairs they did not do.

There is fraud in medicine, too. Some medicines are advertised as a cure for many illnesses. They do not really cure anything. This is fraud.

Most salespeople are honest. Some are not. Always think carefully before you spend your money.

Shop at stores and buy from companies you already know you can trust. When shopping in a new place, ask other people about it. Never be pushed into buying something right now when you are not sure you want it. You may be sorry later. Take your time making up your mind.

Do check prices at other stores. Do not assume that because it is on sale it is cheaper.

Shopping for Insurance

As you become independent, you will need to buy insurance. Some types of insurance are

- health insurance.
- car insurance.
- home owner's insurance or renter's insurance.
- life insurance.

Health insurance. Health insurance pays for all or part of doctor, hospital, dental, and medicine bills. Health insurance may not seem important when you are well. But you could get sick or have an accident. Then the bills can add up very quickly. Insurance can keep you from having to sell your property or take out a loan.

Shop carefully for health insurance. Different policies pay for different things. Some pay so much a day. Some pay a percentage of your total bill. The **premium,** the amount you pay for insurance, is different for different types of policies.

The company where you work may offer health insurance. This type of insurance is usually cheaper than insurance you buy yourself. Your employer may pay part or all of the premium.

Car insurance. If you own a car or motorcycle, you will need car insurance. Car insurance policies include some different kinds of insurance. Ask a trusted insurance agent which kinds you need.

One of the most important kinds of insurance is **liability** coverage. Liability insurance covers your responsibility to others. Suppose you are in an accident. Perhaps someone else is hurt in the accident. Your liability insurance will pay for repairing the other car. It also pays for the injured person's medical bills. Many states require car owners to have liability insurance.

Other types of car insurance are *collision, comprehensive,* and

A fire, storm, theft, or accident can cost you a lot of money if you don't have insurance.

uninsured motorist. Collision pays for damage to your car as a result of a collision, that is, a crash or wreck. Comprehensive pays for damages other than those caused by wrecks. Uninsured motorist covers you when the person at fault does not have liability insurance.

Shop around for your car insurance. Different companies charge different premiums. The more coverage you buy, the higher your premium, too.

Home owner's insurance. A home is usually the biggest purchase a person makes. You cannot afford to lose your home by fire or storm. Home owner's insurance will protect you against the loss of your home. It will pay for your home if it is damaged or destroyed. Home owner's policies sometimes include liability insurance. This coverage will pay for medical care if someone is hurt in your home. Contents insurance pays for your furniture and other things if they are destroyed or stolen.

You may live in an apartment. If so, you can buy a policy that covers just your belongings. If there is a fire or theft, your insurance would pay replacement costs. It would pay for such things as new clothes and furniture.

Life insurance. Life insurance pays money to your family when you die. This money can help pay medical and burial expenses. There are many different types of life insurance. Talk with an insurance agent about the different kinds.

Your employer may offer life insurance through your workplace. Like health insurance, it may be cheaper to buy life insurance this way.

With any kind of insurance, read the policy carefully. Be sure you understand it. Know what it will pay for and what it will not pay for. For example, know the highest amount your liability coverage will pay. Suppose your TV is stolen. Will your insurance pay you what you paid for the TV, or a smaller amount?

Ask questions of your agent. Talk with other people about insurance. Ask someone who knows about insurance to read the policy before you sign.

Check Up: ✓✓ True or False?

1. Checking for quality and shopping sales will save you money in your clothing budget.
2. The best shopping value is usually from a door-to-door salesperson.
3. Comprehensive coverage pays for damages to your car if you are in a wreck.

Shopping for a Car

When you start making your own money, you might want to buy a car. A car can be a big help if you live far from work. What if no buses or trains pass near your home? Then a car would be very important.

Think of the many things you have learned about shopping. How can these tips help you buy a car?

First, decide if you want a new or used car. You may not be able to afford a new one. But maybe you can save enough for a used car. Decide how much money you need to buy the kind of car you want.

Comparison shop. Look at different models. Talk about prices with different dealers. Consider buying a car from someone who is not a dealer, but has one to sell.

After you have picked out a car, you should have it checked. Have a friend or a mechanic you trust drive the car. Have him or her look at the engine. That will help you know if the car is in good shape.

Then think about how you will pay for the car. Do you have enough money to pay cash? Will you need to take out a loan? If so, do you have enough for a down payment? Can you afford the monthly payments?

Think about the added expenses of owning a car. You need a driver's license. You need car license plates. You need gas and oil. You may have repairs. You must buy car insurance. Will you be able to afford all these extras?

A used car can be a good buy if you know the engine is in good condition.

When to Get Help

Managing your money and being a smart shopper are not always easy. But there are many people you can turn to for help.

Your parents, a teacher, or another adult can help you manage your money. You may be spending too much money. Ask one of these people to help you write a good budget. They may be able to tell you a good place to bank. They can help you start a savings plan.

Your employer may be able to help you with some money matters. He or she can explain your tax withholding. Your boss may be able to recommend a bank near your workplace. He or she might help you start a savings account or buy insurance where you work.

Workers at your bank can help you, too. Ask about anything you do not understand. Clerks can teach you how to write a check. They can tell you how much money is in your account. They can help you find a mistake in your check register. They can explain savings plans.

Sometimes you may not be happy with a product or service. If this happens, tell the person who sold it to you. Talk politely and explain your problem. Usually your item will be fixed or replaced. In some cases you will get your money back. If the person refuses to help you, talk to the store manager. If the manager will not help you, call your local Better Business Bureau. Also write to the manufacturer.

In some cases you may want to hire a lawyer. You may want to write a contract for work you will do. You may need a lawyer to read a contract before you sign. Or you may have a contract that the other party is not honoring. In each case you could seek the help of a lawyer.

Find out the lawyer's fee before you hire him or her. Sometimes you can find free legal advice. Look under "Legal Service" in your phone book.

Check Up:✓✓ True or False?

1. There are more costs to owning a car than the purchase price.
2. Taking your time making buying decisions may help you avoid fraud.
3. The only time you would ever need a lawyer is if you are arrested.

REVIEW

REMEMBER WHAT YOU LEARNED

The words

Listed below are the important new words that you learned in this chapter. Next to each word is the page on which you will find the word in bold, black print. Turn back and read again the paragraph in which you find each word. Then write the word and its meaning on a sheet of paper. Also write a sentence of your own using each word.

1. consumer (292)
2. contract (301)
3. down payment (299)
4. fraud (305)
5. goods (292)
6. guarantee (297)
7. installment plan (298)
8. liability (306)
9. premium (306)
10. services (292)

The facts

1. What is the difference between goods and services? Between needs and wants?
2. Name four questions you should ask yourself before buying something.
3. Name four things that influence your buying.
4. Tell four ways to find the best shopping value.
5. Tell three ways to pay for an item. Give an advantage of each.
6. Give three examples of an unwritten contract. Of a written contract.
7. What three things make one product cost more than others?
8. Name three grocery shopping tips. Name three clothing shopping tips.
9. Name four kinds of insurance. Tell what each one is for.
10. Name three sales tricks. Explain how to avoid each one.

What's right here?

ADD TO YOUR KNOWLEDGE AND SKILLS

Talk about your ideas

1. Have you ever bought something you wished you had not bought? Describe the experience.

2. If you won a million dollars, what would you do with it?

3. When is it okay to take out a loan for something you want to buy? When should you pay cash? What are the advantages of each?

Do some activities

1. Check the price of your favorite candy bar at a grocery store. Then check the price at a discount store and in a candy bar machine. Be sure all three bars weigh the same. Are they all the same price? Why, or why not?

Compare the prices of three other items, too. Write the price of each item at two different stores. What have you learned from comparison shopping?

2. Make a list of everything you bought during the past week. By each item write an "N" for need or a "W" for want. Write what was the biggest influence on your decision to buy each item. What can you learn about your shopping habits from studying your lists?

Improve your basic skills

1. Read the ads in your local newpaper. Cut out six. Explain how the ads are different from each other.

1. Suppose a visitor from another planet is coming to stay with you. You are to show him or her around your town. Write a letter to your guest. Tell your guest what money is and how to be a smart shopper.

2. Suppose you bought a toaster a month ago. It is guaranteed for a year. Last week you moved to a different city. You are not near the store where you bought the toaster. The toaster quit working. Write a letter to the manufacturer. Explain your problem. Ask what to do.

5×7=?

1. Jack is shopping for canned fruit. One can of sliced pineapple costs 60¢. It contains 20 ounces. Another can costs 48¢. It contains 15 ounces. Which can of pineapple costs less per ounce?

2. Suppose you want to borrow $500 for a year. You check the interest rates at two banks and one S&L. The rates are 12%, 12½%, and 13%. How much interest would you pay at each rate?

Chapter 16

Living on Your Own

What's wrong here?

Words to learn and use

You will learn several new words in this chapter. The most important words are listed below. Do you know the meanings of these words?

utilities	lease
companionship	crisis intervention
independent	commitment

Build on what you know

You already know. . .

- how to set work goals.
- how to find a job.
- how to be a responsible employee.
- how to manage your money.

In this chapter you will learn. . .

- how to choose the best place to live.
- how to manage your time well.
- how to take care of your transportation, food, clothes, and household chores.
- how to live as a responsible adult.

In Part 4, you are learning about everyday living. You have read about your paycheck deductions and tax return. You have learned how to handle money and be a smart shopper.

Soon you will be employed full-time. You may think about living in your own apartment. Living on your own requires choosing a place to fit your lifestyle. It requires managing your time and money. Living on your own also includes accepting adult responsibilities. This chapter will help you develop the skills to do all these things.

Where Do You Want to Live?

When you get a job, do you want your own apartment? Would you rather live at home? There are good reasons for wanting an apartment. There are good reasons for living at home, too.

Living at Home

Many young people live at home after they finish school. Many live at home even after beginning work. One reason is that it costs less than living on your own.

At home you could share expenses. This would cost less than paying all your own bills. You could pay your share of the rent, food, and **utilities.** Utilities are services such as gas, electricity, and water. Most people pay for these expenses once a month.

There is another advantage to sharing expenses at home. You would be helping your family.

By living at home you may not need to buy expensive items. For example, you could save the cost of buying and owning a car. Maybe you could ride to work with a family member. Or you could share the family car. You also would not have to buy other expensive items. Some of these include appliances, a TV, and furniture.

Another reason to live at home is to share the work. By living with your family, you could share the household work. You could take turns cooking, cleaning, and doing laundry. You would not have to do all these chores by yourself.

Living at home gives you the **companionship** of being with another person. It is fun to talk and eat with someone. Living alone can be lonely.

Living in an apartment of your own is a step toward independence.

Living Away from Home

Suppose your job is in another city. You may *have* to live away from home. Your job might be in your hometown. You may *want* to live away from home.

One reason for living away from home is to be independent. Being **independent** means making your own decisions and being responsible for your own actions. It means not relying on other people for the things you want. You may get a good feeling from earning your own money. Making your own decisions will feel good. And doing things for yourself will build your confidence.

Being independent also means not being controlled by other people. You would not have to share a room with brothers or sisters. You could eat and sleep according to your own work hours. Your schedule would not depend on your family's schedule.

Being independent can be difficult. Can you earn enough money? Will you remember to do everything on time? Will you remember even when there is no one to remind you? Can you manage shopping, cooking, and cleaning along with your job?

Think about the good points of living away from home. Think about the bad points. Then decide which is better for you.

Having a Roommate

Suppose you decide to live away from home after you get a job. You may want to share an apartment with a friend. Think about these questions.

- How independent do you want to be?
- Do you want someone to help pay for rent and food? Do you want to share the chores?
- Will you like having someone around much of the time?

Sharing your place with a friend has both good and bad points. You would be more independent than if you lived at home. But you would be less independent than if you lived alone.

You would not be as lonely. Your friend could help you shop, cook, and clean.

There are some bad points to think about, too. You may have disagreements. Your friend may not want to do what you want to do. You may not like the same foods. You may like different TV shows.

Choosing the right roommate is important. Plan ahead. Decide how you will divide the expenses and the work.

There is no one best place or way to live after you get a job. Think about how *you* want to live.

Finding a Place to Live

Suppose you decide to live away from home. You might choose to live in an apartment or a mobile home. Or you could rent a room in a house or a hotel. Which place will be best for you?

Where to Look

How will you find the place you want to live? One way is to ask your family and friends to help you. Someone may know of a room, mobile home, or apartment for rent. Or someone may be willing to share their home with you.

Another way to find a place is to read the newspaper want ads. Look in the FOR RENT section. Do you want a place with furniture in it? Then look for APARTMENTS: FURNISHED.

APARTMENTS FURNISHED

Available now: 1 bedroom. Nicely, furnished apt. 706 W. Church, C. 1-862-7135 information.

Available now: nicely furnished 2 bedroom apts. Close to downtown Champaign. Carpeted, AC, off-street parking, water paid. 452-3321 after 5:30 pm.

Available now: 3 rooms near Lincoln Square, first floor, heat furnished, private bath and entrance, $265/mo. 267-6396.

Avail. Aug. 15. 2 furn. efficiency apts. in bsmt of older home @ 610 W. Church. Rent includes util., or both could be rented together as large 1 bedroom apt. Call 359-1892 for more information.

Avail. Now, 1 bdrm furnished $230 mo. plus utilities. Off street parking. 259-2735, 284-5717.

1 bdrm $250 heat pd & new paint or eff. $195 new carpet. 1st & Healey. Avail now. 356-7871.

1 bedroom at 403 W. Green, C. $275 includes all utilities. Property.Management Center, 352-5286.

2 bedroom. Carpeted living room. Ceramic kitchen & bath. Disposal. A/C. Laundry. $310/month. 2007 Philo Rd., Urbana. 356-7711.

1 BR Apt Near Beckman Institute & Mercy Hospital, $280/mo includes utilities. Lease. Deposit. Available immediately! 384-4978.

Close to Market Place; Lg 1 Br. off st Pking & Ldry. immed $235. 251-5111 LANDMARK PM.

COUNTRY FAIR
APARTMENTS
Large 1 & 2 bedroom furnished & unfurnished. HEAT & WATER PAID! 2106 W. White, C. 358-3713. Hours: Monday-Friday 9:00-5:30, Saturday 9-12.

Deluxe On Campus
1 & 2 bedrooms for fall
Dishwasher, balconies, air conditioned, security intercom. 328-3771. Bankier Apartments.

EFFICIENCY
Air conditioned, near campus. Call 352-5388 or 352-4132.

Fully furnished 1, 2, 3 or 4 bedroom apts. avail 5/15-8/15 or longer. 2 full baths, cent. ac, microwave, dishwasher. HR Realty, 359-0202.

GREAT CAMPUS LOCATION
Available for August occupancy
Furnished 1, 2, 4, 5, 6 bdrm apts.
All units include dishwasher
Many with microwaves
Great campus location
102 E. Gregory, C
For information, call 356-2297.

LINCOLN PLACE APARTMENTS
2 & 3 BEDROOM APTS.
Call 328-0135.

LONG OR SHORT TERM RENTALS. Utilities, cable, linen furnished.
Motel Thomasboro Apartments
Rt. 45 N. 1-643-7220

APARTMENTS UNFURNISHED

4 August: new 1 bdrm apartments w/A/C. Close to campus, off street parking. Call 328-7101 or 359-7943.

AVAILABLE NOW: Spacious two bedroom, large bathroom, fully equipped kitchen, carpet, central air, laundry facilities, lighted off-street parking. 444-9126.

1 bdr in S. Champaign
Available June 1, $260.
2 bdr near downtown Champaign.
Available May 1. $325
3 bdr near downtown Champaign.
Available May 1. $360.
Dawson Property Mgmt.
359-1220

1 bdrm apartment in Champaign. All utilities paid. No pets. $285/month. 356-2364.

1 & 2 bdrm luxury apts. in Urbana. Most have washer/dryer in apt. Fully equipped kitchen, patio, central air. 384-4953.

Beautiful, cozy, 1 BR apt, carpeted, ac, heat/water/garbage pd, dwntwn Ch, $305. 351-1881.

2 bedroom apartment. Carpeted, good location. $310. Call after 6pm, 351-3521.

2 bedroom apartments. $295 plus deposit and lease. No pets.
SWISS CHALET APTS. 384-1903.

Luxury 4 bedroom, 2 full baths, $780/mo. Available June.
Gower Rentals - 352-2447

Modern campus apartment. 105 E. Green, C. Small one bedroom, full kitchen, carpeted, ac, parking available. $210. Year lease. Sorry, no pets. 352-3564, 356-5954.

NEW 2 bdr. apts. Water paid, dishwasher, microwave, washer/dryer. No pets. Short term leases available with immediate occupancy. $425/mo. CENTURY 21. Heartland 352-4288.

Quiet, 1 bdrm apt with garage. Ideal for 1. $285 plus deposit lease. Call 251-9100 or 359-8922.

2 room efficiency, close to downtown Champaign. $165 plus deposit & electric. No children, no pets, 356-4772.

3 Room Furnished apt. heat, water, and garbage paid. $290/mo. 352-1236 for appt.

4 room 1st. floor apt. Water & garbage furnished. 204 N. Gregory, Urbana. 688-2436.

MOBILE HOMES FOR RENT

2 bdrm, air conditioned, no pets, references, & deposit in our spacious country lot. Call 892-9741.

2 bdrm unfurnished in quiet Urbana Park. Lot rent included. Deposit & references required. $250/mo. 337-1135 ask for Nancy.

In country.
Unfurnished DW 3 bedroom.
No pets. $275. 359-5640.

What information can you learn from these ads? What questions might you want to ask before looking at an apartment?

If you want to get your own furniture, look for APARTMENTS: UNFURNISHED. Many apartments listed as "unfurnished" have a stove and refrigerator. Some have a washer and dryer. Mobile homes may be listed with apartments.

If you are interested, call the number in the ad. Ask if the apartment or room is still for rent. If it is, ask when you may see it.

Another way to find a place is to ask a real estate agent. Real estate agencies are listed in the yellow pages of the phone book. They may have places to rent. But they may not put an ad in the paper.

Spend at least two or three weeks to find the best place for you. Do not rush this important decision. Finding a place takes *time.*

Abbreviations Often Used in Newspaper Ads

AC = air conditioned

appt. = appointment

apt. = apartment

avail. = available

bdrms. (BR) = bedrooms

bldg. = building

cent. air = central air conditioning

dep. = deposit

eff. = **efficiency** (a one-room apartment)

eves. = evenings

frplc. = fireplace

furn. = furnished

immed. = **immediate** (right now)

incl. = includes

ldry. = laundry

lg. = large

mgmt. = management

mins. = minutes

mo. = month

neg. = **negotiable** (to be agreed upon)

occ. = occupancy

ref. = references

refrig. = refrigerator

req. = required

rm. = room

sq. ft. = square feet

unfurn. = unfurnished

\+ util. = you pay the utilities

wkdys. = weekdays

wknds. = weekends

Things to Consider

You will want to think about a number of things before you rent a place to live.

Where the place is can be important. How far is it from work? How will you get to work? Perhaps you do not have a car. Then you must be able to walk or ride the bus to work. Is there a bus route near? Does the bus travel at times that fit your work hours?

The best place to live would be close to many places you need to go. Is it near the grocery and other stores? Is it near family and friends? How far is it to places you go for recreation?

The house or building should be in good repair. It should be safe. Look for fire escapes. Are the stairs safe? Are there locks on windows and doors? Are there plenty of lights inside and outside? Also, look at the neighborhood after dark. Ask police if the area is safe.

Consider the rent. How much can you afford to pay? To find out, write a budget. You learned how to do it in Chapter 14. Compare your expenses with your net pay. Do you have enough? Or is the rent too high?

Is there a lease you must sign? A **lease** is a written contract. It states the amount of the rent. It says what you can do in a rented place. It also tells what you must do before you move to another place. Usually, you must agree not to move out for six months or a year. A lease may be hard to read. Ask an adult friend to help you study it. Do not sign a lease until you understand it.

Remember to set aside some money. You will need enough to buy items for your new apartment. If it is unfurnished, you will need some furniture. Even if it is furnished, you will need bedding and kitchen supplies. Use smart shopping skills to buy these items.

List the things you want to check before you rent.

Planning Your Transportation

You must get to work on time every day. If you live close to your job, you can walk to work. But you need to go many places besides your job.

How you get to places depends on how far away they are. If they are close to home the easiest way is to walk. Walking saves money, too.

Riding the city bus is a good way to travel. If you will be riding often, buy a pass. This will save you money.

For long distances, riding the train may be best. Maybe you will live near a city and work downtown. Then you could ride a commuter train to work.

Living close to your place of work can save transportation costs.

Another way to get to work is to join a car pool. You would then ride to work with someone else. You would pay part of the cost of driving to the owner of the car. If you have a car, you can take turns driving.

Riding a bike is often a good way to get around. However, a bike is not safe in heavy traffic. Bike riding is also dangerous and difficult in bad weather.

A motorcycle or a car can travel in city traffic. You may want to buy one of these. Remember, a motorcycle or car costs a lot to buy. Either is also expensive to own. You must buy a license, gas, oil, and insurance. And do not forget the cost of repairs.

How you get from place to place is part of your lifestyle. It is also part of your budget. You will need to plan your transportation carefully.

Check Up:✓✓ True or False?

1. Everyone should live alone after high school.
2. You may find an apartment by asking a friend, reading the want ads, or calling a real estate agent.
3. You must figure transportation costs in your budget.

Managing Your Time

You will have many things to do when you live away from home. You may find it hard to get everything done. You can learn how to manage your time wisely.

Plan Ahead

You must use your time in the best way. Try to plan each day. Make a list of what you must do. Write how long each activity will take. Your list may look like this:

work	8	hours
eating	2½	hours
rest and sleep	10	hours
dressing	½	hour
housekeeping	1	hour
transportation	1	hour
recreation	1	hour
	24	hours

Would you want to follow this plan every day? Maybe not. Then you must plan ahead for special things you want to do.

Suppose you want to go to a movie. You will need two hours. How could you change your plan so you could go to the movie? Work hours must stay the same. The hour to go to and from work must stay the same. Where can you find time for the movie?

Here is one way. You could skip your recreation one day. You could use that hour to do housekeeping. You could do extra jobs, such as laundry and taking out the trash. Then you could skip housekeeping on the day you go to the movie. You would have two hours for recreation that day.

This is one way you can make time changes in your plan. You may think of others.

Use Your Calendar to Remember

It helps to use a calendar when you plan. Get a large one with space to write on each date. Write the special things that you do on certain days.

Which day will you buy food? When will you do your laundry? And when will you get your hair cut? Mark days for special things, such as parties, meetings, or religious holidays. Also mark when you will not work. These days give you time to do special things not in your plan.

Use your calendar to help you remember to pay your bills. Mark the date you need to pay rent. Also mark dates your phone, gas, electricity, and water bills are due.

JULY						
SUN	MON	TUE	WED	THU	FRI	SAT
1	2 rent phone	3	4 Holiday Picnic 6:00	5 groceries	6	7 laundry movie 7:00
8	9	10	11 choir 7 p.m.	12 groceries	13 dentist 4:00	14 laundry pick up drycleaning
15 mom's birthday	16 gas water	17 haircut 5 p.m.	18	19 groceries	20 Sally's party 8 p.m.	21 laundry
22	23	24	25 choir 7 p.m.	26 groceries	27 dentist 4 p.m.	28 laundry
29	30	31				

Your calendar will also help you remember doctor and dentist visits. Whenever you make an appointment, write it on the calendar.

Look at your calendar each day. See what you have to do that day. Look ahead. See if you need to do anything ahead of time. Your calendar will help you be on time and pay bills on time.

Use Your Time Wisely

Learn to be a smart user of time. For example, you could run several errands in one trip. That would not take as long as going out several different times. Stop at places close together. Run errands on your way home from work.

Keep a shopping list and an errand list. Then you will not forget something and have to go back.

Do two things at once. Take your bills and checkbook along to the laundromat. Pay bills while your clothes are washing. Wash the dishes while you watch TV or listen to music. Do not get behind on your chores. Things are easier to clean if they do not get too dirty.

Plan to run several errands in one trip to save time.

Eating on Your Own

Many young people believe meals are the hardest part of being independent. Planning meals, grocery shopping, cooking, and cleaning up are big jobs. You may not be used to doing these things for yourself.

Choosing Foods

What you eat is important. You know what you like to eat. But you also need to think of foods that keep you healthy. Everyone needs food from four different food groups every day. These groups are

- milk products.
- meats.
- fruits and vegetables.
- breads and cereals.

Milk Products. This group includes milk, yogurt, cheese, ice cream, and many other products. Teens need *four* or more servings a day from this group.

Meats. In this group are meat, fish, eggs, poultry, dried beans, and nuts. Eat *two servings* from this group each day.

Fruits and Vegetables. Green leafy, yellow vegetables, and all fruits belong in this group. Eat at least *four servings* from this group each day.

Breads and Cereals. This group includes white and whole wheat bread, whole grain and breakfast cereals. Eat *four servings* from this group each day.

Your food for one day might be like this:

Breakfast:	
orange juice	toast
egg	milk
Lunch:	
cheese sandwich	carrot sticks
apple	milk
Dinner:	
beef	bread
potatoes	ice cream
lettuce salad	milk

Make sure you get the right amount from each food group. To do this plan ahead. Write what you will eat for the coming week.

Generally, eating at home is cheaper than eating in a restaurant. Sometimes it is easier to eat the right foods at home, too. Fast-food restaurants often do not offer many fruits and vegetables. And they offer mostly fried foods.

When you eat a meal out, eat healthful foods. Think about the food groups. Which ones will you be having during the rest of the day? Order foods in the restaurant that will fill in what you need.

Preparing Food

Cooking can be fun, but it can take a lot of time. Start by making easy-to-fix dishes first.

A beginner's cookbook might be a good thing to buy. It will tell you how to prepare and cook foods.

Some foods do not need cooking. Other foods need to be cooked to become tender and tasty.

Most foods in the milk group do not need cooking. This makes it easy to get your required servings from this group each day.

Foods in the meat group need more cooking than those in other groups. To save time, cook meat for several meals on your day off. Then store it carefully in the refrigerator. Use it for lunches and dinners for the next day or two.

You can buy fresh, frozen, or canned vegetables. Wash or peel fresh vegetables. Some, such as lettuce, cabbage, and celery are usually not cooked. Others, such as carrots, broccoli, and spinach can be eaten raw or cooked. And some, such as potatoes and corn, should be cooked. Frozen and canned vegetables need only a little cooking. Fresh ones take a little longer.

It is easy to eat two, three, or four servings of fruit each day. Fresh fruit needs no cooking. You can buy canned fruit that is ready to eat.

Cooking is easy when you follow directions in a cookbook.

Bread is usually baked before you buy it. But you may buy frozen dough to make rolls or bread.

Most cereals are ready to eat. They are quite expensive, though. You can save money if you eat cereals you cook.

Check Up:✓✓ True or False?

1. Planning your time schedule can help you get everything done.
2. Writing things to do on your calendar should help you remember to do them.
3. There are six basic food groups.

Food Safety

You can get very ill from eating spoiled food. Take care of food properly so it will not spoil. Follow these safety rules.

- Only buy food in sealed, clean, containers that are undamaged. Never buy a bulging or rusty can. Do not buy a leaky bottle or a torn bag.
- Store foods properly in cupboards, the refrigerator, or the freezer. Keep them tightly wrapped.
- Read the label on every package of food. Follow the cooking directions.
- Always wash your hands before preparing or eating food.
- Wash all fresh fruit and vegetables carefully before eating them.
- Thaw frozen meat in the refrigerator. Or start to cook it while it is frozen.
- Keep food that spoils easily very hot or very cold. Do not keep it out of the refrigerator more than two hours.
- Wrap leftovers. Put them into the refrigerator as soon as you finish a meal.
- Keep cold sandwiches cold.
- Wash dishes in hot, sudsy water. Rinse in hot, running water.
- Use clean towels to dry dishes or wipe tabletops.
- Keep insects and pets out of the kitchen. They infect food.
- Do not ever handle food carelessly!

Store foods properly to prevent disease and spoilage.

Taking Care of Your Clothes

Taking care of your own clothes is your responsibility when you live on your own. Read the care label in each piece of clothing. It may say "Dry Clean Only." Take that item to the cleaner when it is dirty. If it is washable, wash it according to the directions.

Before you wash your laundry, sort the clothes. Put the whites in one pile. Put the darks in another. Separate the heavily soiled pieces from the others. Wash each pile separately. Pretreat stains. Mend rips and sew on loose buttons.

Set the machine for the correct water temperature. Whites can be washed in hot water. Darks should be washed in cold. Set the machine for the right speed. Wash jeans on the setting marked "Heavy." Wash delicate fabrics on "Gentle." Wash most other items on "Normal." Add detergent according to the directions on the box. Do not fill the machine too full of clothes. Otherwise, they will not get clean.

Dry your laundry according to the directions on the care labels, too. Set the dryer to the setting that is right for each load. Take clothes out of the dryer as soon as they are dry. Fold or hang them up neatly. Press the pieces that are wrinkled.

If you do your laundry regularly, you will always have clean clothes to wear. The job will not seem so big either.

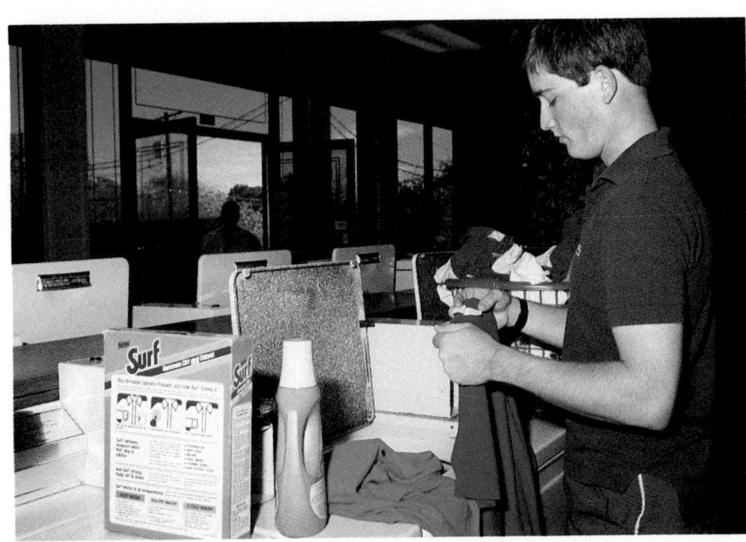

Care labels tell you how to wash and dry your clothing if it is washable. Otherwise, the label will tell you to dryclean the item.

Cleaning Your Apartment

You can be proud of having a place of your own to live. It will make you feel good. You will want to show it to your family and friends. Keeping your home tidy and clean will make you even prouder. Besides, it will make your home safer and more healthful.

Doing your cleaning chores often and regularly will make the job easier. First, keep things picked up. Hang your clothes in the closet. Hang your towel on the rack. Put trash in the waste paper basket. Rinse and stack dirty dishes right after you eat.

Dust regularly. Dust the furniture, of course. Do not forget the places where dust collects. Window sills and air vents are examples. Use furniture polish or wax on wood furniture once in a while.

Vacuum the carpets and large rugs once a week, too. Shake the throw rugs outside. Sweep or dust mop the floors once a week. Scrub them when they get dirty. Wax them occasionally.

Clean the bathroom at least once a week. Scrub the toilet bowel with toilet cleaner and a brush. Scour the sink, tub, tile, and counter top. Use scouring powder or a bathroom cleaner.

The kitchen is probably the biggest cleaning job. Wash the dishes after every meal or at least daily. Wipe off the counters and table top when you do the dishes. Wipe up spills when they happen. Scour the sink every few days. Scrub out the inside of the refrigerator and cupboards when they get dirty. Clean the oven and stove top often.

Never ask a stranger into your house unless you were expecting the person. Call the worker's employer if you are not sure you should open the door.

Protecting Your Safety

In Chapter 9 you learned about safety on the job. You know you can help make your workplace safe and healthful. You can also prepare for accidents that might happen.

Many of the same rules apply at home, too. By following safety rules, you can make your home safer from crime and accidents. You can be prepared in case of an emergency.

Preventing Crime

No one is totally safe from crime. But there are many things you can do to protect yourself. Follow these safety rules at home:

1. Use a door lock that opens only with a key. Keep your door locked day and night.
2. Put a chain lock on the door. Open the door with the chain in place until you know who is there.
3. Never hide your key outdoors.
4. Do not leave your house key in your coat pocket or in your car.
5. Lock your windows. Use the kind of window lock that opens with a key.
6. If you live alone, do not put your first name on the mailbox or in the phone book. Use your initials and last name.
7. If you hear a strange noise outdoors, call the police. Do not go outdoors.
8. Leave a light on while you are away.
9. Tell a friendly neighbor if you will be away overnight.
10. Stop mail and newspaper deliveries if you will be away more than one day.

Follow these safety rules when you are away from home:

1. Always tell someone where you are going and when you will return.
2. Try not to walk alone, day or night.
3. Walk near the curb. Keep away from doorways and alleys.
4. Do not answer questions or give directions for anyone you do not know.
5. If someone follows you, walk into a store. Call the police.
6. On a bus, sit behind the driver if you can. If someone bothers you, tell the driver.
7. If someone tries to touch or hold you, *run away*. Scream "Fire." People stop and look quickly when they hear "Fire." Run to a place where there are people to help you.
8. *Never* accept a ride with someone you do not know.

Preventing Accidents

"Think safety" is good advice for the workplace. It is also good advice for the home. First, make your home as safe as possible. Second, act safely while you are at home.

Falls. You can help prevent falls by keeping your apartment tidy. Do not leave things where you might trip on them. Keep stairs clear. Keep floors clean. Do not use throw rugs that slide easily.

Pay attention to what you are doing when you work or relax at home. Be careful getting in and out of the tub. Do not stand on a piece of furniture that is not steady.

Fires. Check your home for fire safety. See that there are not too many appliances plugged into one outlet. See that all electrical appliances and cords are in good repair. Do not leave clutter, such as rags and papers, where they could catch fire. If your apartment does not have a smoke alarm, put one in. Have a fire extinguisher handy.

Practice fire safety, too. Know how to use gas stoves and heaters. Always put a match to a gas burner before turning on the gas. Be careful when you cook. Do not leave the kitchen when foods are cooking at high temperatures. Keep towels, clothing, and pot holders away from the heat. Do not leave candles burning when you are out of the room.

Poisons. Read the labels on cleaning supplies, bug sprays, and other chemicals. Use them safely. Store them away from food. Never store a poison in a food container. Someone might accidentally eat or drink it.

Guns. The best rule for guns is not to have them in your home. If you do, however, keep them unloaded. Keep the shells stored far from the gun. Know how to use a gun safely before you touch it. Never clown around with a gun.

Keep your home clean and neat. Use appliances carefully. You will have fewer accidents.

First Aid

You can be as careful as possible. Still, accidents are bound to happen once in a while. Know what to do if an accident happens.

If the injury is serious, call for help. Then do what you must to restore breathing, stop bleeding, and treat shock. See Chapter 9 for the right procedures.

You may be able to treat small injuries yourself. Buy a first aid kit. You can get one at a drug store. Perhaps someone at the store can help you pick out a kit. Ask how to use the materials in the kit. If you use up any of the supplies in the kit, replace them. That way you will always be ready in case an accident happens.

Most city health departments will give you a first aid guide. Ask for one and read it. Keep it where you can look at it quickly.

Burns. What will you do if you burn your hand on an electric iron? Quickly put your hand into cold water for five minutes. Carefully dry the burned spot. Then keep it dry for several days. If the burn is large or the skin is broken, see a doctor.

Small cuts. If you should cut yourself, wash the cut thoroughly with soap and water. Cover it with a bandage. Keep it clean and dry until it heals. If it gets red or puffy, see a doctor or show it to the nurse at work.

Something in your eye. If you get something in your eye, do not rub it. Instead, try to wash out the object. Pour water into one corner of your eye. Let the water run out the other corner. You may be able to see the object. If so, try to touch it carefully with the corner of a clean, wet cloth. Then lift it out. If these methods do not work, get help.

Insect bites. An insect bite may cause a bump on the skin. It may itch. Wash the bite with soap under running water. Put ice on it. Most bites are gone in an hour or two. See a doctor if the spot becomes red and large.

Check Up:✓✓ True or False?

1. You should wash all colors of clothes together to be sure they get clean.
2. A clean, tidy home is a safer home.
3. Rubbing your eye will help get out a piece of dirt or an eyelash.

Getting Help in an Emergency

Suppose something bad happens. You may sprain your ankle and be unable to walk. Or you hear a prowler at your window.

In any of these situations, planning ahead may save your life. Your telephone could be the key.

Know whom to call in each emergency situation. Start by becoming familiar with your phone book. See if emergency numbers are listed on the first page or two. If so, read through them. Think whom you would call for different emergencies.

Suppose emergency numbers are not listed in the front of your phone book. Make a list of emergency phone numbers. Keep it near your phone. Your list might include fire department, police, rescue, doctor, hospital, poison control center, and crisis intervention. **Crisis intervention** simply means help in an emergency.

Your town may have a special number for any emergency. If you cannot find the right phone number, dial 0. Calmly explain your problem. The operator will help you call the right place.

Some phone books have a section called *The Green Pages*. This section lists many different services. One of these services could help you in an emergency.

Learn how to get help by telephone.

Do not be afraid to call for help. Most public agencies offer free services. Getting help shows you are smart. You are taking care of your problem.

You can get help for almost any problem. For instance, you might be lonely and just want to talk to someone. The person who answers your call will talk with you. He or she will listen and be your friend.

You might have a family problem. The person who answers your call may help you solve the problem. Or he or she may tell you how to get help.

You might be ill and need a doctor or food. Someone will come to help you or explain where to get the kind of help you need.

Accepting Adult Responsibilities

When you decide to live on your own, you take on many responsibilities. You choose your place to live. You take care of your home. You work at your own job. You pay your own bills. You decide what you will do with your time. You take care of yourself, your clothes, and your food. You watch out for your own safety.

Living on your own also involves being part of your community. You have already learned that as a worker, you are a taxpayer. You pay your share of money to the government. Then the government can do its work. And you, in turn, benefit from government services.

There are some other things you will do when you take on adult responsibilities in your community, too. One is by obeying the laws. Be a good, safe driver. Do not steal from other people or harm anyone. Do not litter or damage property.

Being a good neighbor is part of living in your community. Be friendly to those who live near you. Help them whenever you can. Do not be a bother to your neighbors by being too noisy. Help keep your neighborhood clean and neat.

Voting is another adult responsibility. When you vote you must be eighteen years old. You must be a citizen of the United States. You must have lived in your home for a certain length of time.

If you meet all of these requirements, go to your election office. There you can register to vote. You will receive a voter's registration card. Find out where you go to vote each election.

Whom should you vote for? How will you decide? Talk with your family and friends. At voting time, listen to the radio and TV. You will hear and see news reports about people in the election. Listen to what they say. Do you think they are right? Is what they say what you want? Then decide whom you want to vote for.

As a registered voter, you may be picked for jury duty. As a juror you would go to a trial. You would listen to what is said. You may decide who was at fault in an accident. You may decide if someone is guilty of a crime.

You may want to be involved in your community in other ways. Perhaps you would like to do volunteer work. You might become involved in politics. You could work for a certain candidate. You could work for a special issue—such as drug prevention, clean air, or saving a historical site.

A Desire to Succeed

Dealing with Disability: Marsha Saxton

Marsha Saxton says that she was born "not quite finished." What happened is that her spine did not grow completely together. This birth defect is called *spina bifida*.

As a young child, Marsha was in the hospital many times for surgery. Many of the other children in the hospital could not walk. Marsha was able to walk, so she helped them. Still, she felt frightened and lonely.

During her stays, Marsha went to classes held at the hospital. It was hard to keep up with her studies.

Everyone in her family was very understanding. She says, "My family didn't make a big deal out of my being disabled." Marsha took care of herself.

Until she was twelve, Marsha wore leg braces. When the leg braces came off, Marsha was very excited. At school, though, a girl made fun of her skinny legs. From then on she always wore clothes to hide her legs.

Marsha also has a bladder control problem as a result of her birth defect. She needs to use a catheter to urinate. As a child, she was afraid her classmates would laugh at her. For this reason, she did not talk about that problem.

Marsha went to college. She worked as a speech therapist in a hospital.

Then Marsha joined a peer counseling group. In this group people with similar problems talked about their experiences. Marsha learned to share her feelings. And she told about her handicaps. She found peer counseling helpful for herself.

Marsha wanted to help others in the same way. She started a peer counseling program at the Boston Self-Help Center.

Marsha works very hard for disabled people. She wants them to understand themselves. She wants able-bodied people to understand those who are handicapped.

Living as a Family

You have been learning a lot about work and good money management. Your decisions about these things will help form the lifestyle you want.

For many people an important part of their lifestyle is marriage. In fact, most young people today plan to marry. Many of them hope to have children.

Getting married is a big responsibility. For one thing, living as a couple costs more than living on your own. You and your partner will need a bigger place to live. It costs more to feed two people than just one. You will have more bills of every kind.

Second, and even more important, marriage is a lifetime commitment. A **commitment** is a promise. When you marry, you make a promise to love your partner. You promise to help each other. You promise to work together to build the life you want.

Marriage is an important lifestyle decision. Before you decide to marry, ask yourself many questions. Are you able to take on the financial responsibility? Are you willing to make a commitment for life? Are you willing to do your share of the work? Are you willing to work together even when things go wrong?

You need to make plans before you marry. Just as with work, you need goals for your marriage. You and your partner may each have career goals and other personal goals. But you will plan some lifestyle goals together.

Talk over these things.

- What personal goals do you each have?
- Are your values the same?
- Can you accept your partner's feelings when they are different from yours?
- Do you agree on a lifestyle?
- Will you both work?
- Do you want children?
- Who will take the various responsibilities?

Adding children to a family is a responsibility, too. Children bring much joy to their parents, and many changes to their lifestyle.

Marriage and children are important steps that need lots of planning.

Check Up:✓✓ True or False?

1. Calling someone to help may be a good way to handle a crisis.
2. You must register before voting.
3. Marriage requires planning.

The words

Listed below are the important new words that were used in this chapter. Next to each word is the page on which you will find the word in bold, black print. Turn back and read again the paragraph in which you find each word. Then write the word and its meaning on a sheet of paper. Also write a sentence of your own using each word.

1. commitment (333)
2. companionship (314)
3. crisis intervention (330)
4. lease (314)
5. utilities (314)
6. independent (315)

The facts

1. What are two reasons for living alone after you get a job?
2. Name three ways you might find an apartment to rent.
3. How can you use a calendar to help manage your time?
4. What are five things you should think about when choosing a place to live?
5. Name the four food groups. List three foods from each group.
6. What are five rules to follow to keep food from spoiling?
7. What does a care label on clothing tell you?
8. Name at least five housekeeping chores. How often should you do each one?
9. What are five ways to protect yourself in your home? What are five ways to protect yourself away from home?
10. What are two things to consider before you decide to marry?

What's right here?

ADD TO YOUR KNOWLEDGE AND SKILLS

Talk about your ideas

1. Do you want to live at home or away from home now? Why?
2. How might you avoid conflicts between persons living in the same apartment?
3. Do you eat foods from the four food groups every day? How could you improve your eating habits?
4. What do you think it means to accept adult responsibilities? Are you ready to accept all those responsibilities? Explain.

Do some activities

1. Pretend you are looking for an apartment. Cut out newspaper ads of places for rent. Choose at least five that seem to fit your needs. Compare what is offered in each apartment.
2. Keep a record of what you do each day for a week. Write each activity. Write how much time you spend doing each activity. Study your list. Are you happy with the way you spend your time? Could you manage your time better?
3. Imagine an emergency in your home. Decide whom you would call and what you would say. Role play making this call. Ask a classmate to tell how he or she would respond to your call.

Improve your basic skills

1. Read through the beginning pages of your phone book. Notice if the phone book has a "green pages" section. What agencies are listed?
2. Find a first aid book at the library. Read one first aid procedure. Explain it to the class.

1. Write a list of questions you would ask if you were calling about an apartment for rent.
2. Write a page telling how you feel about one of the following ideas: being independent, being an adult, or living on your own.

1. This recipe for boiled rice serves six people. Change the amount of each ingredient so the recipe will serve two people.

   3 cups water
   1 ½ cups uncooked rice
   1 ½ teaspoons salt
2. Your grocery bill total is $35.67. How much sales tax will you pay if the sales tax rate is 3%? 5%? 5½%?
3. Your meal at a restaurant costs $7.95. Your drink is 55¢. You want to give the waitress a 15% tip. How much money should you leave?

Glossary

A

Abbreviations. Shortened forms of words.

Absenteeism. Missing days of work.

Accommodating work. Work done to serve other people, such as that of airline steward.

Adaptable. Able to change.

Addictive. Habit forming. Hard to quit.

Adult education. Schooling offered to people over the age of 18.

Al-Anon. A group that helps families of alcoholics with their problems.

Alcoholics. People who cannot on their own stop drinking too much alcohol.

Alcoholics Anonymous (AA). A group that helps alcoholics learn to control their drinking.

Amusement. Work done to entertain others.

Appearance. How a person looks.

Applicant. A person who applies for a job.

Application form. A form giving personal information that a job-seeker must fill out when applying for a job.

Apprentice. A person who learns a skill by working with someone who already knows that skill.

Appropriate. Proper.

Aptitude. The ability to do or learn something easily. Talent.

Artistic work. A type of work having to do with the arts. It includes writing, painting, acting, etc.

Attitude. A person's outlook on something.

B

Balance due. An amount of money still owed after other payments have been made.

Bank balance. The amount of money a person has in a bank account.

Bank statement. A printed list prepared by a bank of all the deposits and withdrawals made in an account.

Benefits. Things workers receive when working for a company, such as paid vacation, sick leave, etc.

Body language. Body movements that send messages to others.

Braille. A system blind people use to read. Raised dots on the page stand for letters or words.

Budget. A plan for managing money.

C

Card catalog. An index of all the books in a library.

Career. The work a person does and the jobs a person holds over a number of years.

Career goals. Decisions about the type of work you want to do.

Check register. A booklet in which a record of a checking account is kept.

Collective bargaining. When workers in a union try to come to an agreement with an employer over such things as pay.

Commitment. A promise.

Comparison shopping. Looking at different products before you buy.

Compromise. Coming to an agreement after each side gives in a little.

Consumer. A person who buys goods and services.

Contract. An agreement.

Cooperation. Working together well with others.

Cost of living. The amount of money it takes to live and pay for food, housing, etc.

Crisis intervention. Help in an emergency.

Criticism. An explanation of what is wrong with something.

Cursive writing. Handwriting in which the letters are connected. The opposite of printing.

D

Dependable. Able to be counted on.

Deposit. Money put into a bank account.

Dignity. Pride.

Discount. A marked-down cost.

Down payment. Part of the money paid on a purchase when you buy it. The rest is paid later.

Driving under the influence. Drunk driving.

Dyslexia. A learning disability that makes reading difficult. Words or letters may appear backward or mixed up.

E

Eager. Looking forward to something.

Electronic Fund Transfer (EFT). Services offered by a bank through an automatic teller machine.

Emotions. Feelings.

Empathy. Seeing the other person's side of things.

Employee's Withholding Allowance Certificate (W-4 Form). A written statement giving an employer information affecting a worker's income taxes.

Employment agency. A business that matches workers and jobs.

Endorse. To sign your name on the back of a check.

Enthusiasm. Eagerness. Excitement.

Entitled. Having a right to something.

Equal opportunity. Every job being open to all people regardless of race, sex, age, or beliefs.

Evaluation. A written report saying how well a person is doing a job.

Expensive. Costly. High priced.

Experiences. Activities a person has already tried.

F

Fact sheet. A sheet containing facts about a person's education and work history that should be carried to job interviews.

Federal government. The government of the United States.

Federal income tax. Money paid to the U.S. government to use for all the services it provides.

Fee. An amount of money charged for a service.

FICA (Federal Insurance Contribution Act). Social Security tax. Money paid to the government toward a worker's retirement and other benefits.

Fire extinguisher. A container filled with chemicals that put out small fires.

First impression. The first feeling or idea people have about a person.

Fixed expenses. Things a person must pay for regularly.

Flammable. Able to catch fire.

Follow up. To finish or take the next step.

Foreman. The boss of a job.

Form 1040. The form for reporting federal income tax.

Fraud. Cheating someone by selling the person something other than promised.

Fringe benefits. Special pay or services given by employers to workers.

Full-time work. A job worked for 40 hours a week.

G

Goals. Things a person plans to achieve.

Good grooming. Being clean and neat and dressing with good taste.

Gossip. Talk about others' personal lives.

Gross pay. The full amount of pay for a pay period.

Ground. Connecting an electric tool to some other object so that any escaping electricity will flow to the ground. This prevents shock.

Guarantee. What a manufacturer will do if something goes wrong with a product.

Guidelines. Rules or steps to follow.

H

Handicaps. Things that limit how well a person does something.

Help wanted ads. Ads in a newspaper telling of job openings.

High voltage. A large amount of electricity.

Hospitality services. Work done to make people feel welcome or at home.

Humanitarian work. Work done to take care of someone else.

I

Identity. The personal qualities by which others know you.

Independent. Making your own decisions and being responsible for your own actions.

Industrial work. Work done in factories.

Influencing work. Work that involves convincing others to do something.

Informational interview. A talk with someone at a company about the type of work done there.

Installment plan. A type of credit. The buyer can use the item while paying for it.

Interest. Money earned on savings. Or money paid for the use of money.

Internal Revenue Service. The federal agency that collects federal income tax.

Initiative. Doing things without having to be told.

Inspectors. Factory workers who check the work done by others.

Interest areas. Groups of interests that appeal to workers.

Interests. The things a person likes to think about or do.

Interview. A talk with an employer about a job.

J

Job. All the tasks a person does to earn a living.

Job lead. Information about a job opening.

Job lead card. A card used to keep information about a job lead.

L

Labor contract. An agreement between a union and employees as to hours of work, wages, etc.

Learning disability. The physical problems that make it hard for a person to learn.

Lease. A written contract for rent on property.

Leisure. Free time when a person is not working.

Letter of application. A letter that asks for a job.

Letter of thanks. A letter to an employer thanking him or her for an interview.

Liability coverage. Insurance that covers a person's responsibility to others.

Life science. Science involving plants and animals.

Lifestyle. The way a person lives.

Lifestyle pattern. The pattern formed by the way a person lives. The importance a person gives to the parts of his or her life.

Long-term goals. Things a person plans to achieve in the future.

Luxuries. Things you would like to have but do not really need.

M

Materials control. The shipping, receiving, and storage of materials and products.

Mechanical work. A type of work having to do with tools and machines.

Minimum-wage laws. Laws that say all workers must be paid at least so much money per hour.

N

Negative. Lacking confidence. Thinking about the bad side of things.

Net pay. A worker's gross pay minus all deductions. "Take home" pay.

O

Occupation. All the tasks a person does to earn a living. Job.

***Occupational Outlook Handbook* (OOH).** A book published by the U.S. government that tells about jobs.

Occupational Safety and Health Administration (OSHA). The government department that makes sure work conditions are safe.

On-the-job-training. Learning a job while doing it.

Opinion. What someone thinks about something.

Oral communication. Information passed along to others by talking.

OSHA. Occupational Safety and Health Administration. A government department that makes sure work conditions are safe.

Overdraw. Writing a check for more money than is in a bank account.

Overtime. Hours worked that exceed 40 per week.

P

Part-time job. A job worked for less than 40 hours per week.

Payroll deductions. Money taken out of a worker's paycheck for taxes, insurance, etc.

Pay stub. The section of a paycheck that a worker keeps for his or her records.

Pension. A salary paid to workers after they are retired.

Pension plan. A savings plan for a worker's retirement.

Performance test. A test given to learn if a person has the skill to do a certain job.

Performing art. Art that is meant to be watched, such as a play.

Permanent. Lasting.

Personality. The combination of attitudes, values, behavior, and other things that identify a person.

Personnel department. A department within a company that hires new workers.

Physical science. A science involving the study of the earth.

Placement office. A school office that helps students find jobs.

Positive. Confident. Thinking about the good side of things.

Premium. Money paid for insurance.

Production work. Work usually done in factories to make something.

Private employment agency. A business that matches workers with jobs. Private agencies charge a fee.

Profit. The money a company makes from doing business.

Profit sharing. When companies give a part of the money, or profits, made to the workers.

Promotion. A change within a company to a job with higher pay and more responsibility.

Protective work. A type of work done to keep people or property from harm.

Public employment agency. An office run by the government that matches workers with jobs.

Q

Qualifications. Skills and experience that help a person do a certain job.

Quality control. The inspection, testing, and sorting of products or materials.

R

Raise. An increase in pay.

Reader's Guide. A listing of magazine articles published throughout the year.

Recommendation. A statement to an employer that a person can do a certain job.

Recruiter. Someone who tries to interest others in a school or job.

Reference. A person who can tell an employer that an applicant can do a good job.

Refund. Money returned when an overpayment has been made.

Relating. Getting along with or understanding others.

Reputation. What people think of a person or thing.

Respect. To honor someone or something.

Responsible. Able to be trusted.

Responsibility. Trustworthiness.

Resume. A summary of facts about a person that may be of interest to an employer.

Retirement. Quitting work forever. This is usually done after age 65.

Right-to-work laws. Laws that allow a worker the choice of whether or not to join a union in order to work for a certain company.

Rumors. Stories that may not be true.

S

Safety glasses. Glasses made of strong, clear material that protect the eyes.

Scholarship. A gift of money to a student for further education.

Scientific work. A type of work involved with solving problems or finding a better way of doing things.

Seasonal. Only at certain times, or seasons, of the year.

Self-concept. How a person sees himself or herself.

Self-employed. Being your own boss.

Self-esteem. Feeling good about yourself. Pride.

Self-respect. Liking or feeling good about yourself.

Sense of humor. The ability to see the funny side of things.

Service charge. A fee charged by a bank to manage a checking account.

Services. Things you pay others to do for you.

Short-term goals. Things you plan to achieve now or in the near future.

Sick leave. Paid time off when an employee is sick.

Social security benefits. Money paid by the U.S. government to a worker when he or she retires. The money comes from a fund created by both workers and employers.

Social security card. A card issued by the U.S. government that assigns a worker a social security number.

Stability. The ability to be the same day after day.

Standard English. Words used in such a way that they mean the same to everyone. The opposite of slang.

State income tax. Money collected by a state government for all the services it provides.

Stress. A feeling of physical, emotional, or mental strain.

Supervisor. The boss of a job.

Suspended. Removed from a job for a certain length of time.

T

Talent. The ability to do or learn something easily. Aptitude.

Tardiness. Being late.

Task. A single work activity.

Technicians. Scientific workers who use tools, such as microscopes, in their jobs.

Temporary. Lasting only a short time.

Trade. A job that takes skill with tools, such as welding.

Trade school. A school that teaches skills for certain types of jobs.

Traffic violation. Disobeying a law while driving a car.

Training. Directions and practice doing a job.

"Take home" pay. Net pay.

Taxes. Money paid to a government so it can do its work.

U

Unions. Groups of workers who band together for such things as better pay or working conditions.

Union steward. A person selected by the workers in a union to speak for them.

Utilities. Services such as gas, electricity, and water.

V

Values. A person's ideas about what is important.

Vapors. Gases.

Vending. The sale of items from machines, such as soda pop machines.

Vendor. Someone who sells things from a small stand or moving cart.

Ventilated. Allowing for the free movement of air.

Vocational school. A school that teaches a person a trade.

Visual arts. Art work that is meant to be looked at, such as a painting.

Volunteer work. Work done for no pay.

W

W-2 Form (Wage and Tax Statement). A form filled out by an employer that tells the government how much money a worker has earned.

W-4 Form (Employee's Withholding Certificate). A written statement giving an employer information affecting a worker's income taxes.

Wage and Tax Statement (W-2 Form). A form filled out by an employer that tells the government how much money a worker has earned.

Withdraw. Take money out of a bank account.

Work. Any useful activity.

Work experience program. A school program that allows students to work while still in school.

Work permit. A state form saying that a person under the age of 18 can work at a job.

Written contract. A legal, written promise.

Index

Q

R

S

Credits

ACF Industries, 207
Dave Anderson, 10, 22, 24, 45, 48, 63, 74, 76, 92, 114, 134, 136, 152, 156, 176, 178, 194, 196, 212, 214, 228, 230, 246, 250, 266, 290, 310, 312, 334
Jeff Andrew/Keystone, 78
Apple Computers, Inc., 6, 8

Frank Bolle, 29, 35, 80, 83, 99, 118, 139, 140, 144, 150, 170, 171, 172, 174, 181, 185, 188, 193, 209, 210, 222, 223, 224, 232, 234, 242, 268, 280, 295, 298, 318, 323, 330

Colt Industries, 205
CECO Industries, Inc., 170

Eric Dusenbury, 82, 95

James R. Gaffney, 26, 27, 33, 60, 66, 70, 79, 89, 119, 161, 184, 189, 217, 259, 292, 296, 319, 324, 328

Hewlett-Packard Company, cover, 56, 227
Charles Hofer, 32, 34, 40, 85, 87, 133, 173, 201, 243

Robert McElwee, 39, 51, 57, 62, 122, 193, 198, 206, 218, 235, 237, 272, 278, 281, 284, 297
Motorola, Inc., 54

N. A. Peterson, 154
Brent Phelps, 6, 17, 20, 28, 38, 84, 101, 123, 147, 191, 192, 202, 204, 211, 221, 243, 261, 262, 265, 274, 281, 292, 293, 302, 308, 314, 326
Elizabeth Purcell, 13, 107, 116, 121, 127, 149, 245

Jon Sall, 52, 86, 180
Dave Simpson, 95
Staley Continental, Inc., 65

UAW, 162
Unisys Corporation, cover

Victor Equipment Co., 68

Rod Walker/Vail, 160
Jervis B. Webb Co., 190
Ann Wright, 15, 31, 53, 55, 58, 61, 71, 81, 105, 126, 236, 243, 271, 304, 305, 321, 325

Duane R. Zehr, 5, 18, 37, 72, 94, 104, 138, 148, 164, 186, 221, 244, 249, 258, 282, 286